LAST TRAIN FROM BERLIN

Howard K. Smith worked for UP and CBS in Berlin and then returned to the States to a long career as one of America's most distinguished radio and TV correspondents, working with Ed Murrow among others.

Also by Howard K. Smith

The State of Europe

The Ruble War

Events Leading Up To My Death:
The Life of a Twentieth-Century Reporter

The News Media:
A Service and a Force (with Osborn Elliott and
Merriman Smith)

Washington, D.C.

The Story of our Nation's Capita

LAST TRAIN
FROM BERLIN

Howard K. Smith

*With a new
Introduction by the author*

**PHOENIX
PRESS**

5 UPPER SAINT MARTIN'S LANE
LONDON
WC2H 9EA

A PHOENIX PRESS PAPERBACK

First published in Great Britain
by The Cresset Press in 1942
This paperback edition published in 2000
by Phoenix Press,
a division of The Orion Publishing Group Ltd,
Orion House, 5 Upper St Martin's Lane,
London WC2H 9EA

A CIP catalogue record for this book is available
from the British Library.

Printed and bound in Great Britain by
Butler & Tanner Ltd, Frome and London

ISBN 1 84212 214 2

CONTENTS

INTRODUCTION

It is now sixty years since I used a *laissez-passer* cajoled from the German Foreign Office by the American embassy and was allowed to leave Germany for Switzerland in mid-war. I saw myself as the bearer of a message. I had been a reporter assigned to Germany for Hitler's two best years, 1940 when he conquered western Europe, and 1941 when he won the east and was 500 miles deep in the USSR. The great world may not have cared to admit it but I am sure the consensus, silent in some cases, was that Hitler was going to win this war. Europe would then be converted into a German powerhouse and made the base for wider events. My message was—not so fast; the tide is about to turn. The day—the hour—I entered Switzerland my message became more credible. The Japanese bombed Pearl Harbor. Days later Hitler obliged his Asian ally by declaring war on America. Britain, dreadfully alone a little while ago, had been given as allies two hitherto lethargic giants who were about to become the two strongest nations in the world. No wonder Winston Churchill, with much blood and tears still to pay, is said to have uttered, "So—we have won!".

Dennis Cohen of Cresset Press in London telegraphed requesting a book. With my boots still damp from German snows I rented a room and began typing. In two months of night and day work it was done. The American legation in isolated Switzerland refused to transport the manuscript in its diplomatic pouch; the musty air of isolationism took awhile to be cleared from my country's institutions. The British legation obliged without demur.

I had expected my hasty first draft of a transition in History to be read by a small British audience. Asked where to send any royalties, I suggested Mrs. Churchill's fund for refugees. Dennis Cohen disregarded my suggestion and opened an account in London in my name to receive proceeds, for they began to be substantial. I confess that I was pleased to hear of his deception after the war, for I had begun to create a family on nearly "nothing a year" like the couple in *Vanity Fair* and discovered that it didn't work; money was needed.

After a sell-out in Britain the book was published in most free western countries. In America it appeared on the *Times* best-seller list. In occupied Denmark it was duplicated on an office copying machine and distributed hand to hand. In England a tiny fragment was translated into French, made into match-book sized books, re-titled "Un Temoignage" and dropped from airplanes over occupied France. A Hollywood studio bought the title and designed a movie around it to star Gary Cooper. My employer at CBS News was hired as consultant. I have seen the scenario and am relieved to say it was abandoned before shooting began.

Over time it acquired some compliments that were pleasing. Bill Shirer, author of far the best Berlin book of the war, *Berlin Diary*, returned late in the war to visit me in Europe and told me, "A pretty little WAC met me at the airport and said, 'Oh, Mr. Shirer, I am so pleased to meet you at last. I read your book, *Last Train From Berlin*, and thought it quite the best book of the war.'"

Another involved Willi Brandt, the socialist mayor of Berlin after the war. The occasion was the premiere of the film *Judgment at Nüremberg*, held in Berlin. I was one of a party of Americans flown over to witness it. At a cocktail reception before the showing I chatted with Brandt about the war and he said that one American wartime journalist showed a particularly shrewd understanding of the Nazis in his writings, but Brandt could not remember his name. I suggested the name of Shirer and several other eminences of the time, but the mayor shrugged each off as not the one. When we sat down in the theater, he in the seat just in front of mine, he turned his head back to me and said, "he wrote a book called *Last Train From Berlin*, but I cannot remember his name."

Finally, forty years after the book was written, a German publisher asked to translate it into German and publish it in Germany. "I think we are just about ready for it," he said.

It is a personal matter, but in a way relevant here for it strongly affected the substance of the book and the personal experience from which the book was drawn. Yet it was never mentioned in the manuscript, lest it harm a loved one. I did not tarry in Switzerland with the purpose of writing a book. I wrote a book while enduring my main aim which was waiting for a lovely girl. She was tall, with magnificent limbs, with hair of a redness the luckiest leaves get in the Fall, and a persona that compensated for each of my many faults. She was 20 and an apprentice journalist for a Danish newspaper. After a courtship of four days (Life was hurried; I knew I was to go south but did not know whether it was to be to Switzerland or to Dachau) I proposed and she accepted. But being under age she had to go back to Denmark for written parental approval.

No sooner had we separated, with Germany between us, than America came into the war. The German occupation forces in Denmark now flatly refused to give her a permit to cross Germany in order to marry one who, always hostile, was now a certified enemy. So the impasse stood for months until, when seemingly permanent, it was resolved the way fairy stories are. Her father was a country lawyer, highly esteemed in Denmark. He appealed to the Queen of Denmark! She became interested and summoned the German ambassador and told him of her royal wish that the young lady receive the requisite permissions. With so many other problems on their hands, the Germans hoped Denmark would remain quiet, so they yielded and sent the girl flying to her lover and commencing the process of living happily ever after—or at least for six decades so far.

I confess that in the hard winter of that year my sureness that the tide was turning was still diluted with a large admixture of just hoping I was right. Hitler still had a reputation for swift recovery from setbacks and for delivering harsher blows than before. Yugoslavia was a recent case. It had turned on him, and he had struck back and smashed it to smithereens, and gone on to seize Greece in addition. The coming of spring in Russia might see a similar German recovery. The Soviet Red Army was still the army that had lost more officers to Stalin's own domestic bloodlust than to Hitler's attack from outside. It could commence re-collapsing with dry weather. And America, the super-isolationist, was an unknown value as an ally, particularly since it faced a more immediate military challenge in Asia.

My doubts were misplaced. In 1942 there was not just a change in Hitler's fortunes. New actors on the scene started thinking new thoughts, doing new things. There was in the whole world what Shakespeare dubbed a sea change, a shift of basic attitudes and assumptions. Hitler had to be whipped, but that was not enough. Almost all the great events-forcing decisions made in the first half of the century were seen to have been dreadfully wrong and had led to trains of disaster. In 1942 wherever people were free to engage in it there began a surge of resolve in heart and mind to start over and get it right this time. Leaders began actively learning from History. I claim a lot, but hear the evidence.

To me in Switzerland the first sign of change was the catching-on of the new thought that Hitler could be beaten. The Nazis lost their armor of invincibility. Defeated peoples in occupied countries nearby began organizing resistance they had not dared before. CBS kept me on in Switzerland to try to establish contact with those organizations and to become, in fact, CBS's underground Europe correspondent. I did so with rewarding results. My greatest success was tapping into a regular underground courier service between Switzerland and Yugoslavia over North Italy. I was soon able to brag that I was the first journalist to reveal the identity of the partisan leader Tito to the public. Alan Welch Dulles, chief of America's Intelligence in Europe, asked me to put him in touch with the partisans. I accepted it as a wartime patriotic duty, and something of a compliment, to bring Dulles together with a partisan leader in my apartment safe from observation. Later I, alone of journalists—how reporters love that boast!—was able to cross the Swiss border into Nazi-occupied France and spend a week with two French underground armies in the alps. In a thrilling episode my hosts flushed out a German prison and made the Gestapo guards kneel and answer questions from me.

The change of 1942 was actually best displayed by my own country. In 1937 when I left America it was a beaten nation, whipped by a Depression to which there seemed no end. The dictators were stomping the earth unappeased and unopposed. When we should have been joining, leading, the opposition, we shrank away, our legislators seeking protection in a dirty, dangerous world by designing our own special Maginot Line—the neutrality laws. Hitler could not touch us because it was against the law.

With student jobs hard to come by, I signed up with the National Guard, a part of what armed forces we possessed. Then, advised that I had won a valued English scholarship that would give me two years in Europe, I begged the recruiter to intercept my enlistment papers and destroy them, which he did. But I had a glimpse of what we had to offer on the cusp of a time of military trouble, and it was pitiful. When Neville Chamberlain was scolded for not seeking help against Hitler overseas he said, "You can expect nothing from the Americans." He was right.

Now, back in Europe and in mid-war, D-Day happened. The Germans vacated the exits to Switzerland and I was able to go out and see the new U.S. Army just landed. I was assigned to cover the U.S. Ninth Army headquartered in Holland but slated to take Berlin. I looked upon a revelation. It was now a 12-million man army, trained, expertly officered, equipped as none other on earth. It was the beginning of one of the massive shifts of the century—the transformation of an isolationist army the size of Rumaniala into a most interventionist army with more than 2,000 military bases in 32 countries.

But the change in spirit was more impressive than that of size. "This time we're not going home and pull up the drawbridge behind us. This time we're going to stay and be responsible for what comes out of this," so a young officer put it. The Japanese and Hitler had dealt a fatal blow to isolationism. The change would be even more impressive in the aftermath of the war. With our European allies too battered to defend themselves, the Truman Doctrine was issued to make America responsible for doing so. The Marshall Plan would enable Europe to rise from impotence to peace-time output levels in less than a decade. The North Atlantic Treaty Alliance would put an end to the French-German habit of warring one another and begin the uniting of Europe. Our worst, bellicose, enemies Germany and Japan would be converted into prosperous best friends and forces for peace in the world.

These were all America-initiated actions, with enormous power to back them up, and producing trains of well thought-out, good consequences. (By the end of the century, Europe would for the first time be made up, almost entirely, of democracies; it doesn't make things perfect, but it does make them easier.) They were so different from the decisions of the first half of the century which produced World War One, fought it with strategies that maximized slaughter, ended it with treaties punishing and discrediting Germany's first democratic government and, via appeasement in Europe and isolation in America, allowed Hitler to grow strong and to launch the biggest war ever.

My experience with the Ninth Army was bracing. I guess living with advancing, victorious armies always is. Briefly, Hitler gave us the experience of a beaten, retreating army; he packed two panzer armies in the Belgian mountains and let fly at a poorly defended arc. It was the so called Battle of the Bulge which developed into the biggest battle Americans ever fought anywhere in any war. After several weeks we regained control and resumed our successful advance.

The Ninth Army did not go to Berlin. We were across the Elbe and were on the way but Eisenhower called us back: Leave Berlin to the Russians. The same day the Germans surrendered to him in Reims, France, Eisenhower received a message from his Russian counterpart,

Marshal Georgi Zhukov, who had just taken Berlin. Its burden: Reims is not enough; the Germans must also surrender directly to us in Berlin. Zhukov was concerned that there be no Nazi myths, no myth, for example, that the Nazis had surrendered only to the western allies, not to the Russians, a legend that would deny the Soviets a place at the peace table. Next day, Eisenhower sent a high delegation winging to the German capital for Zhukov's ceremony. They took along a couple of journalists of whom I was one. Thus did he who had left Berlin on the last train go back on the first plane.

It was high adventure. Berlin was probably the most destroyed city in Europe. As we flew over its still smoking corpse, the view illustrated what Churchill meant when he said we would bomb and re-bomb until we "make the rubble bounce." That night, with Zhukov directing, Nazi Field Marshal Wilhelm Keitel was brought into a room to sign an unconditional surrender. His face was taut. Behind him his adjutant stood taut also but with rivers of tears pouring down his cheeks. Keitel was then taken to Nüremberg for the trials which would consign him to death on the gallows.

(The building in which the Berlin surrender ceremony was held was set aside as a Museum. A half-century later the Germans produced an epic TV documentary about it including a re-enactment. To take part they flew back Russian, English, French and German officers who had been present, but discovered that the only American present at the time and still alive was—me. How did I represent my great nation at one of its great moments? Quickly, before anyone who knew could object.)

I covered the Nüremberg trials later in 1945. Among other attributes, they were a university-level class in hitherto secret recent German history. We came into possession of storehouses full of official records, excruciatingly detailed, with responsibility certified by signatures of officials in charge. Criminality was established by Hitler's strange neglect to remove a sentence in every German soldier's paybook. It ordered every German soldier *not to obey* orders by superiors to do illegal acts like those listed in many of the documents.

After the trials my home address was moved to London, where Edward R. Murrow appointed me to succeed him as chief European correspondent of CBS. Simultaneously a new factum came to dominate the news and life: The Cold War.

The U.S. Army grew into a remarkable fighting force over a period of half a decade. The Soviet Red Army did the same in what seemed overnight. That was the biggest change in 1942.

When the Soviets stopped the Germans outside Moscow in 1942, the Red Army was stamped as the least effective army in World War Two momentarily saved by the early onset of a very bad Winter. It had performed abysmally when it attacked Finland in 1939, and did worse against the early German invaders in 1941, ceding Hitler complete armies containing three million soldiers in mass surrenders. Hitler proclaimed, "I declare today and I declare it without any reservation, that the enemy in the east has been struck down and will never rise again." In America, General Staff experts notified favored American editors that there would be a total Soviet collapse within weeks.

But when that same year 1942 faded again into Winter, the Red Army was on the way to victory in the nearest thing to a decisive battle in WW II—Stalingrad—thanks to brilliant strategy and incredible power and morale. A little later it engaged the Germans in the biggest tank battle in military history around Kursk, and won. From these two blows Hitler never recovered. Among the lesser consequences: my report that the tide was turning for good was rendered truthful.

What produced this most dramatic change? Hitler himself was the principal cause. Before the offensive he called his generals together and told them to divest themselves of traditional notions of war; he was preparing a hell on earth for the Soviet people. Goering predicted 30 million of them would simply be starved to death as the Germans removed or destroyed all means of survival. Every German officer from lowest grade up was given the right of judgment and execution against any who dared resist or object. As it is easier for tired lieutenants to shoot prisoners rather than guard and feed them, this was an invitation to slaughter. Hitler thus offered the victim people the stark choice: win, or die, terribly.

A special event allowed them to start winning. In Khrushchev's famous secret speech to the Soviet Communist party in 1956, after Stalin's death, he told that when the Germans first came sweeping into the Soviet Union, Stalin went to pieces. "He said, 'All that which Lenin created we have lost forever.' After this, Stalin for a long time did not direct military operations and ceased to do anything whatever." John Erickson said the tyrant locked himself away for days but was still shaky when he re-appeared. However long, it was shock enough to persuade him to stop killing his professional officers and start depending upon them. Luckily, there were still very good ones left, Georgi Zhukov in the lead.

Zhukov first won note by thrashing the Japanese thoroughly in one of their war-sized skirmishes in the Far East. In the winter crisis of 1942 he was called upon to set up the defenses that kept the Germans out of Moscow. Then, with the Army staff, he worked out, and carried out, the plans to turn the war around at Stalingrad.

In 1945 I saw Zhukov and his army at the peak of their triumph, the end of their unique journey of 1500 miles from Stalingrad to Berlin, fighting all the way. They were forests of ants teeming over the ruins of Berlin, but orderly ants, order kept and traffic movement maintained by women, very large, very young women, berets on the backs of their heads and in short skirts and boots, who gave snappy signals and got instant obedience, and grinned with pride at the efficiency of their command. Next to numbers and women, the big impression was transportation. America supplied them with 13 million pairs of socks and boots to march in, trucks and Jeeps to drive and thousands of miles of rails to roll on, but it was not enough for this nation in movement. Everywhere were horses, oxen, even cows resting by the side of the roads between assignments.

Surrender night, when Keitel had been removed, squads of ants cleared the room, produced long tables, piled them with forests of bottles and plates and produced a military band kept invisible behind veils of cheesecloth, and Marshal Zhukov gave us a party to end parties. It was probably the last time allies of east and west were civil to one another. Safely victorious, his prestige high due to a phenomenal military performance, Stalin reverted to his preferred role as champion of world proletarian revolution. All over Soviet-occupied Berlin signs appeared bearing slogans denominating Stalin as Germany's protector against Nazism and its twin, Imperialism. Imperialism was short for Britain and America. We were subjected to vicious tests aiming to drive America out of Europe and Asia—the Russian blockade of us in Berlin and a cruel aggressive war in Korea.

We withstood both, but the tension and bloodshed tied the two new great powers and their allies in the biggest, dearest, most dangerous arms race in history. The Cold War, as the contest became known, lasted half a century, cost national fortunes and kept the world on the edge of terror. Berlin attained new fame in a different struggle. With American and Russian tanks meeting muzzle to muzzle there, the city was regarded as the Cold War's epicenter. And the huge, ugly, gun-crested Berlin wall, constructed by the Russians to stop the steady, draining westward flight of east Germans, became its symbol.

The Cold War has little relation to this book. Its story, with its fantastic ending in the utter collapse of the Soviet Union without a shot being fired, is for later books. Here I shall mention only its one relationship with wartime Germany that was decisive. The Cold War settled satisfactorily the thorniest question that emerged from the war—what to do with this troublesome German nation once peace was forced. Europe needed for its recovery also a recovery of the strongest unit within it, Germany. But Germans would not work to this end without full economic rewards and freedom from outside dictate. And such freedom might become a re-play, a third effort by Germans to conquer by force. What to do? Europeans found their own answer. They discovered that dealing successfully with Germany required exactly the same policy they were applying to meet their other main missions: organizing themselves to resist Russia in the Cold War and restoring battered Europe to great power status: European Union. Roughly, let Germany be something like a big Texas in a union that leaves it free, but under the over-arching discipline of that union and all its members. So far, it seems to be working, but prayer is still appreciated by its proponents.

HOWARD K. SMITH

PREFACE

This book contains what American correspondents in Berlin have been trying to tell the world between the lines of their dispatches since last autumn. So far as I know it is the only record of the sweeping changes which have taken place inside Germany since the beginning of, and due to, the Russian war. I am able to write it because, after spending the better part of almost six years in Germany, I was the last American to get out of the country. Just after I crossed the Swiss border, Germany declared war on America, and my fellow reporters were locked up by the Nazis.

One world of explanation: The first part of the book is a personalized history, in conscious application of a principle I think is good. One does not have to be an apostle of Bishop Berkeley to know that impressions are not spontaneously imprinted on him who observes, but are conditioned, sometimes even determined, by the observer himself. For example, consider the case of Russia. Before the war, a quarter of a million people used to visit that land every year. The range of personal sentences passed on that favourite object of invective and praise by people who saw virtually the same things should clinch the point.

In this book the facts and verdict are, I sincerely believe, important. They constitute about the only report available on the present condition of the enemy. They are written down at a moment when the greatest conflict in history has not yet been decided, but when the atmosphere induces the feeling that a decision is at hand. *Under these circumstances, it would be next to criminal to have a share in arousing false hopes or causing false despair. That is why, from the very outset, I want to lay my own cards down on the table—in so far as they concern Germany—and lay bare my own personal prejudices, predilections, sophistications—or lack of them—on this particular subject. If, however, the reader has neither the time nor the desire to consider these, then let him turn to Chapter III for the story of Germany since June 22nd, 1941.*

INTIMATE HISTORY OF AN ATTITUDE

FOR REASONS my own household gods must have determined, Germany became, precisely in the year of our Lord, 1936, the cheapest country in Europe in which an American could travel. I know because I figured it out that spring to the pfennig, the centime, the centavo and the last ha'penny. A year later and France would have been cheapest and I would have gone to France. But it was 1936, and summer, and I had to adapt myself to my personal circumstances. I had just finished University in New Orleans, and longed to see a spot of the outside world before I settled down to a $15 a week job on a local newspaper. For the first time in my life I had earned $100 all in one smack by writing a short story. And a steamship company agreed to give me a job as deck-hand on a cargo boat sailing for Europe. Since $100, or $90, for I had to buy a passport, could last longer in Germany than anywhere else, I decided to go to Germany. For a decision of the kind people call "fateful" it was made on remarkably indifferent grounds. But fateful it was, for I have only just now escaped from its consequences, on the last train. But, to get back to the chronology.

It was 1936 and I was a student; officially graduated, but a student in spirit still. I was full of American zeal to see Europe, and College-Graduate zeal to study the same. Europeans make game of both zeals: They say they can always spot an American from a mile away because he always has a camera, with which to freeze his memories on cardboard, lashed by a leather strap to his shoulder, and carries a guide-book in one hand and a diary in the other. But I think both zeals are good things. Properly applied, they indicate the attitude of the student, of which we could have more. Anyhow, that is the attitude with which I was approaching Germany.

It was to be a tour at first. But then my friends converted it into a sociological mission: My friends were a little, unofficial fraternity of penniless students who spent part of their student-years in the university and the other part driving trucks and washing dishes to make enough money to get back into the university. We had found our way together in four years of higher education on the basis of a common interest in World Problems, with capital letters. We studied little, but we read quantities, which in retrospect appear amazing, of literature on World Problems, and spent most of our time just shooting bull, chewing the rag, debating, but always with the purpose of finding the constituents of the magic word— Solutions, with a big S. People make fun of that attitude, too, but again, I think it is a good one. That is how people learn. It is the essence of Liberalism. Naturally Nazi Germany was one of our problems. We filled the atmosphere of many a study room with pipe-smoke and weighty words arguing about the new, novel government of Germany, whether it was workable, if it afforded solutions to problems we had in America, whether it necessarily meant war—or all boiled down to a single Britishism: was Nazi Germany a Good Thing or a Bad Thing?

A liberal education naturally prejudiced us all towards rejecting dictatorship, but the atmosphere of those times, when the world had not yet recovered from its most serious economic depression, was to test all theories and welcome a consideration of all ideas (readers whose memories are blurred by the rush and hardness of more recent events are cautioned not to think it naive and academic that these questions should be considered debatable. It should be remembered that, at that time, great and powerful governments were forming their policies around the assumption that these questions were debatable. At least two governments assumed that, far from debatable, they might even be answered in Hitler's favour). To a group eager even for good second-hand information on any subject, my plans to get first-hand information on Germany were welcomed as a common good fortune. Since my friends were too concerned about getting and holding jobs to imagine going to Europe, whereas I, thanks to my short story, was just able to go, I was charged with representing all of them.

The idea of being thus a one-man fact-finding commission intrigued me. Like a political Descartes, I tried to wash all preconceptions and prejudices out of my mind. For background I read everything on Germany I could find, including several compendious histories, written and a-gathering dust while Adolf Hitler was not even a prospective accident in his great grandfather's wildest reveries. With the noble highsounding aim of "polishing up my cogitative processes" I re-read two of Harold Laski's books on Politics and States in general. I am sure the host of prominent and professional investigators who are sent out on commissions of world import every year by governments and big institutions never felt, even collectively, their obligation to history and their commissioners more weightily than I did. Nor were commissioners ever more exacting. Jointly, we spent long evenings and great pains compiling a list of things to be looked for and questions to be put. My old German instructor got busy and procured me a scholarship with which I could spend a month, cheaply, at Heidelberg. Then, having filled my cardboard suitcase with half a dozen fat, blank, notebooks, I sailed.

The voyage lasted twenty-one days, but every eventless day filled three or four pages of a notebook; it was my first and, taking into account the return voyage, my next to last time on the high seas, and I was determined to store up enough memories to last me the rest of my life. Nothing, absolutely nothing, happened. The days were all of a pattern: calm, endless seas; hard work, "soojying" bulkheads, scraping decks, washing dishes. The only variation was when I committed the classic error of tossing garbage overboard into the wind: I never made the mistake again. But from the volume of notes I took, one would have gathered it was the most exciting voyage since Odysseus. When the silent, blinking light of Lizard Rock hove into sight off our port bow early one morning, I sent squeals of glee moving across our timber-laden deck which startled the captain out of a fast sleep and earned for me a calling-down I shall never forget. I regret that I could not maintain that original enthusiasm for seeing new things and places, for, second to intelligence, it is the best quality a reporter can have. But I have long since passed the stage described by Mark Twain in *Life on the Mississippi* when new worlds lose their lustre, things once odd become everyday, and diaries conscientiously launched, begin to sputter and finally stop altogether.

Germany captivated me before I set foot inside it. Crawling up the Elbe from Bremerhaven, we passed one fancy-tickling miniature town after another, all spotless with rows of toy houses and big, sunny beer gardens along the river bank. By the time we docked, I had scrubbed off twenty-four hours of grime, shaved off three weeks growth of beard and put on my Sunday and only suit. I was the first ashore. Although I was anything but averse to drinking, I renounced the traditional first-night-in-port drunk and went sight-seeing alone; hours were too brief, valuable and irretrievable to waste the next twenty-four of them nursing a hangover. That night I walked, just walked alone, up and down mediæval streets, watched lights sparkling in the windows of the old *Rathaus* wide-eyed as a child early on Christmas morning. Twice I stopped in taverns for beer. Once, at four o'clock, I breakfasted at a street-corner lunch-counter on *Bockwurst* and mustard served in a little paper trough. At six, tired but still enchanted, I reached the ship again and went to sleep. At noon the next day I was out on the streets again. It was four days before I came out of this original trance. Then, with some effort, I shoved what is called in tourist bureaux the charm of the old world back among my secondary interests, obtained my discharge papers from the ship's captain, and, recalling my obligations back home, settled down to the businesslike job of studying, not Germany, but *Nazi* Germany.

With a sheaf of railway tickets I left Bremen for Heidelberg. There, my equilibrium again wobbled a little, as it was bound to in that lovely little town, and the trance returned, but I soon had the situation under control again. I lived there a month for a pittance in the *Studentenheim*, and ate whopping meals at fifty pfennigs in the Students' *Mensa*. Then, for another wonderful month, I crammed, strictly *à l'Americain*, Germany's six biggest cities into a single tour.

About the whole experience, I want, from the outset, to distinguish between two different sets of impressions one could get. First, there were the impressions connected with the "research" I was doing to satisfy the intellectual demands of me and my patrons. They were *active* impressions, involving consciously looking out for certain features and asking certain questions according to a plan laid down in advance. They had to be combined by an active mental process into corollaries which might be different with different observers. Their mark of distinction was that they were *active*. But alongside these were a set of *passive* impressions which one got whether one sought them or not, which required no special effort on the part of the observer, but which came simply as a result of living and travelling in that atmosphere for a period of time. Unlike the active impressions, these followed a pattern of progress which, I have since noted, was almost universal among foreign visitors to Germany. The first set dealt mainly with political and economic phases of German life; the second with the "Culture"—in the broad sense of the general spiritual atmosphere —of the new Germany. It is on these latter that I want first to dwell. The fact that their pattern of progress is similar for all visitors appears to lend them more authority than the others; but, whether or not that is true, they are interesting for their own sake.

Now the only variations in the pattern of passive impressions was the rapidity with which different individuals completed the entire scale of them. Some people, sharp and sensitive, could run the entire gamut in a week, which is unusually good. Some, it took several years, and only the outbreak of war forced the last stages on their minds. There are even some who never get beyond stage one, which bespeaks the sensitivity of a rhinoceros's hide and the profundity of a tea-saucer. (The tea-saucer depth-rate was especially high among the young American schoolgirls in Heidelberg. The principal obstacle in the way of their further progress was, I think, the fact that German men are handsome and wear uniforms.)

The first and most general of these passive impressions was good beyond all expectation. On first glance, Germany was overwhelmingly attractive, and first impressions disarmed many a hardy anti-Nazi before he could lift his lance for attack. Germany was clean, it was neat, a truly handsome land. Its big cities were cleaner than big cities ought, by custom, to be. You could search far and wide through Berlin's sea of houses or Hamburg's huge harbour district, but you could never find a slum or anything approaching one. On the countryside, broad, flourishing acres were cut into neat checkerboards, and no square foot of land was wasted. People looked good. Nobody was in rags, not a single citizen. They were well dressed, if not stylishly dressed. And they were well fed. The impression was one of order, cleanliness and prosperity—and this has been of immense propaganda value to the Nazis. There is a great fallacy here, and it is a mistake which an unfortunately large number of young American students I met in Heidelberg made and retained for a long time. The fallacy is in connecting this admirable order, cleanliness and apparent prosperity with the Nazi government. Actually, and this was pointed out to me by a German dock-worker on my first magic day in Bremen, Germans and Germany were neat, clean and able to do an amazing lot with amazingly little long before Hitler came to power. Such slums as existed were removed by the Socialist government and replaced with neat workers' apartments while the Nazis were still a noisy minority chalking swastikas on back-alley fences. The German people are, by their very nature, clean and thrifty and can make their Sunday suits last and look new for triple or quadruple the time an American or an Englishman can. But no matter; that is general impression number one to every visitor to Germany, valid or not.

The second impression, a more specific one, followed hard on the heels of the first, if it was not coeval with it. It was—uniforms and guns; the amazing extent to which Germany, even then, was prepared for war. It took my breath away. I had read about Nazi rearmament, but to me it was still a word, not a sense-idea. In New Orleans I could sum up in a figure of two integers all the uniforms I had ever seen. Before our boat docked in Bremen I saw a big multiple of that figure, sailors of Germany's war navy, walking up and down the long wharves. The railway station in Bremen, and later every railway station I saw, was a milling hive of soldiers in green uniforms in full war-kit and with rifles, getting off trains and getting on them. Farther inland, towns looked like garrisons, with every third or fourth man in uniform. On trains, all day long, one passed long railway caravans of camouflaged tanks, cannon and war-trucks lashed to railway flat cars, and freight depots were lined with more of these monsters hooded in brown canvas. In large towns, traffic had to be interrupted at intervals on some days to let cavalcades of unearthly machines, manned by dust-covered, steel-helmeted Men-from-Mars roar through the main streets in manœuvres.

The reaction that belongs to stage number two was one of titillation. Or, more than that, it was downright exciting. It was a brand new experience, rich in colour and thrilling action, to hoard up in my memory and describe later to wide-eyed, envious listeners at home.

Imagine the best example of it, standing at a window in Nuremberg, as I did later, watching a broad undulating river of ten, twenty thousand men in uniform, stamping in unison down the cobble-stone street below, flooding the valley between the houses with a marching song so loud the windows rattled, and so compelling your very heart adopted its military rhythm. In the thin margin between the houses and the men, helmeted messengers on motor-cycles sped up and down from mysterious grey staff cars ahead to staff cars in the rear, their cut-outs ripping raucous, jagged edges in the air. As far back as you could see were men in uniform, their ranks broken only occasionally by grey, motorized anti-aircraft guns nosing up at the sky; and you knew that beyond where you could see were thousands and thousands more.

Seeing vast numbers, great masses or infinite expanses, like a sea or an endless plain has a way of inducing philosophic moods and making one wonder about things like Time and Space and individual components of them. Seeing a mass of armed, uniformed men called into movement by a single laconic command, one inevitably began to grow curious about the individuals that made it up. Along these lines, in Germany, you could arrive at a new genus; *homo militaris*, it might be called. And you could with almost no active application, in that land where the genus abounds, observe and classify its "habits and customs" as a botanist observes and classifies flora. The outstanding property of the *homo militaris*, you discovered, is the readiness with which he can change personalities. For example, follow a couple of soldiers off duty down the street, any street in Germany. You admire their bronzed, smiling faces and the way they walk loosely and gracefully as athletes. They're completely human beings. Suddenly a certain stimulus is applied to the objects of study. For purposes of investigation, it might be called the stimulus of "officer in sight". In an instant, the two soldiers freeze into solid blocks of machinery; lightning-like they snap their arms, in unison, to their caps and their faces harden and lose expression. The stimulus is removed, the officer passes, and the young men collapse into humanity in an instant, and are again walking loosely and gracefully as athletes, as though nothing had happened.

Or take another example. In Heidelberg, on the parade ground outside the barracks. You stand and watch fifty or sixty of them drilling. Since you have lived there several weeks, and seen many of them on the streets, you know they are human beings. But on parade ground they have switched off humanity and are being trained for several hours at being machines. They react to incomprehensible, monosyllabic commands as a new slot-machine reacts to a shiny coin. They are simply having their reflexes drilled, so that they can move without thinking. On stimulus one they snap to rigid attention. On stimulus two they present arms.

On stimulus three, all, like a single machine, raise their left legs high before them and begin goose-stepping. And you know that if stimulus four did not come to stop them, reaction three would carry them over a cliff, if one were there, and on the way down into the abyss, their expressionless faces would not change and their legs would click up and down in the air like a mechanical toy until they crashed at the bottom.

These were not observations for a dilettante. For they had meaning. As the novelty of anything inevitably wears off, so the novelty of militarism does with time. And as newness loses its grip on your faculties, your brain silently muscles in on territory that had belonged entirely to your senses. The impression is still a passive one; the thought process involved is no more active than a reverie. And this, in one form or another, is just the way almost every visitor to Germany I met slid imperceptibly from stage two of his passive impressions to stage three. You began to grasp that what was happening was that young humans, millions of them, were being trained to act merely upon reflexes. And you inevitably came to wonder, what, after all, is the ultimate, the final reflex toward which all this drilling is directed? Obviously, to kill, as a reflex. To destroy "according to plan". On terse commands which altered their personalities more neatly than Doctor Jekyll became Mr. Hyde, they were learning to smash, crush, destroy, wreck. Not one of them would harm a fly while he was Doctor Jekyll. But apply the proper stimulus and they would fall into the military trance, blast the guts out of the first person in range of them or drop big fat bombs on peaceful homes and blow them to smithereens. That, of course, is the nature of the military man in any country; but to understand their full effect, it must be remembered that these impressions came when the rest of the world, my nation in the fore, was sleeping in the delusion that its only problems were far less formidable than those of war. In that setting, the reaction that accompanies this stage is one of uneasiness.

When I first arrived in Bremen, I met a young naval rating named Otto. He was about three years younger than I, handsome, pink-cheeked and always smiling. He came aboard our ship and I gave him a packet of cigarettes. After that he became my inseparable companion for all the time I stayed in Bremen; showed me everything in town and took me to beer-halls where we ex-

changed treats, sang songs together and had a wonderful time.
When I left, he would not let me carry my bag to the station, but
insisted on carrying it himself. When the train departed, I thought
he would weep. He stood on the platform a solitary, blue figure,
smiling sadly and waving his handkerchief until I was out of sight.
When I returned to Bremen two months later, Otto and I were
happy as a couple of kids to meet again at the station. Arm in arm,
we marched off, grinning and chattering, to the station restaurant
for a couple of reunion toasts to start off a big evening. But sadly,
by that time my brain had muscled in on my senses, and when we
passed an officer I watched Otto closely for the first time. In a
flash his boyish face grew rigid and cold, his eyes fixed and glassy,
and a cruel strain burned through his expressionless face; his whole
demeanour was that of a robot, lifeless and dependent on command for movement. In another instant, the trance broke and
Otto was my good old, smiling Doctor Jekyll again. But it was all
over after that. Against my will the charm had been broken. I distrusted Otto. I knew that as Otto, he would fight anybody who
spoke roughly to me. But I also knew that as military man number
743914-X he would harden, turn on me and slash my throat. We
never again achieved that easiness that pals have. Lovable, pink-
cheeked Otto, who would not harm a dog on the streets, has probably, figuratively speaking, cut many human throats by now.

From uneasiness in stage three, the reaction in stage four could
turn to one of a strange, stark terror. It happened to me only once
on my first trip to Germany. Actually nothing very unusual called
forth this reaction; it was simply that it was due to me in my allotted
scale of reactions, and it came one night in the town of Worms,
on the river Rhine. A few months before, the Germans had, in
defiance of the Versailles treaty, marched into the Rhineland. A
friend of mine and I bicycled to Worms to see what we could see.
The town was not in war, yet, but it was the best imitation of a
town-in-war I have ever seen. The streets were filled with soldiers.
On every corner forests of new sign-posts told the way to parking
grounds for motorized units, regimental headquarters, divisional
headquarters, corps headquarters, field hospitals. We elbowed our
way the length of the main street and saw not another man in
civilian dress. That evening we spent in a beer-hall, in whose
upper stories we had rented rooms. The beer-hall was packed with
fine-looking young officers, drinking, shouting, and singing. The

tables were wet with spilled beer and the air hazy with blue cigarette smoke. I do not know what it was, except that the turn of this reaction was logically due—it was perhaps partly that the beer had loosened up my imagination—but watching the faces of these men, my own age, my own generation, caused me to think of their military culture, for the first time, in terms of me and my culture. For the first time I thought of Germany, not as an academic subject studiously to gather facts about for discussion at home, but as a real, direct and imminent threat to the existence of a civilization which gathers facts and discusses. A schism deeper than the Grand Canyon separated my world from that of the young man across from me, whose face bore fencing scars and carried a monocle over one glassy eye. The fetishes of my world, the values it worshipped, if it did not always attain them, were contained in words like "Reason", "Think", "Truth". His fetishes and his values were "Feel", "Obey", "Fight". There was no base pride for me in this involuntary comparison; rather, a terror like that which paralyzes a child alone in the dark took hold of me. For, my world, with all the good qualities I thought it had, was, in terms of force, weak; his was mighty, powerful, reckless. It screamed defiance at my world from the housetops. One had to be deaf not to hear it.

After that my senses sharpened and I guided them to fill out my impressions. I watched propaganda in the newspapers, placards on street-corner billboards, listened to it on the radio; I took closer note of the trends and tone of lectures in Heidelberg, listened more attentively to conversations with university instructors, chosen for their ability as propagandists rather than as teachers, at Saturday night social gatherings in the Institute for Foreigners. Everything I saw and heard confirmed my new-born fear. I had now gone through all the stages save one—that is when fear has matured and been converted into political action. In its own way, that came later.

The individual human will is a wonderful thing. It can accomplish deeds that are theoretically impossible, overcome serious illnesses, win governments. A nation of millions of human wills united in the determination to achieve a certain, definite end is that many times more powerful. A whole nation, for instance, which is unified as to means, methods, and an intense desire to abolish poverty and create abundance for all, could make the grandest civilization we have ever known, in a single generation.

By the same token, a whole great nation which is unified in means, methods and will to carry out the single purpose of waging war could, if its neighbours were not equally determined, flood the world with blood and misery unequalled. That last is what I saw in Germany. I saw it before a month was out. My non-partisanship had slipped badly.

Every fibre and tissue of the social fabric was strained towards that single needle-point goal of war. Newspapers screamed belligerency and hate every single day. The objects of the belligerency altered with expediency, but the screaming tone was unvaried. "We have been wronged by A; we are being threatened by B; we will right those wrongs and eliminate that threat, and Heaven help any misguided individual who stands in our way!" Children were taught it in schools; we were given a milder dose of it in the university. Soldiers had it drilled into them as another reflex. Art was nothing but war posters. Germany clearly and unequivocally wanted war and told the world so in tones so distinct that it was criminal to disbelieve them.

My Great Adventure continued, and I scrupulously gathered masses of active impressions to stand by the passive ones. Germany was a fortunate choice for this sort of kerbstone research, for every German I met leaned over backward to oblige; everyone was friendly and most were downright voluble. When the end of the second month rolled around I arrived in Bremen penniless. I could find no place on a ship there, so I sold the two new shirts I had not yet taken the pins out of to an American sailor, and bought a railway ticket to Rotterdam on the sailor's tip. There I found a freighter and went home.

By the time my ship (she was a groaning, antiquated barge named *Meanticut*; she struggled hard to make the last miles to New Orleans, and after I left her she sailed back out into the Atlantic and, in a storm off the Azores, cracked in half and sank. I have never since complained about my luck) turned into the mouth of the Mississippi, my "report" was organized. It was a long, unwieldy document, shot through with dozens of incidents and illustrations for every point made. The thread of its reasoning was, however, relatively simple and exploded in a final verdict so definite and uncompromising that I fear it was a slight shock to the liberal sensibilities of my friends. The result for me of the active impressions was: National Socialism was quite decidedly a

Bad Thing. It offered no solution to any problem. For the very
reason that it could solve no problems, but only postpone them, I
held that Nazism absolutely, inevitably, and even, in the terms of
our debating question, *necessarily* meant war.

The active impressions reduced to only their most essential filtrate were composed something like this (I regret the *McGuffy's
First Reader* style, but the point to be made is essential to this book).

First: the object of any government in any state in the world is
to maintain and increase the well-being of the people living in it.
And on their success or failure at this, governments must be
judged.

Second: Hitler took over a nation in which the well-being of the
people was prevented from being well by several serious problems.
The principal problems were:

(*a*) a low standard of living;

(*b*) millions of unemployed workers; and

(*c*) an economic crisis was in course, in which industry, which
furnishes the people with the necessities of food, clothing and
shelter was virtually paralyzed.

Third: Hitler's success or failure must be judged on the extent
to which he has solved, or failed to solve, these problems.

Now, on the basis of what I saw, heard and checked wherever
possible—and I strained to be impartial—these are the results.

Problem (*a*), *Standard of Living.* First impressions indicate a good
standard of living. That, however (as I pointed out above) is illu-
sory as a judgment of the progress of the standard of living since
Hitler. For it is an ingrown, admirable quality of Germans that
they make the most out of every little bit, whether governed by
Hitler, Wilhelm Hohenzollern or Bismarck. The only way to tell
whether a standard of living is rising or falling is to see whether
people are getting more and better things to eat and wear for their
incomes, or less and worse things.

Now, in 1936, I made as thorough a check as possible on prices
for consumption commodities—shirts, shoe-polish, tooth-paste,
razor blades, sausages, soap, etc. With a little difficulty, I also
gathered prices for the same commodities in 1933, when Hitler
came to power, from people on the streets and in taverns. The result was, in every case, a steady and continuing rise in prices.
Some, like that for cooking-fat, had gone up fifty per cent in three
years. Meanwhile, testimony was unanimous that the quality of

most of these articles had gone down. The conclusion is that what people got for their money was more expensive and less good.

The other element in the standard-of-living complex—individual incomes—remained, meanwhile, in terms of money, the same. A law clearly inscribed in Hitler's law books calling for what is termed a "wage-stop" is all the evidence needed for this.

In short, money wages were stabilized in 1933 at a low, depression level; prices had risen steadily, and—this, too, is obvious in Hitler's law books—hours of labour had increased without a compensatory increase in payment. The only, inevitable conclusion was that people were getting less and worse things for their income than they were when Hitler took over in the depression of 1933. The standard of living had not risen but dropped, and severely.

Problem (b) *Unemployment.* To begin with, what is the cause of unemployment? There are as many theories about this as there were hairs in Samson's head before the shearing. But this is one which, in its wording, no economist, I think, from J. M. Keynes across the scale to John Strachey, can find fault with: unemployment exists because the people do not possess sufficient purchasing power to keep industry and all its workers fully employed, simply by their daily purchases of goods they need and want.

In Germany (that veritable empire of appearances) the problem of unemployment superficially appeared to be solved. Certainly no German was without work. Hitler created this appearance simply by drafting all the unemployed workers into industries where they best fitted into his plans, and spreading the real wages of all thinner so that all might be paid. (There is nothing in the "wage-stop" law, referred to above, to prevent decreases in the real wages of workers already employed in 1933.)

Hitler did not even begin to attack the real economic problem of expanding *mass* purchasing power. For him, the problem of unemployment was "solved", according to his lights, by increasing *government* purchasing power (by exacting more of the people's income through exorbitant taxes and "voluntary" contributions to phoney schemes). And this government purchasing power was exercised to buy armaments—utterly useless to the consuming masses, a loss to the whole economic system—in order to keep industry functioning. To solve unemployment on the basis we have set down means to solve it so that the solution redounds to the well-being of the people. Hitler's "solution" had the opposite effect: first, it forced the people to work more for less income, and, second, it diverted resources from the production of things they could eat and wear to ends, armaments, that were useless to them. In short, on our basis, Hitler did not solve the problem of unemployment.

Problem (c) *Economic Crisis*. What has just been written merges into this. An economic crisis occurs when industry, which makes things people eat and wear, does not function. Hitler's solution to the crisis was not by making useful goods, but by producing the greatest aggregation of arms, which nobody can eat or wear, in all history. (He could make industry go this way by buying at prices fixed by the government and the armaments industries all the arms the industry could produce. It is irrelevant to this analysis, but interesting that prices were fixed by the government agency for armaments, the *Wirtschaftsgruppe Schwerindustrie* and the arms factories. Since Krupp was the biggest arms producer and at the same time the dominant bureaucrat on the *Wirtschaftsgruppe Schwerindustrie*, these prices, with "reasonable profit" included were fixed by Krupp in conference with Krupp. Mischievous tongues allege that there is some relation between this and the fact that the Krupp works after making a loss in 1933, enjoyed record profits in 1935 and broke the record in each successive year including 1941!) So, from the outset, Hitler has not solved the problem of economic crisis in our sense, for he has not added to, but subtracted from the quality and quantity of consumers' goods which existed in 1933.

But, let us accept his solution and trace it to its logical conclusion. Economically speaking, there are two possible conclusions: first, Hitler can choose to make only so many armaments and then call a stop to it. Or second, he can increase the production of armaments *ad infinitum* until all industry produces arms, and no industry produces bread and shirts. In the former case, mass unemployment will break out the moment the arms factories cease production, and crisis, aggravated by delay, will come. In the second case, everybody starves and a worse crisis exists. The economic conclusion in both cases is crisis.

There was one way out for Hitler, if he did not face either of these economic consequences of his policy, and that was war. War to conquer new lands and new markets which could keep his industry going. To me, this was the crux of the whole analysis.

The issue was so immaculately clear to me that I would not even brook alternative interpretations people suggested to me merely for sake of argument. I was overcome with an utterly un-liberal impatience at my friends who tried to keep the matter in that rare-fied academic stratum of opinion and counter-opinion. No matter which way I looked at the question, it ended with the same answer. The mere atmosphere of the place was one of a nation at war with the world. Germany's propaganda shouted it quite plainly. Economic analysis showed Germany was being *driven* to war. And, clearest of all was the simple fact that the guns were there in un-heard of numbers, plain for all to see. What was he going to do with them? Not use them? In which case all these beautiful fruits of years of industry would be wasted; or use them, which again, and finally, meant war. For me the moral question of Nazism's rightness or wrongness was settled beyond hope of alteration. For me the *moral* question yielded place to the only remaining ones: the purely *technical* questions of, what is the best way to stop Hitler? How strong is he? Is there hope he will crack before he throws the world into war?

There was no little satisfaction in having arrived at a point of view regarding the moral question. It cleared the air for me. But the rise of the technical questions soon doused this satisfaction with new worries and fears. This evolution, this additional scale of Reactions to Germany, too, turned out later to be on a pattern most others followed—from debating whether Hitler was really a Bad Thing, to concluding that he was, then to the frustrating fear that perhaps it was too late; perhaps Hitler had gone too far, gathered too much momentum to be stopped. As one of my friends said to me when I conjured up visions of a Nazi conquest of the world: "It sounds bad, and if it is that bad, we would impoverish the nation trying to catch up with him; I'd rather not, thanks." He was an intelligent man. He was an outright anti-Nazi fanatic compared to the others in my home town who smiled at the thought of "little Germany" ever conquering big America. Even more disturbing was a kindred sensation which stole over me at the same time, that there was something magic about Hitler, and that he was as little comprehensible in natural terms as Dracula. When you reviewed his record, even then, it seemed there truly was a charm over him that defied defeat. It is only by the most

fantastic combination and concourse of circumstances imaginable
that a second-rate, psychopathic carpenter with a third-rate
intellect could become head of a nation of 66,000,000 souls, in
which he, after all, was a rank foreigner. But for Hitler the circumstances had fitted themselves together as though impelled to do so
by some evil, omnipotent sorcerer. With a background and a
theory of politics which were anathema to socialist-minded and, at
that time, anti-militarist Germany, he not only built a political
party but made it strong. With a minority party which had
already reached its peak of popularity and was heading into swift
decline, he became chancellor, then unbridled dictator of all
Germany. Head of a defeated nation which was surrounded by
strong and suspicious neighbours, he defied the peace treaty which
had been dictated by the victors and marched his troops against
the French border with utter impunity. And inside Germany,
one had to admit, for all his *wrongness*, he had constructed for
himself a foundation that was inordinately strong. Among a
people the majority of whom were not only against him at the
polls, but violently so (it is now easy to forget that in Hitler's
most successful election campaign the Nazi Party won only
slightly more than forty-five per cent of the votes balloted),
he had accomplished the impossible task of stifling all articulate
opposition. In a society with a large and influential intelligentsia,
he easily choked most of the intellectual class and brought the
remnants into line with his anti-intellectual culture. Though he
had overstrained Germany's never abundant resources to build a
war machine, economically his system was pervaded by an uncanny strength and stability, whose existence one had to admit.
I reasoned, and, I believe, with justice, that this was the stability
of a man on the treadmill, or that of Alice in the Looking Glass
when she had constantly to run twice as fast as before in order to
stay in the same place—an impossible sort of stability. But the
hair-raising thing was that to Hitler it was possible; Hitler always
did succeed in running twice as fast as before! You know the feeling
now. For it, the world has created a name: the "Hitler Myth",
one of the most insidious forces that has ever tried to creep unwanted into my psychological make-up. Later, this purely
psychological force crept over whole nations, and eventually
threatened the morale of the world.

*   *   *   *

By way of incident, I earned a precarious living working as a leg reporter for the *New Orleans Item*. By carefully manœuvring, I eventually managed to work my way into a department of the newspaper where my main duty was rewriting foreign dispatches from the news agencies and writing features on foreign affairs—mainly about Germany. My trip had tied me hopelessly to that subject and I suffered an unendurable itch to go back again and see more. That lucky star which made the old *Meanticut* wait until I had left her to crack in half and sink, shone down on me in January. I applied for a Rhodes scholarship, to study in Oxford, and I won it. The scholarship became valid in October, but I couldn't wait that long to go back to Europe. I pinched pennies, borrowed more, and in May I quit my job and—this time I travelled in style, paying $50 for transportation on a freighter—returned to Bremen.

A few small things had changed. From a mutual friend, I learned Otto was no longer around: he had gone to Spain as a "volunteer" to cut throats. I asked about a Communist dock-worker I had met before and learned he had been placed in a concentration camp for trying to talk up a dockers' strike for higher wages. Prices had gone up since last summer. There were still more uniforms, for Hitler had lengthened the term of military service for those already having their reflexes drilled, and called more classes to the colours. Inside Germany Hitler strengthened his grip on boys and girls, following the "Get 'em young" strategy, by making membership in the Hitler Youth compulsory. For those whose muscles were bigger and reflexes quicker, he set up "Adolf Hitler schools" to train this *élite* for service as obeying, feeling, fighting members of the Gestapo and the S.S. In the foreign field he was winning the first leg in World War II in Spain, giving his brand new airmen practice by ordering them to raze undefended Guernica to the ground, and his shiny new navy (including Otto) had warmed up with a bombardment of the Spanish port of Almeria—the first of the later notorious "reprisal actions". Perhaps more important, he was by way of repairing the only weakness in his armour, the absence of allies, by signing a friendship agreement with Italy, which was called by the German papers for the first time an "axis"; and later in the summer he had the Italian leader decorated with the German Grand Cross of the Order of the Eagle—all events which should have called the world to arms against him, but actually only evoked paper protests couched in the flimsy language of diplomacy. That Hitler could tell the world so plainly what he intended to do and then proceed about doing it calmly and naturally as Mr. Chamberlain took a walk in St. James's Park, was almost incontrovertible evidence that his stars were blessed.

Frankly the main object of my "research" this time was to try and find a fissure, a tiny crevice somewhere in his glorious monument to the Rightness of Might: a crack through which might flicker a spark of the light of encouragement that National Socialism was human and subject to the laws of compensation. I cast my nets far and wide over the Reich. But the haul yielded next to nothing. The only thing I won was further confirmation of my original judgment, that Hitler and war were synonymous terms. I travelled by train, and when my funds ran low, I began hitch-hiking. Hitch-hiking was exceedingly easy. I simply draped a small American flag over my single bag and those simple, friendly people stopped every time. When they could not take me along because they were turning off a half-mile farther, they stopped to apologize for the fact. The friendliness, the overwhelming hospitality of Germans to foreigners—and especially to Americans— was phenomenal. The *penchant* for Americans was, I think, induced by the showing my countrymen made in the Olympics in Berlin the year before. At any rate, for one reason or another, Americans appeared to be the German people's favourite foreigner.

I went to Munich, for the opening of the season's exhibition of seeded Nazi paintings in the "House of Art". Originally, I went in the hope of seeing, at long last, the Great Man himself, but he had come, seen and gone by the time I arrived. The exhibition was interesting in itself, however. It featured a comparison between pre-Nazi, "decadent" and "bolshevist" art and the clean photographic canvases painted at the behest and for the propagation of the Nazi faith and species. Nazi art drew from two themes, and two alone: Pornography and Militarism. Both had purely political purposes which the canvases shouted down at you from the walls. The pornographic art, naked women and men with not a detail, not a single hair left unemphasized, was aimed to induce in observers the urge to go right home and take measures to increase the race. And the other was aimed to demonstrate what a beautiful thing war can be—all the heroics of men with sweaty, grimy faces in muddy trenches holding an enemy at bay or, with "will power" and determination written in every sinewy wrinkle of their clothing, going over to attack in a blaze of glory. But there was not a dead man, or a crippled one, or one with a bleeding stump left in place of an arm, to be seen. War did not involve that sort of mess. You got a patriotic lump in your throat, if this disconcerting, last-named eventuality did not occur to you. Which was, after all, the purpose of the paintings.

From Munich I went to Berlin. I had a letter from the managing editor of the *New Orleans Item* to Fred Oechsner, head of the United Press in Berlin. Oechsner was a native of New Orleans, had studied in my university and had once worked on the *Item*. He was full of information and more than congenial during my stay there, but the full value of his acquaintance did not become obvious until later. He gave me his card, which I put in my passport and thought no more about it. Then I hitch-hiked to Kiel on the Baltic Sea, met a friend there and together we hitch-hiked across the border into Denmark for a much-needed breath of fresh air.

In Copenhagen I bought a few copies of an anti-Nazi German-language newspaper to take back to friends, and we returned. At the border I was stopped and searched, the papers were found and I was arrested. I stayed in prison in Flensburg on the border three days until a Gestapo officer, going through my passport found Oechsner's card in it. He immediately called me from my cell, apologized for the detention and set me free. He told me that if any further information about me were needed, he would call on Oechsner. Those were the fine spring days of Nazi history when Germany hoped to keep America out of its coming *débâcle*, until America's turn should come up, and, consequently, treated newspaper men and people who knew them as though they were diplomats.

Materially speaking, the Flensburg interlude was not too unpleasant. My shoes, belt and watch were taken from me (the rules stated this had to be done lest the prisoner, in despair, should use these articles, or a part of them, like shoestrings, to commit suicide!). Food was scanty and bad—two pieces of brown bread and thin soup thrice a day, and I was made to pay fifty pfennigs for each meal when I was released. On the wall was a sign informing me that by virtue of being an inmate I was no longer entitled for the period of my detention to make use of the German greeting "Heil Hitler"!

That was not a particularly hard blow. As to the other little privations, the warden did all he could to make up for them by allowing me a ten-minute smoke every morning and lending me a German translation of "Huckleberry Finn" to read. But the mere experience of seeing nothing but four grey walls twenty-four hours a day (I could not sleep due to the utter uncertainty of my situation; no charges had been made, the warden refused to let me contact the American consulate in Hamburg, and I was given no hint as to how long I would be held) left, as such experiences will, a bad taste in my mouth. In the best of circumstances, Germany is hard to bear for more than a month or two in a single dose, and after this, though my curiosity and interest in that country were genuine and insatiable, I took the first train from Kiel and resolved to go directly to France without a stop-over. In Munich, I changed trains—and plans.

Hitler was in Munich. I was told by a waiter in the Loewenbraeu beer cellar near the station, where I was having a beer while waiting for my train. The Fuehrer's white and red standard had been waving over the Brown House, the Nazi Party headquarters, since early morning. A friend of the waiter had told him that Hitler had come to see the opera that evening, a special gala performance of *Aïda*. I left my bag in the Loewenbraeu, indulged in the luxury of a taxi to the State Opera House and bought one of the last tickets in the pit.

I have seen Hitler many times since then, and in grander settings, but I have never been as excited as on this first visitation of the holy teutonic sacrament. Nothing could have convinced me so far beyond doubt that Nazism was black magic and he a weird, incredible wizard as this. Hitler arrived late, after the curtain had risen, certainly for reasons of safety. The audience rose as soon as the light flashed on in the royal box below me where I could not see him, and cheered and shouted the Aryan greeting I had lately temporarily been deprived of. From that moment the true stage was in the rear, in the red-plush box which once framed the person of the mad Ludwig and his coterie, not in front where the singers were. At the end of the first act, when the prima donna, borrowed from La Scala in Milan especially for the occasion, had made her fifth bow, two ushers carried to the stage an enormous bouquet of three or four dozen roses from which hung a broad red sash bearing Hitler's name in gold. I rushed downstairs to the entrance to the royal box and elbowed my way through a milling throng of Teutons all of the same mind. But the door to his box was closed, and beside it stood two tall black-uniformed young men on whose sleeves was embroidered in silver, "Adolf Hitler". They were the *Leibstandarte*, the bodyguard, the cream, or better the very scum off the cream of Aryanism, with magnificent reflexes and no brain at all.

I sat tortured with the pains of Tantalus through the next act, able to feel the presence of the Almighty, but not to see him. When the curtain fell, I rushed around the tier to a place on its left arm, and broke a space between two portly Germans on the balustrade. There, about thirty yards below me, like a flash of light from the hammer of Thor stood Siegfried, in tails, leaning on the railing of his box and smiling out at his subjects. It was without doubt the single most impressive spectacle I have ever seen. The spectacle was impressive because Hitler was not. Had he been a heroic figure like Washington, Gladstone or Bismarck, it would have been different. But he was not. He was a short, very short, little, comical looking man. Had his eyes had the firm, warm glow of Lincoln's, or the dash of Kaiser Wilhelm's, it would have been different, but his eyes were beady little black dots with timid circles under them. Had his moustache the boldly turned up ends like that of Hindenburg, it would have been otherwise. But his was a laughable little wisp of hair not as broad as his crooked mouth or the under-part of his nose. That was what, after you smothered your first unconscious smile, alarmed you, and brought back in its fullest strength the haunting fear of the Myth. *This* was the thing that had built a party in impossible circumstances, taken over control of a nation and created the mightiest army in the world. This, the "apotheosis of the little man", was what I saw as the blood-spitting, fire-breathing monster of the future. This funny little figure with its crooked smile, flapping its hand over its black-coated shoulder in salute, was God the omnipotent and infinite, Siegfried the hero of Nordics, and Adolf Hitler, the coming ruler of a destroyed world. That was Hitler in 1937, before he evolved from the Little Man to the Conqueror, and his appearance, demeanour and manner altered to fit his new role. Then, in 1937, he was not entirely sure of himself; and you could read it in his whole make-up.

Hitler then retreated to the back of his box for a lemonade. I watched him back there sipping it and talking to a man in a brown uniform, then I left for the station and France, then the boat-train, London and Oxford.

*   *   *   *

Oxford was bad medicine. My American liberals had been difficult with their adoration of the ikon of "open-mindedness", but their attitude was downright rash compared with the stony calm with which that breed called "Oxonians", both dons and students, heard my stormy predictions and awful warnings. I acquired the reputation of a "harmless but annoying zealot", as one young gentleman put it, my first night inside the grey walls of Merton College.

The impression I created was an exaggerated one due to two misfortunes. First, by some cruel mischance I was taken to the rooms of the stuffiest, most exasperatingly shallow elements in the college, a kind of atmosphere which always makes one doubly aggressive in argument. Second, I assumed that British beer could be poured into one in the same quantities and the same tempo as light German lager, and acted on that assumption to my own undoing. The heat of the argument that ensued was all on my side, not theirs, and was due not to any particular factual dispute but to the frustrating ineffectiveness with which my remarks shattered against the stone wall of their ingrown British casualness. They chastized me in fatherly tones for taking "the thing" seriously, which was simply pouring oil on an already waxing fire. At length, unable to grow madder or suffer more, I stood and wobbled to the door, where I shouted with a flourish they would rue these days of taking Hitler lightly, and took my leave. Outside, I abandoned a quart or so of undigested beer in the quadrangle and wobbled up to my room. Next morning, suffering from a bitter hangover I resolved to leave; I was either a misfit or wasn't, but was in the wrong element. At lunch time, Karl Price, from Kentucky, came up to my rooms and told me he had a hangover, didn't like the place even when he was sober, and thought he would pack up and go home. That was no end of relief to me. Together we then visited a second-year American student who, with very little struggle against our waning wills, prevailed on us to stay. We did, and it took us about three days to be glad of it. In those three days I discovered there were also Englishmen, even in Oxford, who could be classified as human beings, and in another week I had found my way into an amenable milieu, and in a month I felt as though I had lived in the cloisters of Oxford all my life. The reputation that institution of learning has in America, and this prejudiced me against it at first, of being the ultra-ultra of snobbism is greatly out of date. It may have been once a valid verdict, but since the first world war an increase in free scholarships, especially those endowed by the British trade unions, has multiplied the number of students from the working class who study at Oxford. Several of my best friends there were penniless young men and women from the distressed areas of Wales.

Academically, Oxford was almost totally wasted on me. It was saved from being a total academic waste by some conscientious application to economics. I suffered from an affliction which affects many American Rhodes scholars; after four years of university in America I was a little weary of academic life, a little impatient at the tireless conservatism, weighing of every possible point of view, and the refusal to adopt conclusively any one of them, which liberal education necessarily involves. During the first term, I applied myself diligently, but academic diligence gradually gave way in the face of my German experiences which constantly shouted at me to Do Something! Inevitably, I gravitated to the extra-curricula political clubs. I visited the Conservative Club, a tiny ineffectual group of wealthy students, numbering about one hundred members, then the Liberal club, with about three times as large a membership but still a little too equivocal for my tastes. Finally I settled in the Labour Club, a live and thriving branch of the British Labour Party, which took its politics seriously, believed in action far outside the radius of Oxford and had the unbelievable membership of a thousand students.

The Labour Club was an incredible organization. It was less a part of the university than a competitor of it. It maintained its own classes and lecture courses, with its own roster of tutors and lecturers, including men of the calibre of G. D. H. Cole, Sir Arthur Salter, R. H. S. Crossman, A. D. Lindsay, and a score of others. Its curriculum included four times as many lectures, five times as many lecturers as my own college, Merton!

To an American, accustomed to belonging to political clubs
with membership totalling ten or twelve, the scale of the Labour
Club meetings was startling. Meetings were not meetings, but
mass demonstrations attended by as many as two or three thousand
people. The quality of the speakers justified the audiences: Sir
Stafford Cripps, Harold Nicolson, Professor Harold Laski, John
Strachey, Captain Tom Wintringham, Herbert Morrison,
William Gallacher, and dozens of others. In London, people were
paying pounds to hear Paul Robeson sing, but he came to Oxford
to sing before the Labour Club for no fee whatever.

The energy of the students who made up the membership was
something to wonder at. The leaders of the Club became, in plain
language, Labour Party organizers rather than students. Besides
arranging big socials, publishing a newspaper, planning mammoth demonstrations and parades on the streets of Oxford, they
also helped organize trade unions in the Morris motor-car works
and in the adjoining Pressed Steel factory. At week-ends the
Club chartered buses and carried several hundred students to
London to march, carrying banners and posters, down Oxford
Street to Whitehall, to demonstrate in Trafalgar Square or before
No. 10, Downing Street.

I drank deep of the political spring, and had more fun than I
have had before or since. As I had, in America, been an able
keeper of score-boards at football games to augment my personal
funds, my first assignment in the Labour Party was as a member of
the poster-drawing squad. From this I was graduated to writing a
column of comment in the weekly magazine, and then to inclusion
on the list of speakers who every week made the rounds of colleges
to propagate the faith (principal theme: Germany). My progress
was eventually so good that I was proudly chosen to become a
member of little groups who stole out of college in the wee hours
of morning on missions of painting political slogans like "Chamberlain must go"! and "Throw out the men of Munich"! on
prominent spots in town. The marks of one of these escapades are
still printed big as day on the pavement before the headquarters of
the Oxford police, unless the town fathers have found some way to
remove creosote and tar which we did not think of when we determined to use that medium of political expression. On several
occasions, I joined in trips to the House of Commons where, in
small groups, we called our local M.P.s out of the chamber in the

middle of sessions and presented them with oral petitions to vote against Chamberlain. On another I picketed the Prime Minister's residence at No. 10 Downing Street, wearing a sandwich board and shouting in unison with others, "Throw the rascals out"! All this was, of course, for me, illegal, which made it more fun than ever. For American students entering Britain were made to sign a pledge they would not accept "employment, paid or unpaid", and this catch phrase the Home Office interpreted rather broadly, to include, on one occasion, unpaid employment of an American student in the London School of Economics on a Socialist newspaper. He was asked to leave the country.

A Rhodes-scholar institution was tea with Lady Astor at Cliveden once a year. I was prejudiced against Cliveden for the role it was playing in British politics at the time, so my reaction is a foregone conclusion. With Lady Astor in the lead we made a tour of the estate viewing points of interest. Then we returned to the mansion and sipped tea and plucked crumpets from bouquets of them and other goodies on enormous silver platters. The Grand Finale was a one-lady show by Lady Astor, who donned a feathery hat, crammed a set of protrusive false teeth in her mouth and gave us an "Imitation of an English woman imitating an American woman". Lady Astor also gave several tea-parties for us in London at which George Bernard Shaw and Mr. Chamberlain were invited. Mr. Chamberlain and I regretfully to declined the invitation to the tea arranged for him; he had a date with the Cabinet and I had one with the Labour Club—patrolling No. 10 Downing Street in sandwich boards.

Vacations, which were frequent and long (there were three a year and they totalled six months), I spent mostly in Germany. Once, however, I broke my routine and took a trip to Russia. That land impressed me disgustingly favourably for an individual who was still more Liberal than Socialist. Contrary to the development of my reactions in Germany, Russia looked better the longer I stayed and the more I saw. Russia was not neat, clean and orderly. Russia was dirty and disorderly. But the spirit of the thing got me. The Bolsheviks did not inherit cleanliness and order; they inherited a wrecked feudal society, and in a relatively short period wonders had been done. The edges were rough and the effort was amateur. But that was just it; it was amateur, everybody was building it. You got the impression that each and every little individual was feeling pretty important doing the pretty important job of building up a State, eager and interested as a bunch of little boys turned loose in a locomotive and told to run it as they please. It showed promise like a gifted child's first scratchings of "a house" on paper. *Klein aber mein*; a little but mine own, as the proverb goes. What is more the standard of living was definitely rising, not falling. The whole picture was not as pretty as the German one, but the atmosphere, utterly devoid of any trace of militarism or racial prejudice, was clean and healthy as the streets were dirty. I knew all along the atmosphere reminded me of a word, but I couldn't think what it was until I got back to Germany. The word was "democracy". That, I know, is a strange reaction to a country which is well known to be a dictatorship, but the atmosphere simply did not coincide with the newspapers' verdict. There are a multitude of objections to arriving at any fixed conclusion. I travelled with Intourist; I did not speak Russian as I did German; I saw only part of Russia and stayed only a month. I know the objections, and for that reason, I did not arrive at a conclusion. I postponed it. But that, in itself, speaks well for Russia. I couldn't postpone fixing a point of view about Hitler. Those who tried got fooled, horribly fooled, and Hitler ultimately had to make up their minds for them in a rather forceful manner.

Watching the incredible succession of events in those years was like an experience I had once in a hotel in Holland, gazing blankly from the window of my room and smoking a pipe; suddenly across a canal, I saw an empty parked automobile, its brakes apparently jarred loose by passing cars, begin to roll slowly, very slowly and calmly down the incline towards the un-protected edge of the canal. It was a strange little feeling watching the car edge downward with studied, easy deliberation, with not a soul but me to see. I shouted weakly at nobody for somebody to do something. It took only seconds, but it felt like several minutes until the little car toppled over the edge of the canal and splashed into the water. Hitler walked into Austria. At an interval of a month, I followed his path to desolate Vienna; its streets were empty, its population reduced at one blow of the Gestapo by one-fourth. While the notorious committee for the non-intervention of foreign nations in Spain pondered long and deeply, Spain succumbed to the intervention of two foreign nations, against the expressed will not only of the Spanish people, but of the overwhelming majority of the American, British and French people. Munich Happened. I did not go to Germany then or the vacation afterwards; I didn't believe I was quite up to taking the insolence and boastfulness of a nation fresh from achieving one of the biggest easy steals in history. Not only the general direction, but also the specific strategy of Nazi policy was becoming clearer. By a process of elimination one could arrive at two possible strategies: first, the Nazis had taken Austria to pincer Czechoslovakia, then taken Czechoslovakia to pincer Poland to get a contiguous border for a war against Russia (and this, I think, many members of the British ruling classes expected and hoped for at the time, but by no means all of them), or they were following the same procedure to clear their rear for an attack on France, then England.

At the end of my second year in Oxford, I was elected head of the Labour Club. Since I was the first American student ever to hold this position, and took it seriously, I rushed off to Germany at the end of term to sharpen up my zeal. Nothing made me hate Nazism, fear it, and long to do some little thing to destroy it more than a few, long, deep breaths of its own atmosphere. I returned to Munich. The main new feature was that the blank space, in which the German press wrote its particular hate of the season, was filled in big red letters with the name of Poland. That fitted well into the logical sequence of conquests. But what I had not reckoned with was the increasing intensity of attacks, in the press and on street-corner placards, on Britain. Something unusual was brewing and my German friends warned me of it: "*Dort im Osten ist etwas los*", they said with a shake of their fingers at me. Something was happening with Russia. I could not believe it although the indications became plainer every day. Nazi newspapers which had, daily for six years, carried flaming attacks on Russia and Communism, had suddenly ceased even mentioning those two subjects. One newspaper which published over an account of the British-Russian negotiations for a mutual defence pact, the headline "London bows its head to bloody Moscow", was confiscated an hour after the edition had reached the news-stands. The weekly Nazi magazine, *Die Woche*, was publishing a series of articles on Britain and Russia entitled "Gentlemen and Bolsheviks through two decades", in which the British came off a bad second best in comparison with the Russians. In bookshop windows the barricade of viciously anti-Soviet books became conspicuous by their sudden disappearance.

Confused, I returned in August to London. The morning after I arrived the news was published in the London papers: the one element which I had hoped to see rip a fissure in my perfect Prussian monument to war had been eliminated. Russia had agreed not to engage in war against Germany. There is no attempt here to place the blame for the failure of the British-Russian negotiations. Russia's individual demands on Britain were apparently severe. At the same time the real reason why any negotiations between two parties break down is not over any individual specific points so much as because of a mutual distrust, and at this time, the reputation of the British Government in international affairs was a good deal worse and more conducive to distrust than that of the Soviet Government. The decision can, however, be left to history. To me, the point was that once again, Adolf Hitler had succeeded in running twice as fast as the moment before. The funny little man had manœuvred the world into war; and more than that, he had manœuvred the world into a position at the beginning of the war in which all the advantages were on his own side.

I confess another false calculation. In this moment of depression, I felt certain the Chamberlain Government would not take up Hitler's challenge, and that Hitler would destroy Poland unhampered by a threat from another quarter. Next he would have France, next Britain, next Russia—*ad infinitum et ad nauseam*. In that I was wrong. I lived, worried, in a students' home in University Street in London, and one fine autumn morning after Hitler had attacked Poland I took a bus and went to the *News of the World* building off Fleet Street, to the United Press office. Inside, I asked for Webb Miller, the U.P.'s chief correspondent. Webb Miller came outside to see me and he was nervous and excited. I asked him, if war should come between Britain and Germany, might I have a job. He said I could come in and take a desk. War had just been declared.

II

MYTH'S PROGRESS

THE HITLER-CAN'T-BE-LICKED Complex is an unpleasant leech on your spirit no matter which way you take it. But—always assuming you have climbed, or descended, the requisite number of stages to become fully aware of it—it is a lot more enervating when you have to suffer it in its own specially created environment inside Germany, than when experienced from a goodly distance and over a number of frontiers *via* newspapers and radio sets. In America and England, one can always forget it for periods, even in war-time, by taking in Ginger Rogers and Fred Astaire at the Capitol, or turning on Eddie Cantor instead of the news. In Germany there is no easy escape. Films never miss an opportunity to drag it in somewhere. You can see a perfectly good movie in which the hero gets his woman and things are working up to a fine happy ending and just when you're beginning to congratulate yourself that the Nazi angle has been left out, at the very end, Hero and Heroine are married, have a child and visit him in school and he greets them in a Hitler Youth uniform, and instead of saying "Hello, Mother and Dad", snaps to attention and shouts "Heil Hitler"! You can twist your radio dial until it breaks and you won't get anything else. You can't even take a quiet walk in the park without running into a yellow sign on a bench announcing that "Jews are forbidden" to sit there, which carries you straight back to it. When I went to work in London, whose communications with Germany were cut forthwith, I was certain that the queer, irresistible sort of sadism to which I had subjected myself for three years was over for good. I could never again see Germany until the battle was lost and won; until either the Hitler Myth had expanded to its logical, all-enveloping conclusion and the swastika waved over Whitehall and Washington, or some dilatory silver bullet had found the heart of the National Socialist system. But the ways of Fate are proverbially strange. Certainly the strangest single thing it ever did was so to arrange circumstances that a wall-paper hanger could initiate a second and greater World War. To me, the second strangest thing was the way not even world war could keep me out of Germany. It was along these lines that my thoughts were wandering when my train drew into Stettiner Bahnhof, Berlin, on New Year's Day, 1940.

After three months in London, Webb Miller had sent me to Copenhagen by aeroplane to be on tap in the event of hostilities breaking out between Russia and Finland. After I had spent two months in Copenhagen, Fred Oechsner, in Berlin, demanded an addition to his staff, and, since I could speak German, Miller ordered me to go to Berlin.

In London, the mere fact that the Chamberlain Government had at long last been moved into creaky action against Hitler had stirred a faint breeze of hope inside me. But, after my first glance at Berlin, the night-and-day contrast between the ways the two nations had entered the war destroyed that mite of alleviation as completely as Hitler destroyed the Polish army. Aside from the black-out, Berlin had slid smoothly and almost imperceptibly into a state of war, with that exasperating calmness and stability in which every circumstance is reckoned with and each eventuality provided for. London, on the other hand, was pitiful with confusion and unpreparedness. The axiom that the British Government is one of amateurs never seemed truer than in those first months of the war.

As an appropriate beginning, some damned fool mistakenly turned on the air-raid sirens a quarter of an hour after Mr. Chamberlain's voice, declaring war, had died off the air, and sent seven million people running to the cellars with frightful Wellsian visions of ten thousand Nazi bombers hurdling the cliffs of Dover and pummelling London to ashes in a single blow. I was forced into an underground dance-hall by a zealous air-raid warden who had apparently read all the books published on his new profession by H.M. Stationery Office. Under the heading "Panic —how to avoid same", he had obviously read that the perfect warden always smiles so that his spirit will become contagious and reinforce the spirits of all. Also, patrons should be made to sing. For an hour we sang desperately about Packing up our Troubles in our old Kit-Bag, and a dozen other themes equally cheerful. When the all-clear sounded, and I came out into the light of day again, it was, I confess, almost with disappointment that I observed not a single window-pane was broken after sixty minutes' expenditure of nervous energy by seven million souls and bodies.

Prices went up like rockets. Trains were overcrowded and passenger traffic in near chaos. A million London children were
evacuated to the country and in little more than a month or two
most of them had wandered back home, for one reason or another.
Rationing was officially introduced, but it was months before the
first crude system was applied.

Most distressing of all at that time was the amateurish struggle
to get a Ministry of Information operating to compete with Dr.
Goebbels' high-powered, 12-cylinder propaganda machine. For
sins I am not yet acquainted with, I was sentenced by the United
Press to service covering the new Ministry in London, and suffered
all the many agonies of its birth and learning to crawl. I wrote
nothing. I spent my days at the U.P. desk in the Ministry playing
rummy with an *Evening Star* correspondent, and trying un-
successfully to teach a couple of cockney messenger boys how to
talk with a Dead-End Kid accent at their repeated and urgent
request. There was no news; or rather there was, but the Ministry
did not release it. What came, reached us in colourless drivels and
hours after it had ceased to be of interest. Censorship was chaotic.
Though the censors were all well-meaning, and some of them, like
K. Zilliacus, extremely intelligent men, ultimate authority regarding what could be passed and what not was indefinite and the result was confusion. My principal job soon became that of getting
stories through the censorship for the United Press with as little
butchery from the censors as possible, a job which involved more
diplomacy than I was capable of.

Of less immediate concern to me, but far more important, was
the incomparable vapidity the Ministry managed, with effort, to
infuse into the propaganda it created for its own people. Propaganda releases were entirely without a trace of imagination or
ingenuity; they were dull tracts on phases of the British war effort,
written apparently by civil servants who knew their fields well but
had no idea as to how to make interesting reading matter of them.
Propaganda photographs consisted of (*a*) a few Bond Street
mannequins in steel helmets (this at least showed a spark of
imagination, just a spark); (*b*) Mr. Chamberlain, with umbrella,
promenading in St. James's Park and being saluted by two soldiers,
and (*c*) a batch of full-dress snapshots of the King and Queen.
War, though a terrible thing, could be made exciting. A defensive
war against an aggressor whom every people in the world feared

and most of them hated, could be made heroic. For years, the Nazis had been making just war in general an exciting and heroic thing with great success; but Britain with a grand cause to fight for did not know how to start taking advantage of opportunities that begged to be taken advantage of. One had to agree with the government's many critics that the old ruling school was suffering from an appalling bankruptcy of ideas.

But the best single point in Britain's case for war, the fact that it was a Democracy, also became the saving grace of the Ministry of Information. People could complain, and they did. The press poured forth reams of criticism, bitter to the point of being insulting to Lord Macmillan, the Minister at the time, but in its ultimate effect, refreshing and cleansing. David Low, the *Evening Standard's* great cartoonist, led off a vigorous campaign by editorial artists against the Ministry. The case of the People *v.* The Ministry of Information was perhaps best put by the illustrated *Picture Post*, which published the photograph of a blacked-out, fenced-in field, before which a signpost warned: "To the British People: KEEP OUT! This is a private war between the Admiralty and the War Ministry on one hand and Hitler on the other". On the following pages was a series of photographs to be compared with those which had been sent to the British Ministry for censorship. The German pictures were moving, full of action and imagination. The British pictures carried captions equally interesting, but in the squares above the captions were only blank spaces— blank except for the tiny notation: "These pictures were not passed by the British censor".

Finally, Lord Macmillan called the entire army of correspondents, foreign and domestic, to a closed conference and invited a frank and open airing of woes. Though that memorable session was secret then, it now belongs to history; the greater part of the Ministry's weakness at that time has been removed, and there is no longer any harm in telling about it. It was the most heartening exhibition of uninhibited, democratic grousing I have ever witnessed. The air was thick with charges, and their tone was bitter in the extreme. But the most heartening feature was the manner in which mere newspaper reporters refused to allow the issue to slip from a high political plane—a height, in fact, which was not often reached in the House of Commons itself. The reporters were not concerned about this or that little technical mistake; this or that error on the part of an individual censor, or the lack of imagination shown in any particular propaganda hand-out. They were concerned about the ingrown attitude of the British rulers which was reflected in the great number and general character of all these errors. The attitude, frozen into the fabric of the "ruling class mind" by years of privilege was one of indifference to the people. Whether the leaders were conscious of it or not, they did actually consider this war was, like the matter of government in general, a purely private affair. When the people were needed, later, to bear the burden of fighting, England would expect them to do or die, but Cliveden had bought the concession on reasoning why, and it was no affair of the people's. The storm broke in a climax with the contribution of W. N. Ewer, the diplomatic correspondent of the *Daily Herald*. Ewer accused the leaders of the Ministry of boring the British people hopelessly stiff, simply because the Ministry was indifferent to the spiritual needs of the people. He declared that when the British people would later be called on to fight this war, they would, if this policy continued, be neither able nor willing to resist Hitler. In a blaze of eloquence, Ewer finished by bluntly accusing the leaders of the Ministry of Information of high treason to the people and recommending that the full penalty prescribed by law for this crime be imposed on the responsible leaders. The words were bold, but the burst of applause which came when he sat down proved how strongly the whole assembly agreed. The session did much. The tone of the Ministry's general efforts changed a great deal after that, and, so far as I know, the change, though it has made considerable progress, has not yet halted. When the meeting was over I felt more encouraged regarding the chances of beating Hitler than at any time since war had been declared.

The German Ministry in the Wilhelmstrasse, which inevitably became my centre of gravity in Berlin, worked with that uncanny smoothness which was so disconcertingly typical of all things Nazi. News gushed promptly and copiously from the ticker-tape of D.N.B., the official news agency. In press conferences, twice a day, once in the Foreign Office and once in the Propaganda Ministry, half a dozen spokesmen, diplomatic, military and economic, sat at tables before reporters and made expansive comments and issued reports meaty with fact. There were always, of course, several layers of propaganda feathers. But that, after all, is the principal demand made on a foreign correspondent especially in time of war—to be able to dig through the feathers and work the remaining meat, together with other information on the particular subject at hand from other sources, into good dispatches. Criticism was, of course, not allowed, but in those days of Nazi high summer there was seldom need of any criticism of the technical functioning of their propaganda machine.

The best of all its many smooth features was the total absence of censorship of press cables. Radio correspondents had to submit their scripts to a triple-barrelled censorship of the Propaganda Ministry, the Foreign Office and the High Command, but for newspapermen there prevailed a liberal policy regarding news transmission which was singular in a state where all else was so rigidly controlled. One had but to leave the text of a story at the cable office or at a special counter in the Propaganda Ministry and it would be sent without delay and without censorship direct to one's home office. Actually, there did exist a check after-the-fact which amounted to a general supervision by the Ministry: if, after the cabled story was published in America, the local German consul found something objectionable in it, he would report the fact back to the Wilhelmstrasse. One of Dr. Goebbels' subordinates would then call in the correspondent who had written the story and punish him according to a scale ranging from a polite wrist-slap to banishment from Germany. However, the system made the job of routine reporting tremendously easier than was the case in London. And it had to be admitted that this policy did bespeak a strength of sorts: but liberalism in these things is a luxury which a winning nation can always enjoy. Later, things were much, much different in Germany.

Berlin was a good spot to work from. In many ways it was probably the best spot in Europe for a journalist. The context of the times must, however, be kept in mind. Those were the days before the catchword of American foreign policy had even advanced as far as "short of war". America was still undecided about the moral arguments of the two warring sides. And Germany, by means of the Propaganda Ministry, still hoped either to keep America undecided or to tilt her favour towards Germany. It was, after all, through the eyes of a relatively small corps of reporters in Berlin that America saw Germany and that large and waxing portion of Europe under Germany's control. The Propa-

ganda Ministry was one great big optometrist's shop which specialized in grinding rose-coloured lenses.

More ardently than any other national group of journalists, the
American corps was courted with a multitude of favours. To get
the Nazi facts and figures on some phase of German life—a story
on food supplies, biographies of generals, the progress of prices, etc.
—it was not necessary to dig through files and wait weeks for ap-
pointments; one simply had to mention the intention to write the
story in the Ministry and within twenty-four hours a list of sources
would be made out, copies of periodicals furnished, and interviews with the personalities involved arranged. A special department of the propaganda organization busied itself arranging excursions to the particular front in existence at any time, to towns
which had been bombed, to aeroplane factories and field hospitals.
The purpose of the excursions was obviously and naturally propagandist; but, again, with some perspicacity, one could always
glean good stuff out of what was offered.

In their private lives, too, journalists were smothered with
favours and special privileges. The Propaganda Ministry maintained a department which rendered the invaluable service of cut-
ting red tape in a country bound up in it: it arranged leases for
apartments, got visas for vacation trips, secured special passes to
big events and tickets at reduced rates to operas and films. Newspapermen were granted double food rations and, while the civil
population was limited to a certain number of "points" worth of
clothing purchases a year, no limit was placed on the amount of
clothing correspondents could buy with special permits from the
Ministry. To fill out already abundant rations, too, the foreign
press and radio were allowed unlimited importations of coffee,
butter and eggs from outside. The pass department of the Ministry
equipped each reporter with a little red identification card which
worked like a magic wand at getting taxis, which grew scarce as
the war proceeded, at smoothing over minor infringements of
law, with policemen, and also allowed the holder the luxury of
listening at will to foreign radio broadcasts.

Lest the gentlemen of the press should not find sufficient good
food and comfort in Berlin's restaurants, Dr. Goebbels invested
half a million marks of the people's money in redecorating and re-
building the old Foreigners' Club on Leipziger Platz into a palatial refuge for journalists. It consisted of a great, ornate restau-

rant, with loudspeakers built in the walls, to page patrons, perhaps
the finest bar in all Berlin, and big rooms equipped with newspapers from all over the world next to other rooms filled with
typewriters and telephones. After the Foreigners' Club was rebuilt
it was not even necessary to maintain an office, for all the con-
veniences of an office, and many more, were provided in the club-
rooms. In competition, Ribbentrop built the *Foreign Press Club* in
the residential west end of Berlin which was smaller but still more
comfortable. On tables lay neat folders containing the day's service from Reuters, D.N.B. and a dozen lesser news agencies, and a
file of the London *Times* was always on hand in the reading room.

Perhaps the best advantage of all was the regulation allowing
foreign reporters to receive money from their home offices at a rate
of exchange two or three times better than the official rate. The
official rate of exchange was two and a half marks for one dollar.
At the special rate, Americans received from five to seven marks
for a dollar, which virtually tripled their income at a loss to
nobody except the German taxpayers.

It is a remarkable commentary on the Nazi system's powers of
attraction that these myriad favours failed entirely of their purpose with men who had no particular reason to be resistant—the
American corps. Of all the American groups I mixed with in
Germany, the journalists were least attracted to Nazism. Students,
business-men and even diplomats, as groups, showed far more
readiness to find a psychological *mode de vivre* with their adopted
environment. With very few temporary exceptions, the whole
American journalist colony not only remained opposed to
Nazism, but grew aggressively so with time. When Wallace Deuel,
of the *Chicago Daily News*, returned to America after seven years in
Germany and wrote for his paper one of the most biting attacks on
Nazism ever written by a journalist, in Berlin the official foreign
office spokesman, Braun von Stumm, wailed with anger. After
Bill Shirer, of Columbia Broadcasting System, published his
Berlin Diary, his name was put at the top of the Nazi list of
unmentionables. Both were called "ingrates" who had abused
"the years of hospitality and cordial co-operation we have
offered them".

The all-round quality of the American corps in Berlin was, in
my opinion, at least, the highest of all the various American groups
in Europe. Otto D. Tolischus, of the *New York Times*, whom I met

shortly before the Nazis politely hinted to him that he had best leave the country, was, I believe, the ablest of the entire original corps. He was a less easy stylist than many of the others, but his stories were conscientious, scholarly and, from a factual standpoint, squeamishly correct. It is impossible to "rank" the others: Wallace Deuel of the *Chicago Daily News*, Bill Shirer of C.B.S., who wrote the best book to come out of war-time Germany; Fred Oechsner of U.P., who unfortunately gave too little time to writing and too much time to being the best office boss in Berlin, and Louis Lochner of A.P. and Pierre Huss of the Hearst papers, both of whom have won the Pulitzer Prize.

One by one, most of these men became nauseated with too many years of fighting their way through the feathers of propaganda, and generally sick at heart—much the same affliction I have already described in my own case—took their leave of Germany for good. I was overcome time and again with the same desire. But the insidious reasoning, that I had stuck it out this long, why not stay just a little longer and see a little more, always held me there—I did not even take a vacation in two years—until the last moment.

The Germany-at-war to which I returned was little different from the Germany-at-peace I had left. In a state created expressly for the purpose of waging war, the line dividing the two conditions was bound to be a fine, almost invisible one. Rationing had been introduced on the first day of war. (*Buerger* who were told England began the war after long, treacherous preparation, were surprised to find their rationing system smoothly functioning, their ration tickets printed and waiting for them a few hours after the first bombs had fallen on Warsaw.) But it was not a measure of immediate necessity, but rather had the purpose of simply parcelling out, according to a schedule, the enormous reserves of foodstuffs Germany then possessed. I was later told by an authoritative source that the immediate introduction of a fairly stiff rationing scheme was, too, partly psychological; for the government wanted to avoid the impact on German morale of having to reduce big rations at a later stage, by introducing rather Spartan rations at the very beginning; he said Germany intended to finish the war within a reasonably short time and with no recourse to any decreases in the people's nourishment. A few amenities disappeared, and their absence was certainly felt—coffee and chocolate, for example—but almost all the others were there in abundant quantities: liquor, beer, wine, cigarettes, etc. That familiar un-war-time-like orderliness, neatness and cleanliness still prevailed, and the whole atmosphere was incompatible with the strain Germany had undergone preparing for war and the new strain involved in beginning one. The mobilization of several million soldiers to fight in Poland, a gargantuan performance, had, it was evident, had no more effect on the German home front than the wash of a motorboat on a giant liner at sea. It was heart-breaking, but it seemed true, when a German officer, at whose side I was strolling down Unter den Linden in the first spring of the war told me: "Look around you, Herr Smith. Nowhere a sign of war. Not the slightest difference from two years ago. Is that not the best argument for our strength? We shall never be beaten". From Berlin, the war *was* something unreal. It was something you read about, happening in another planet. One of the best of Wallace Deuel's many excellent stories dealt with this uncanny feeling. It was an "atmosphere" story describing Berlin in that spring, expressing in better words what we all felt and thought. How, under these circumstances, could the horror of war ever be brought home to the German people? War wasn't so bad. It was not a struggle of life and death. It was becoming the national sport, like cricket in England and baseball in America. Hitler was the all-American coach, and the aviators and submarine commanders whom he decorated with the oak-leaf to the Knights Cross of the Iron Cross, were the all-national team. Even in war, Adolf Hitler was master of his incredible treadmill.

Poland had collapsed in the Prussian gale like a house of cards (actually, from what the world later learned of German military might, Poland's performance was not too bad). From the second front in France, Germany had not even felt the pressure of the pea under the mattress in the story about the sensitive princess. Despite the strain on resources in the past seven years, raw materials for war purposes were still obviously not scarce. All Poland's war supplies now belonged to Germany. To augment them, Goering called on the public to give all their old metal scrap from cellars and attics to the government, and the response was awe-inspiring. In order to write a story on the collection, I visited about a dozen sifting depots and waded through rooms filled with corroded candlesticks, scratched busts of Kaiser Wilhelm and brass pitchers with broken handles—all of which added up to a handsome little reserve for more cannon and tanks. The first winter brought a little inconvenience bordering on suffering for the population—the coldest cold-spell Europe had experienced in half a century. The spell had nothing to do with the war; it was simply that heavy snowfalls and frozen canals hindered transport of coal to cities. I took a special diabolic joy in it, although, for me, it involved writing my dispatches in the U.P. office with gloves and an overcoat on to keep from growing numb.

I lived through that first war winter in a hope that was almost mean that summer and autumn would bring Hitler's delayed peak. No nation's resources are inexhaustible, even when replenished by conquest. And I, with the rest of the world, believed Hitler had at last reached the limit of easy conquest; the rest would be costly. On one side was Russia, whom the Nazis were not likely to attack until they could somehow split France off from Great Britain (which the press struggled all that winter to do through propaganda) and destroy them one by one. On the other side was that insuperable wall of concrete and steel—the Maginot Line. Germany would certainly attack the Maginot Line, or try and circumvent it through Holland and Belgium. But that I looked forward to as the welcome beginning of exhaustion.

Came the spring. One night while I boned over copy in the slot in the U.P. Office a query from New York was handed to me. From indefinite but well informed sources, New York heard the Germans were practising embarkation and debarkation of troops in Kiel on the Baltic Sea; what about it? Indifferently, I contacted all the sources available by telephone, and since they were all official or semi-official, they, of course, denied the report. Next morning, walking down Kurfuerstendamm, I learned in a manner which is shameful for a foreign correspondent, simply by buying a newspaper and reading it, that German troops had invaded Denmark and Norway. My negligence was inexcusable; not that I could have sent out any information of this character beforehand, for that would have subjected me to banishment or even arrest on a charge of "espionage" (one of the thinnest tight ropes a correspondent in Germany had to walk was that infinitely small thread between conscientious military reporting and espionage), but there was no excuse in not being prepared for the news. Knowing something is coming is half of covering it when it happens. There was a knack to covering Berlin—a knack to which I was not yet seasoned—of knowing what things to keep your eyes on, and when. Once the invasion had begun, I recalled lots of little weather-vanes: a woman I knew in Bavaria had written in a letter to me that many of my old friends there had recently been called up for training in mountain warfare; in Berlin for the two months before the invasion the railway stations had been filled with mountain chasseurs in their distinctive caps with *Edelweiss* badges on them. A little combining of facts should have told me the men came from Bavaria and Austria, they were passing through Berlin—obviously the direction of this great hegira was northwards. The sudden disappearance of mountaineers from Berlin, after a long and copious flow of them, should have given me an indication that the time for their action was nearing. And finally, the only place North of Berlin where there were mountains was Norway. One learns by error. I learned much from that one. After that, although I could never predict any specific details of coming events, I learned by keeping my eyes open, to tell general directions with some skill.

For the invasion of Holland and Belgium, most of these sort of indications were unavailable, for Berlin was not a junction in troop movements. But from friends and sources in Western Germany came scraps of information indicating the invasion was not far off.

My hopes sprang to new heights when the attack was launched on May 10. I felt certain that, this time, the great Dictator had overreached himself. For one thing, American opinion would be irreparably alienated by the aggression against neutrals, and American aid to the allies would increase. For another, he was opposed by the armies and resources of four nations, one of which had the reputation of being the greatest military force in the world. Finally, between Hitler and his objective, the conquest of France, stood the most powerful defence works ever created by man; the Maginot Line. Essentially, it was a conflict between the Hitler Myth and the Maginot Myth. (On a visit to the ruins of the famous fortifications just after the Germans cracked it, I determined with chagrin and disillusionment how completely mythical the latter was. Aside from a few palatial underground forts, the might of the fortifications was nine-tenths propaganda and one-tenth real, and the former came out of the conflict more potent than ever.) In four brief months; to be precise, in seventy-four days, those German resources I had hoped to see dwindle to exhaustion were reinforced by the bountiful resources and machines of no less than *five* more conquered nations.

The faster and higher false hopes rise, the faster and harder they fall. The feeling that took hold of me after the French armistice constituted one of the most demoralizing spiritual crises I have ever suffered. Surrounded by something I hated and knew was wrong, smothered by it and stuffed day after day with its indigestible propaganda; then watching it march from one triumph to another, was making dangerous inroads on my psychology.

It is amazing how even minds made of sterner stuff can be affected by experiencing from close up a long, steadily mounting, seemingly endless succession of successes by one man or an organization, and how the conviction imperceptibly steals upon them that these things cannot be beaten. The result is to cripple any will to counter-activity, to want to surrender in the face of something human beings have no control over. For my part, I have always tried, though not always successfully, to discipline my mind in what my old philosophy instructor called the "scientific attitude"; to believe every phenomenon can be explained in acceptable, natural terms, no matter how mysterious it may seem on preliminary investigation. Thus, it is no small confession I make when I admit the Hitler Myth was growing to alarming proportions in my mind. Living outside Germany the impact of the succession of incredible triumphs is not so shattering to one's psychology. Inside Germany, in that hermetically sealed atmosphere, it can become dangerous. It sounds fantastic, but I grew to fear with a terror the pressure of this mystical attitude—that Hitler and his evil progress were not natural—and what it might do to my balance of mind. For that reason, after the conquest of France, I forced myself to become interested in something which had been an utter bore to me before then: soldiery. I wanted to make the reasons, good hard tangible, down-to-earth reasons why Hitler could conquer three nations in forty-five days water-clear to myself as a defence against the encroaching Myth. I bought every book and pamphlet I could find on military strategy and arms in general, and the French campaign in particular. I read Guderian on Panzer war, Rommel's accounts of infantry combat in the World War, and built up a military library of several dozen volumes. The important point here is that a sane individual who at least makes it his aim to be intelligent, should be forced to follow a procedure like this, involving days and nights of tedious work, due to sheer fear of a spectre. If it was this difficult for me, who had satisfied myself of Hitler's wrongness, how virtually impossible it must have been for Germans, who had never been outside Germany, to disagree with the Fuehrer's words when on November 8, 1940, they heard he had barely escaped assassination in the Loewenbraeu cellar in Munich: "It must be the will of God"!

Hitler, himself, I saw many times during the first two years of war. My impression of him changed drastically. It may have been because he now constantly wore a uniform which suited him better than the ridiculous tails I had first seen him in, or it may have been—and there is a strong case for this—that Hitler himself changed. When I first saw him, he was a political phenomenon, but still untried in the field he loved most, the actual mechanics of war and conquest. Austria, his greatest diplomatic triumph at Munich, and the breath-taking military campaigns, were still ahead of him. But now he was the greatest conqueror in world history, the most hated and the most loved man alive. His walk, as he strode, hatless, up to the white rostrum of the Sports Palace to speak, was graceful and confident. Chatting on his balcony with Goering while crowds cheered him on his return from France he smiled, but there was no timidity about his crooked mouth. Once, I stood outside the gates of the chancellery and watched him drive out in an open car. From a distance of ten feet, his eyes appeared no longer the eyes of the funny little man, not yet entirely certain of himself, but were calm, hard and cruel, like the Apotheosis of the Military Man, which he had become. The impression that Hitler is self-conscious, however, remained. In fact, I was convinced that of all the millions on whom the Hitler Myth had fastened itself, the most carried away was Adolf Hitler, himself.

I vegetated on through the long black night of the second war-winter. I was losing my eagerness to see and learn in a tidal wave of despair. My lethargy was not unique. Already old names, long connected with news from Berlin, were disappearing for the simple reason that their owners were sick at heart. Tolischus and Deuel had gone. Shirer went. In the U.P. Office, that most

charming and congenial of chiefs, Fred Oechsner, had grown
fretful, nervous and difficult to work with. At the end of winter,
in suffocation, he followed the others to America for a much
needed breath of air. Brooks Peters of the *New York Times* told me
his turn was coming; he couldn't take it much longer. His fellow
correspondent on the *Times* staff, Percy Knauth, had already
packed up and gone to Switzerland. The pressure that forced
them, one by one, to desert Berlin was finally christened with a
name. Those of us who remained called it the "Berlin Blues".
The name stuck, to describe those awful pits of spiritual depression
each of us fell into with periodic regularity, and which grew
more severe as the war wore on.

There was one bright element in the whole dingy winter—the
R.A.F. Despite Goering's assurance to the populace that the
British would never reach Berlin, British bombers did suddenly
appear late one night, and dropped their loads on Babelsberg,
a southwestern suburb. Next day, the Propaganda Ministry
promptly herded us out to Babelsberg to show us how little
damage had been done. Then the British came again and dropped
bombs in Berlin proper. The Ministry poo-poohed the raid and
told us that henceforth, if these pin-pricks continued, they would
send army cars around to pick us up at our homes an hour after
each raid and we might direct the chauffeurs to take us anywhere
in Berlin and see for ourselves what scanty damage had been done.
Covering air-raids developed into the best fun a reporter could
have in Berlin. The Germans allowed us every freedom. We gave
running descriptions to New York on each occasion. One man
would sit at a teletype machine typing the information straight
to the Zurich office which relayed it without delay to New York,
and another would cover the telephones receiving reports from
other members of the staff who were observing the raid in all
parts of Berlin. Afterwards came the grand tour to see the damage.
I got no end of enjoyment dashing through the black streets of
Berlin at three and four o'clock in the morning from one flaming
building to another, stopping at tavern telephones at each
juncture to relay my description to the office. The Nazis were
still enjoying the luxuries only a winner may enjoy.

Then, one morning in the Ministry, Dr. Karl Boehmer, the
head of the foreign press section, announced that henceforth any
mention in our reports that a raid was going on at the time of

writing would be considered espionage. As the British came more regularly, one little freedom after another was removed. The dawn tours were discontinued. Finally, communications with the outside world were cut off altogether by the High Command during and for hours after air-raids. Richard Hottelet of the U.P. went out alone on several occasions to see what he could see following air-raids and was eventually arrested. The fact was, of course, that the raids were becoming more effective, and the High Command had muscled in on Dr. Goebbels' territory and forbade reporting the facts. In a year, the policy narrowed from one of excessive freedom for reporters to one of absolutely no freedom whatever. The last regulation, and the High Command could go no further than that, required that reporting an air-raid must be limited to sending only the brief, uninformative communiqué that was issued by D.N.B. several hours after the raid. The penalty for overstepping this infinitely restrictive boundary was imprisonment!

The British raids actually never reached the calamitous proportions that these measures would imply. In fact, I think no single British raid on Berlin could compare with any of the milder German raids on London during the great Blitz. The worst was the occasion on which the central area, around Unter den Linden, was peppered with fire bombs which made the famous street a sea of flame, setting afire more than a dozen buildings. On that night a British bomber, flying so low that his plane seemed to be skimming the roof tops, scored a direct hit on Goebbels' *Staats Oper* and burnt it to the ground. Another brilliant attack was delivered by the Russians last year. A single Russian bomber flew several hundred miles over the Baltic sea, then cut in sharply due south to Berlin, flying at a high altitude. Many miles outside Berlin, the plane cut off its motors and coasted down over the outskirts of the city to just a few hundred feet above the Stettiner railway station, where it dropped a whole cargo of explosives, and blasted the railway tracks into fantastic knots of steel. The bomber turned back and was safely away by the time the sirens were turned on ten minutes later. But the Russians made few visits, and the British still fewer, until, ultimately, Berlin was safe as any neutral city.

The decision of the R.A.F. command to discontinue regular raids on Berlin was unfortunate. Although the raids seldom resulted in serious material damage, they shocked civilian morale more effectively than any single feature of the war before the Russian campaign. Mornings after raids, people were in a miserable mood from lack of sleep and nervous strain. When the air attacks began early or lasted until after dawn, traffic was jammed and the whole business of life in Berlin was in chaos until noon and later. Friends parting at night created a new farewell term, in the place of *auf Wiedersehen*, wishing one another *Bolona* which is short for *bombenlose Nacht* (Bombless Night). The number of planes which took part and the damage done were of secondary importance. One single plane, without a single bomb to drop but which merely kept people nervous, afraid and awake in cold cellars for several hours could have done and could still do wonders to the morale of Berlin's grumpy millions. Perhaps there are good reasons for not carrying on a nuisance campaign like this every night.

Aside from these little episodes the second war-winter was a dingy one. The setting of events during and following it was not calculated to lift the gloom. In Berlin, with much pomp, the Japanese ambassador signed a tri-power pact with Ribbentrop and Ciano against America. In America, in a speech, Colonel Lindbergh saw no menace whatever to America, and, if there was, why waste all our armaments by sending them to Britain? In Africa, the British chased the Italians out of Cyrenaica, and Rommel, blessed by the star of the invincibility of Siegfried, promptly chased the British back to the Egyptian border. In the Balkans, the Greeks defied Mussolini and were by way of beating the devil out of him. Then Hitler marched into Yugoslavia and Greece and crushed both in twenty-one days.

While the Greek campaign was going on, I quit. I gave up, unconditionally and absolutely. For the sake of mere sanity, I had to get out. I stopped going to press conferences. I could not bear to go to those ornate rooms in the propaganda ministry and the foreign office and sit through sessions conducted by confident, cocky little bureaucrats who were overbearing with successful importance and generous with nasty remarks about America and England. In the Propaganda Ministry's press club on Leipziger Platz I insulted Doctor Goebbels' chargé for the American press, a crass, pea-brained individual named Karl Froelich, shouted in his face, and broke off relations with the club. My mood was a horrible one. I even got in wrangles with my own co-workers in the United Press, over no particular question, but simply due to disaffection on all our parts. Finally, I handed a letter of resignation to the U.P., went to the Foreign Office and applied for a permit to leave Germany. Oechsner cabled me from New Orleans to reconsider, but I was through for good with Germany and never wanted to breathe its atmosphere again.

That is, I was almost through. But not quite. Walking dolefully through the streets of Berlin one day after I had resigned from the United Press and was awaiting my exit permit from the German Government, I thought I saw one of those little weather-vanes of war pointing in a peculiar direction. It was in the window of a bookshop next to the restaurant called "Alois" which is run by Adolf Hitler's half-brother, on Wittenberg Platz, across from my apartment. Scanning the contents of the window I remarked the conspicuous absence of a favourite volume of mine, which had been on constant display for more than a year in that window. The book that was missing was a little collection of Soviet Russian short stories by Michael Soistshenko, and the title was *Schlaf schneller, Genosse* (the title was taken from a short story about a rickety Russian hotel in which a sign appeared above each bed: "*Sleep faster, comrade*, for another comrade needs your bed"). *Schlaf schneller, Genosse* had been for a year more than a book to me, it had been a close friend. It was the only Soviet Russian book which the Germans allowed to be published in Germany after the signing of the German-Russian pact. Once, for the United Press, I had written a lengthy feature story about it because of this. I had told about how the short stories were all satires on life in Soviet Russia, frank, bold and extremely funny. (For example, there was one story about how Uncle Ivan died, and Uncle Ivan's relatives tried for a month to get a hearse to take his body away and, when the hearse finally came, Uncle Ivan woke up from what was merely a hard drunk, so the hearsemen went away in disgust, and as soon as they had gone, Uncle Ivan collapsed and died of alcoholic poisoning, so his relatives, in frustration, simply put his body in the bath-tub which was never used anyhow and that was all there was to it. That was the style of these charming *feuilletons*.) I wrote that the Nazis permitted this book alone of all Soviet books because it was obviously unfavourable, and according to their calculations its publication would, at once, show that Germany was not afraid of Communist literature, and it would cast a bad light on Russia. I added that the result was a little alarming to the Propaganda Ministry which an official in that institution confirmed to me, for the little book was sold out three days after the first edition had reached the bookshops, and several more editions had to be printed. Germans were delighted, and one German woman who borrowed my copy, because the edition had been exhausted when she had tried to buy a copy, told me afterwards: "It's unbelievable. Why no German author could say things like that about Germany. He would lose his head." It raised Russia's stock far higher than the book censors had calculated.

Well, the volume was missing from the window, for the first time in a year. I wandered on home, but the observation stuck in my mind all that day and the next morning. So the following afternoon I went back to the bookshop, went inside, and, working on a hunch, told a salesgirl I wanted something on Russia and what did she have? My hunch was a square hit. She took me to a shelf filled with political books and pointed to my old friends with the screaming titles, which had lived in storage for almost two years: "The TRUTH about the Soviet Paradise", "The Betrayal of Socialism", "My Life in the Russian Hell". My friend, *Schlaf schneller* was nowhere to be seen. I told the salesgirl no and returned home.

There is in Berlin a handful of men who constitute a strange breed of animal, called on the expense accounts which American correspondents send home to their offices, "tipsters". Sometime some one should write a book about them, if he can ever determine with certainty on which team they were playing. They are smooth, charming, and say "Heil Hitler"! in public and tell strange stories about the Nazis, individually and collectively, in private. They work for the American press and enjoy a remarkably wide-open entrée to every office in the Wilhelmstrasse. But, as I once learned, the Wilhelmstrasse, on the other hand, has such a remarkably detailed dossier on each American reporter in Berlin, filled with facts that could only have been obtained from someone intimate with them, the breed must remain suspect. By far the most charming of them was a man called B. Since I am not yet sure who B's ultimate employers were, I cannot reveal his name. At any rate, I got in touch with B. right away. He said he was eating in the

Club that evening, so I, putting my recent resolution not to visit that place again deep down in my pocket, went there to meet him. Yes, he said, there were rumours: Hitler had presented a list of demands to Stalin. The most important was the lease of the Ukraine to Germany for ninety-nine years. It was rumoured that Stalin had accepted, for he thus avoided war and overthrow which was imminent anyhow, as everybody knew.

The next day I cancelled my plans to leave, and asked Harry Flannery of the Columbia Broadcasting System if an offer he had made me when I left U.P. was still open. Harry had a chance to go to Crete, which was then being attacked, and needed someone to cover Berlin so he took me on.

A few days later, Ivan Filipoff, the head of Tass, the Russian news agency in Berlin, called on the telephone. I was a special friend of Filipoff's for, in his first days in Berlin when Germans ignored him and other reporters stared at him as a red curiosity in this brown environment, I paid him a visit and offered to help him get adjusted if I could. He wanted to talk to me and suggested lunch in the Hotel Eden near my place. We met in the Eden restaurant and he told me the Russian language newspaper *Novoye Slovo* which the Nazis published in Berlin for *émigrés* had taken a sudden unfriendly line towards Russia in its editorial comments, and wild rumours were circulating. Had I heard anything? I told him the wee bit I had observed and the rumours B. had passed on to me. That was funny, he said; B. had sought out a correspondent on his staff and told him the same rumours. That, we agreed, made the air much clearer. It was obviously a new application of an old Wilhelmstrasse gag—to plant rumours where they might do some good. Filipoff had direct connection with Moscow. He would transmit these rumours in a news story to Moscow, writing that it was learned from sources close to the Wilhemstrasse that war and overthrow of the Soviet government might be avoided by the granting of the Ukraine to Germany. The Kremlin would be somewhat prepared to get in a lets-talk-this-thing-over-at-the-conference-table-before-we-do-anything-hasty mood. The rumour was then planted with other correspondents in Berlin in order that they might reinforce Filipoff's fears by telling him casually, Say, do you know what I have heard? and so on. Whether or not this interpretation is correct cannot be proven. But the circumstantial evidence in favour of it is convincing. For any German to tell an American correspondent quite openly and frankly he had heard rumours in the Wilhelmstrasse to the effect that Hitler was taking steps to get the Ukraine would have been a penal offence at that time. In fact, it was a penal offence; no less a personage than Dr. Karl Boehmer, head of the foreign press department of the Propaganda Ministry was removed from his post for making a similar statement, and was tried and sentenced to two years imprisonment a month later. No German could dare mention this question at this time, unless he had received orders from the Wilhelmstrasse to do so.

With unmistakable directness, the coming event proceeded to cast its shadow before. From Poland a young German *Unteroffizier* (something better than a corporal, a little less than a sergeant) I knew had written he would be back in Berlin on leave soon and wanted to see me; then came a letter from him telling me all leave had been cancelled and he would write again soon. How the German field censors ever let this letter, addressed to a name obviously not German, come through I do not know. A young member of the Hitler Youth who used to visit our apartment to practise his English on Jack Fleischer of the U.P., my apartment-mate, told me all party members and Hitler Youth had been ordered to gather in their local party headquarters in the next few days. He had been told he need not wear his uniform as there was to be no demonstration, only directions for changing the line of propaganda. Two German friends of mine told me of letters they had received from men recently called up which revealed they were in Poland moving eastward. From Moscow came a report that German Panzer units had arrived in South Finland, and new rumours of border clashes between the Russians and the Germans were reported from Turkey daily. When a correspondent in the foreign office press conference asked regarding these rumours, they were neither denied nor confirmed, but "nothing is known" about the reports. Hitherto, German spokesmen had always denied forthwith and unequivocally any rumours of strained relations between German and Russia.

I tried to combine several of these features into items for broadcasts, but the censors struck out every mention of Russia. The last tell-tale sign came from Americans who lived in the Adlon Hotel on the corner of the Wilhelmstrasse and Unter den

Linden. Several suites of rooms had been rented by the German foreign office on the top floor of the hotel. A squad of typists and civil servants had entered them a few days ago with barrows of writing paper, and none of them had come out since. The doors were being guarded by armed German soldiers in steel helmets. Obviously, once again, documents were being prepared. The punch was beautifully telegraphed but my efforts to put it on the radio were of no avail.

The punch came at three o'clock in the morning of Sunday, June 22, 1941. I was called out of bed by the foreign office to a special press conference which was to begin at five o'clock. Being called out of bed at three in the morning, I knew from several past occasions, meant but one thing: Germany was going to save the world from somebody again. At this time there were three candidates whom correspondents had nominated in speculative bull-sessions in the Adlon bar after learning about the activity going on in the suites above: the White Peril in Washington, the Heathen Peril of Istanbul and the Red Peril of the Kremlin. After watching weather-vanes for two months, there was little doubt in my mind which had been chosen. I telephoned the United Press office and confirmed my suspicion, that all communications between Germany and the outside world had been cut since midnight. Then, as the subways were not running, I wandered out into the dark, empty streets down to the Wilhelmstrasse.

In the Foreign Office, the handsome little council room, where Bismarck once debated and which is now used for foreign press conferences, was packed with sleepy reporters. From the corners of the room klieg-lights beat down on a little bouquet of microphones on the centre of the table in the middle of the room. At points of vantage cameramen had taken up positions in the crowd. The little corps of sons of the wealthy Prussian caste, who served Ribbentrop as a staff, stood behind the table in the handsome blue, black uniforms and gold sashes of the Foreign Office. From the Propaganda Ministry across the street, Dr. Goebbels had just read before the microphone the Fuehrer's proclamation to the German people to the effect that he was beginning this day to save them from what a few hours ago they had considered a friendly nation. Ribbentrop had just called the Soviet ambassador, Dekanosov, to him in his yellow-coloured home on the Wilhelmstrasse and given him the notice of the Reich government. The foreign minister was now on his way, through the back halls of the foreign office, to us—it was the familiar routine of committing the crime, then justifying it to the world.

Of all Nazi leaders, I hated Ribbentrop most. I think my sentiments were shared by a great mass of the German people. I remember when Ribbentrop escorted Molotov, the then Soviet premier, to the Anhalter station after Molotov had completed his visit to Berlin, I stood outside the station in a large crowd of Germans waiting for the big shots to come out again. One by one, they came, and the crowd greeted each one with a mild cheer. But when the foreign minister reappeared, there was not a single cheer; not even a muffled whisper, just dead silence so complete you could have heard a pin drop. Ribbentrop stood on the platform a few minutes drawing on his gloves and chatting with an underling, then got in his open car and sped away. Then Dr. Ley, the red-faced "Labour Leader" came out and a weak Heil spread over the audience breaking a chill silence of five minutes or so. It may be that my feelings for Ribbentrop are partially caused by the fact that I have been subjected to him more often than I have to the others. However, the attitude may also be coupled with having seen too many gangster films as a boy. Towards the gangsters themselves one tends to be somewhat lenient in condemnation, for, after all, they do the dirty work and take all the implied risks. But nobody loves the shyster lawyer who is assigned to justify their deeds. That was the light in which I saw my favourite hate that morning. He was clean, and natty in a double-breasted brown jacket and black trousers. Not a speck of blood on his hands. He stiffly saluted his underlings, stuffed his right fist in his pocket, picked up a sheaf of papers from the table with his left, turned to us and began the maudlin scene of pleading Germany's spotless innocence before the channels to the incredulous court of world opinion. It made little difference whether the world believed or not; tomorrow the Berlin papers would publish the headline: "The World breathless at Ribbentrop's branding of Soviets" over a few lines of comment from the Rumanian and Bulgarian press which had been dictated by Berlin. His voice was deep and hoarse, and at intervals the little yes-men in blue and gold behind him nodded in approval. Below and beside him crouched his fat, greasy, mongol-eyed understudy Paul Schmidt, the head of the foreign office's foreign press section, grinning like a bloated Buddha. This little uniformed gathering was truly a fine sight, a symbol of the whole institution they belonged to: two ambitious, unscrupulous, intelligent plotters, and a staff of sartorially perfect, empty-headed ignoramuses—the most incompetent bevy of crackpots who ever dreamed of new-ordering a world. (My opinion of the brain-power of the German Foreign Office is extremely low, as a result of first-hand experience. The German foreign office has no diplomatic success to its credit since Munich and that triumph belongs only to a small extent to the Foreign Office. What has passed for the last three years as diplomatic coups are nothing more nor less than the fear in the hearts of other nations of German armed power. On its own, the German Foreign Office is a stupid vehicle. There is little need for a successful or an intelligent diplomatic staff in a state which possesses an armed force as strong as Hitler's.)

When Ribbentrop finished, there was applause from the Axis correspondents. One Swiss Quisling whose name I have never learned, but who knew of my friendship with Filipoff of the Tass agency, whispered in my ear to ask where, on this fine summer morning was Herr Filipoff, ha! ha! Without looking at him, I left the room to stand in line outside for copies, which the Foreign Office staff had been preparing in the Adlon Hotel all the week, of Ribbentrop's note to the Soviet ambassador. Then I wandered home. There was no need to hurry, for communications were still interrupted. I walked down Potsdamer Strasse to the old Landwehr canal and along it past the headquarters of the Supreme Command. After uttering a few imprecations on its portal, I walked on, under the elms by the canal trying to figure the situation out.

On first glance, it was encouraging. Any new opponent was welcome to the flock. To the west of Germany, Britain was undefeated and America was growing more threatening daily despite the queer Appeals to Reason of Colonel Lindbergh and Senator Wheeler. And in the east Hitler had invited a new enemy into the fray. Sheerly on the bases of geography and numbers Hitler had pulled a boner.

But in my state of mind it was not easy to believe Hitler would deliberately do anything so absurd. He was fighting for his chapter in the next Outline of History, and he wasn't going to spoil it as simply as that. The longer I considered, the more method revealed itself in his madness. Suppose—I did not believe it—but just suppose, for argument's sake, Russia *should* collapse after a few hard blows on the frontier. The rest would be isolated combats between a few scattered loyal Soviet divisions and a handful of German Panzers. Russia, with all those fine new factories I had seen, with all her bountiful resources, would be in the hands of Hitler. What blockade could be effective against the combination of Russian resources and German industry? Still a trace in my psychology, too, was the England I had last seen, the England of Munich. I had always been convinced that one purpose of the English rulers at Munich was to steer Germany into a struggle with Russia which would spare England. That struggle was now, at long last, a reality. I could not believe in a separate peace, but I could fear a lessening of British pressure. Then, in America, Roosevelt would be embarrassed by his new and unexpected ally, and might have to yield to his opposition and retrench on his enmity to Hitler. In fair argument I could never have convinced myself on all these points; one has to take in consideration that awful malady, the "Berlin Blues", to understand my reasoning. Under the circumstances, my greater willingness to accept this line than to refuse it is understandable. I could see in my mind's eye Hitler of the graceful walk and cruel eyes again mounting the rostrum of the Sports Palace, three months hence, saluting his beaming partners in crime, then turning to his audience and microphones—the master of all Europe and most of Asia—to scream the crimes the world had committed against Germany at them, and to end in a blaze of new promises and new threats to destroy anyone who stood in his path to the new ordering of the entire world. The Hitler Myth and its logical conclusion.

When I reached home, Jack Fleischer was up, listening to the radio in his pyjamas. Radio reports straight from the eastern front were coming through; soldier-reporters were breathlessly talking about the flashes of shell explosions over there in the Russian lines. The first Russian barracks had been taken. Surprised Russian prisoners were described. That was Nazi, perfectly Nazi. Everything so beautifully arranged that radio reporters in soldiers' uniform had hooked up their apparatus on the front and, long before the High Command issued any communiqué, were describing what was happening blow by blow. The Russians were already collapsing. It wasn't war. It was a national sport and the reporters were right on the sidelines giving a play-by-play description. Frankly, my heart dropped inside me. Harry Flannery called. As soon as communications opened, we had orders for five broadcasts that day and I should get a few hours sleep and then come out to the radio station on Adolf Hitler Platz. I took off my clothes and lay in bed an hour. But I couldn't sleep. I wished I had gone on home to America instead of hanging around. The radio kept giving those damnable reports. I got up, put on my clothes and went out on the streets. The *Voelkischer Beobachter* had issued extra editions. It was the first time the official party newspaper had issued extras. In my bookshop window next to Alois's, they were changing the book-display, putting in those volumes that had lately been shown me. I took the subway, which was packed with Sunday emigrants to the suburbs, and went to the radio station. I made but one broadcast, and Moscow tried to jam it. I was downright ashamed of myself that an ally, in her death-struggle, should have to try and drown out what I must say. Then I returned to the apartment.

At home, measures were taken against the gathering clouds of depression. Jack Fleischer produced a bottle of schnaps and, together, we drained it. But you can't drown troubles that have learned to swim. George Kidd, of the U.P., and his wife, came out to the house to cheer me up (my "case", several shades worse than most others by virtue of my seniority-in-time in Germany, was well known by then over American Berlin), but their argument was fouled by the fact that they had applied for and obtained exit permits to escape just what I was suffering from. Again I swore off press conferences and lopped the Nazi press clubs off my visiting list. Harry Flannery, my boss, was returning to New York, leaving me to take care of broadcasts from Berlin, so I charged him with pushing my case in New York for immediate transfer to anywhere, just to escape Berlin and get out of the night. All Berlin nights were deep and dark, but the one which fell over me and us then was the deepest and darkest of all. It was that particular degree of darkness which, as old wives say, quoting the proverb, comes just before dawn.

*   *   *   *

For once an old wives' proverb was apt. After that Dawn did come up. Swiftly. It was just the way they make Dawn come up on the stage in a Wagnerian Opera. Slowly, at first, a faint diffusion of light over everything, then faster and faster until suddenly its full, blinding glare bursts over the whole stage like a clap of thunder. It was an amazing experience. The rest of this book is a record of it.

History already has its material for the chapter on what Germany did to Russia. Every military communiqué, German or Russian, tells that. This is meant to be a contribution to the still unwritten chapter, *what Russia did to Germany*.

III

DOCTOR DIETRICH GOES TO TOWN

BEFORE THIS time, I had never in my life witnessed a vast social change anywhere. The outbreak of war in England was a novelty and represented a ragged break with peace conditions, but the change was neither swift nor great. The only other change of moment I had been subjected to was the great depression in America, but that experience was wasted on me, partly because I was, in 1929, more interested in football statistics than social ones, and partly because, as happened in the cases of many poor families, a greater drop in prices than in my father's money income as a night-watchman paradoxically made the depression for us a moment of prosperity.

Neither of these compared in any way or degree with the startling metamorphosis of Nazi Germany after June 22, 1941. The individual elements of the metamorphosis are reported in detail elsewhere in this book. The only purpose here is to limn its general outlines. They are clear-cut and develop in perceptible stages. The economic change was coeval with the beginning of the campaign. The mere preparations for this vast undertaking made themselves evident in little lacunæ in the home front's supplies from the first day, but they amounted at that time to nothing serious. Morally, the decline did not begin until after the second month of war. In fact, for reasons to be given later, the actual outbreak of the campaign acted as a strong restorative to spirits that had fallen in the doldrums. When the war entered its third month, however, a moral depression set in which joined the economic decline. The downward movement was slow; then, from the beginning of autumn, both declines gathered speed, reacting on one another. By the end of October it became obvious that this was no mere "seasonal" drop, but a dangerous, perhaps permanent movement. People began grumbling openly, tempers were perceptibly short. This together with the decay of capital equipment caused a levelling off of war production for the first time in Nazi history, then a steep decline in production. The German propaganda machine adopted new tactics, introduced all kinds of new "explana-

tory" propaganda and finally instituted a new anti-Jewish campaign to divert bitterness. The campaign failed entirely of its goal.
From appeasing the people to offering them scapegoats, the
Government then turned to threats and force. The Storm-troops,
the "fighting vanguard of the *Kleinbuergertum*" were in effect
disbanded due to disaffection in their ranks. The Berlin garrison
of the Gestapo was doubled in numbers and the Gestapo took up
strategic positions in residential districts, set up arsenals; and the
number of arrests tripled.

The Nazis took excessively great pains to keep these things quiet.
Probably the most revealing measure they adopted was to muzzle
the American press with an open censorship. This is the first time
censorship of the foreign press has been resorted to in the nine
years of Hitler's power. For the three radio correspondents, of
whom I was one, there had always been a censorship; but when
the Great Depression of late 1941 set in, it was converted into a
veritable strait-jacket. I could not only no longer give a reasonably
accurate picture of what was happening in Berlin; pressure was
even applied to make me tell blunt falsehoods. I was actually
ordered by the Nazis to use their propaganda material! I, of course,
promptly reported these incidents to the American Embassy in
Berlin. The situation was unbearable, and I sent a telegram to
Paul White, director of News Programmes for the Columbia
Broadcasting System, in New York, telling him so. The Nazi censors informed me they would not send the telegram or any other
information containing complaints against them. Then I telephoned White, and told him the facts. Telephone conversations
were still uncensored, but they were listened to by the Gestapo.
All these things I had done in conjunction and agreement with the
two other radio correspondents in Berlin, Alex Dreier of the
National Broadcasting Company, and Paul Dickson of the Mutual
Broadcasting System. The following day we were all informed that
the German radio refused to allow us the use of facilities any
longer, and that we might, thus, no longer work in Germany.
They did not forbid our *companies* from operating from Berlin, and
they did not throw us out. Had they done either of these things,
we would be able to leave the country and to speak freely, once
outside, without fear of reprisals being taken on our companies in
Berlin. But instead, they even refused at first to let us leave. We
stayed in Berlin another month able neither to work nor to leave;

until eventually our companies agreed to send substitutes for us who, in Nazi eyes, would serve as hostages against our talking. On this ruse, I finally received an exit permit. No substitute of course was ever sent to take my place. I crossed the borders while Japanese bombs were falling on Pearl Harbour; an hour later they were closed, and three days later my colleagues in Berlin had been put under house arrest, then interned. That is why these facts have remained unreported until now.

But, while the Propaganda Ministry and the Gestapo were straining their every resource to keep the new developments from ears and eyes of the outside world, unmistakable admissions of their existence were blurted bluntly out by none other than— Adolf Hitler himself! Speaking to old party comrades on November 8, 1941, Hitler, for the first time, mentioned the existence of opposition to him inside Germany. The Fuehrer said: "Should anyone among us seriously hope to be able to disturb our front— it makes no difference where he comes from or to which camp he belongs—I will keep an eye on him for a certain period. You know my methods. That is always the period of probation. But then there comes the moment when I strike like lightning and eliminate that kind of thing". The Fuehrer then stated that the Nazi organization "reaches into every house and zealously keeps watch that there shall never be another November, 1918". Since 1933, opposition to Hitler inside Germany had been a strict "unmentionable" for party speakers and even the Fuehrer himself. The deviation, at this particular time, was significant.

Again, on December 11, Hitler returned to that theme, and this time he was more emphatic. Speaking to the Nazi Reichstag in Berlin about the duty all Germans owe to their Fatherland's tradition, he stated: "Whoever intends to escape this duty has no claim to being held a National Comrade with the rest of us. Just as we were mercilessly hard in the struggle for national power, we will again be merciless and hard in this struggle for the preservation of our people. At a time when thousands of our best men, the fathers and sons of our people, are falling, no individual at home who blasphemes the sacrifice of the front, can reckon with remaining alive. No matter what camouflage covers any attempt to disturb this German front, to undermine our people's will to resist, to weaken the authority of the government or sabotage the efforts of the home front—the guilty one will fall"!

In their settings, these statements are nothing less than sensational. How meaningful they are is indicated by the embarrassed manner in which the Propaganda Ministry handled them. The former speech was never broadcast to the German people. The first condensation of the speech, which was not released until five hours after Hitler had spoken, did not include the statement quoted above at all. Although the second speech was broadcast, the first text of it, released over the ticker machines of the official German News Agency, entirely neglected the passage I have quoted. It was released only the following day, when it was apparently hoped that most people had read the first version and would not bother about going over the second, more complete and less severely expurgated version. The Fuehrer could not be censored directly; but there were ways of doing it indirectly!

The story from here on is what Dr. Goebbels' shears were trying to keep the Fuehrer and the American correspondents—war makes strange bedfellows!—from telling about.

One date stands out over all other possible candidates for designation as the Great Watershed—that point in time before which all was rising and after which all fell, in the history of Hitler and National Socialism. It is Thursday, October 9, 1941. Since that day the morale of the German people has fallen into a black abyss from which nothing on earth can ever resurrect it except a complete, final, decisive military victory in the war. There can be no substitutes of propaganda and no substitutes of bold military successes which are astounding but not decisive. On that day, German propaganda destroyed itself as an effective means of moulding opinion, spirit and morale; and a callousness to military victories set in which nothing less than a real, tangible *decision* in this war can remove. If the decision does not come soon, I hazard the prediction that Germany will lose the war. In that case, I believe the perspective of history will call October 9 not only the watershed of Nazi History but of the entire conflict determining—to borrow a leaf from Hitler—the destiny of the world for the next thousand years. The world took little note of the occasion, principally because its ultimate consequences turned out to be exactly opposite to every indication at the time. The story is an interesting one. This is it.

Known circumstances permit a chronological reconstruction. The Russian war had hit the doldrums. The Red Army simply refused to collapse under a series of mighty blows. Winter was approaching. The situation inside Germany was, as a result of overlong strain, not so good. In a month of quiet on the central front before Moscow, Hitler, secretively as possible, drew up every soldier and every gun, big and little, which he could extract from the Reich and spare from the other fronts. He compressed millions of men and weapons tight up against the Russian lines, like the spring of a giant catapult, for a final blow no army in the world could withstand. This was the consummation, the concentrate of all Prussian military skill and power. The might with which he blasted holes in the Maginot Line was not to be the equal of this. To quote Hitler's own official newspaper of a later date, writing of this occasion, "This time, it was really all out!" ("*Diesmal ging es aufs Ganze!*") On October 2, Hitler drew the latch and the mighty mass sprang forward. Already on the first day, the advance was impressive, but the issue was not yet certain. On October 4, Hitler went from his eastern headquarters to Berlin to make a speech at the opening of the Winter Relief Campaign. The occasion was a melancholy one. At the beginning of the year Hitler had promised victory in 1941; and here he was back in Berlin opening the third war-time winter relief campaign. The Fuehrer had ordered total silence about the new offensive. But the occasion demanded a branch of hope; so the Leader made known to his people, for the first time, the fact that this mighty new offensive had been launched, and he prophesied that it would bring the Eastern war to an end before winter. That was helpful, but, after he had returned to the front, the people became restive for specific news. On October 8, the Fuehrer issued a High Command communiqué, the first news, telling of progress. And on the morning of October 9, after poring over his maps and pronouncing what he saw on them good, he called in his lipless little press chief, Dr. Otto Dietrich, from an adjoining hut in the headquarters. Removing his horn-rimmed glasses which he wears in private but sedulously guards from the range of court photographers, the Fuehrer became expansive before the Doctor, bidding him to go to town and reveal all. The period of "strategic silence" had ended. Dietrich caught the bright, "historical" mood of his Leader and returned to his hut to order an underling to contact Dr. Goebbels in Berlin on the telephone, and instruct him to gather the world press; there was history to be made. Then Dr. Dietrich put on his grey great-coat, kicked the first light eastern snow off his polished boots, and enplaned for Berlin, important as the good horse Roland who carried the joyous news from Ghent to Aix.

When the telephone rang, I was lying in bed with a miserable cold and a skull-splitting headache. It was the secretary of Dr. Froehlich, the Propaganda Ministry's liaison officer for the American press and radio. She was excited, and told me I should come to an important special press conference at noon sharp; something of extremely great importance. No, she did not know what it was about, but, be there on time, for at five minutes after twelve the doors would be barred and guarded.

I had no broadcast that afternoon. And, besides, after two years packed with repetitions of Nazi full-dress shows, I was inured to "history" and indifferent, anyway, to the further progress of a world which has never discovered an effective remedy for the common head-cold. So I turned over and tried to go to sleep. The telephone rang again. It was Guido Enderis, the chief of the *New York Times*' Berlin office, for whom I had been writing on occasion. His man, Brooks Peters, had gone home to escape the Berlin blues, so, would I cover the special conference for the *Times*? He had been assured of its historic import. Reluctantly, I yielded.

I put on my clothes, stuffed two handkerchiefs in my pocket, and took the underground to the Wilhelmstrasse. The red-plush Theatre Hall of the Propaganda Ministry was filled with reporters from everywhere, guessing in a dozen different languages what it was all about. My head throbbed. Before the audience was a long conference table, and around the table in little clots stood a bevy of gorgeous uniforms—green, brown, grey and two shades of blue, well stuffed with Prussian officers, party officials and just bureaucrats of the Ministry, beaming with joy at an opportunity to appear before their daily *Publikum* in costumes which lent glamour to waistlines and limbs made for mufti.

As on all Nazi "historic" occasions—except those in which Hitler is the leading man, for he can afford to risk non-conformity —the central show-piece was impressively and precisely late. At 12.30 on the dot, a few officers rushed through the door into the room, indicating the coming of the Leader's emissary. The clots dissolved into one fine phalanx and in walked little Dr. Dietrich, flapping his right palm back over his shoulder in imitation of his

Fuehrer's salute and grinning as if fair to bursting with the tidings he bore. There was profuse handshaking, sandwiched each time between stiff-armed salutes. Cameras snapped and flashlight bulbs flashed. On the great stage behind the central figure, Dietrich, the red velvet curtains were drawn apart to reveal a monstrous map of European Russia thrice as high as the speaker. The effect was impressive.

Dietrich was introduced briefly and oilily by Dr. Brauweiler, a musty old Nazi party wheel-horse who had been appointed leader of the foreign press section of the Ministry after the arrest of Boehmer, and given a natty blue uniform for having kept his mouth and head shut for eight years. Then the little doctor rose and held forth. I regret I cannot quote him directly. But it is a strange, strange feature of this grand occasion that the text of what Dietrich said has never been published. Unlike most other important utterances of Nazi leaders, his words were never re-broadcast to the German people—a feature which caused inquisitive whispering in German and foreign circles alike. It is just possible, that somewhere among the roses of enthusiasm which blossomed out in uniform that happy day, there was a little, inconspicuous thorn of prudence, some little bureaucrat, who cast the vaguest shadow of a doubt over the mind of Dr. Goebbels, the producer of the show, with dampening references to the uncertain space between the cup and the lip, and with that hateful phrase which is anathema to the best laid plans of mice and men: "But, suppose it doesn't turn out that way?" If there was such a bureaucrat, you may be sure that, however much he may have been considered an unwelcome cold douche on that merry day, he has since been promoted and given a new uniform for his counsel.

For Dietrich said bold words and cast moderating and conditional phrases to the four winds. In the vernacular of the diplomatic correspondent, Dietrich put himself away, away out on a mighty high limb. With an air of finality, Dietrich announced the very *last remnants* of the Red Army were locked in two steel German pockets before Moscow and were undergoing, swift, merciless annihilation. This was sensational. To understand how big the story was one must remember the circumstances. This was the first substantial news about the mighty, new offensive. It came directly from Adolf Hitler himself, and could not be doubted. Dietrich continued: behind the two pockets there stood between the German armies and Moscow just so much space and nothing more. As one correspondent later put it, Dietrich indicated that between Germany and the complete conquest of the untold riches of Russia there remained only "the time it takes man and machine to cover the given distance". After seven short days, the Fuehrer's offensive had smashed the Red Army to splinters, the decision was reached and the eastern continent lay, like a limp virgin, in the mighty arms of the lustful, hungry German Mars. ". . . And on that, Gentlemen, I stake my whole journalistic reputation!" Dietrich shouted, swinging his fist high in the air in a dramatic gesture.

Now nobody will contest the contention that the Nazis tell lies, and great big ones. But it is true that Hitler himself has never told a lie about a specific military fact which can be checked. There are two good reasons for this. First, he does not have to lie about them; you don't have to tell a fib when you're winning. Second, a specific military fact can be so easily checked, and if it were found out that the "Almighty" had told a blunt untruth, especially about something so big as this particular event, it would be disastrous to his position. So we of the fourth estate had no choice but to believe these dramatic assertions were gospel truth. Behind his unrecorded words there arose, in the minds of his listeners, inevitable images. Russia, with her rich resources in Hitler's hands: an increment of almost 200,000,000 units of slave labour to make implements of war, bringing the total of man-power at Germany's disposal to a figure greater than that of England, and North and South America combined. Hitler's armies, ten million men, flushed with victory, eager for more of the easy, national sport, were in the main free to return west and flood England, at long last, with blood and Nazis. The American news agency men, on the first row, were sitting on the edges of their seats, tensely eyeing the door behind which were telephones, leading to more telephones to America and the world. My headache receded in my consciousness and in its place settled the more painful conviction—common to all there—that the eastern war was over; and, perhaps, the decision in the entire conflict already lay in Hitler's hands.

When Dietrich finished tense excitement prevailed. The uniforms gathered round him and pumped his hand as a sort of mutual congratulation on the German victory. The agency men had burst through the doorway and were giving short, hot bulletins over the phones to their offices. Axis and Balkan correspondents applauded and cheered, then stood and raised their arms in salute to Dietrich who sped out of the room to return to the Fuehrer's headquarters and be on hand for the last terrible blows, the *coups de grâce*, the Grand Finale.

I walked down the marble stairs from the Theatre Hall and talked briefly to Oechsner, who had just returned from his breather in America, and Lochner. The mood was grim all round. I went alone, then, up the Wilhelmstrasse to the Adlon bar for alcoholic reinforcement against my cold. The bar radio announced a special communiqué could be expected from the Fuehrer's headquarters in a few minutes; when it came the barman turned up the volume and the specifically military report Dietrich had made in his speech, minus the trimmings and predictions, was announced. I scanned my notes and began writing a tentative lead on the back of an envelope; but it was one of those insidious stories whose implications grow on you as you think more about it. I left the hotel, took a taxi to the *Times* office to get that accessory which is indispensable to clear thinking on my part, a typewriter; although my deadline was still hours away.

My insidious "growing" reaction was apparently universal. Several American bureau chiefs had been invited the day before to leave on October 10 on a trip to the eastern front—the juiciest journalistic plum the German High Command could offer. But so strong was the conviction among us that the end was perhaps a matter of only hours away that Louis Lochner, of the Associated Press, telephoned the Propaganda Ministry, after studying his notes, and informed the proper official that he had decided to relinquish his place on the trip and remain in Berlin. It was too hazardous leaving his base of communications at a moment like this. Then Pierre Huss, of I.N.S., phoned and delivered, with regret, the same message. Oechsner, of U.P., wavered but ultimately decided to take a chance on going to the East. That afternoon powerful pieces, "situationers" reeking with historic implications, went over the wires from Berlin.

But what escaped almost every correspondent was the reaction of the German people themselves. At this time, in the atmosphere of triumph, that feature was, after all, secondary to considerations such as the new strategic and economic advantages the total conquest of Russia offered Hitler. But when that atmosphere dissolved, when the true consequences became clear, the main, and, for Hitler, disastrous feature was, the People.

The little thorn of prudence kept the full strength of Dietrich's predictions from them. The papers published no direct quotations. But they did publish condensed, expurgated, indirect summaries of the "epochal" conference which were strong enough to make German hearts beat faster. Headlines shouted: "The Veil over the New Offensive is lifted!"; "Dietrich: 'Campaign in East Decided'"! The *Voelkischer Beobachter* headline read: "The Great Hour has Struck! Army groups of Timoshenko, Voroshilov encircled—Budyenny Army-group in dissolution". Quoting the Fuehrer's order of the day to the army at the beginning of the offensive, to "strike the last mighty blow, which will crush this enemy before the beginning of winter", and to complete "the last great battle of decision of this year", the official Nazi newspaper commented in bold language, only few degrees less perilously committal than Dietrich's own words: "That order has already essentially been carried out. In the sense of the Fuehrer's order, the strategic decision has already been gained. If ever the concept 'Blitzkrieg' was realized, it is here!—Seven short days have sufficed to deal a deathblow to the largest war machine in the world, a blow from which Russia can never, never recover".

The response was electric. There was visible alleviation in faces that for weeks had been dismally drawn. In Baarz' beer-restaurant behind Unter den Linden, people stood and saluted when the radio, after repeating the High Command communiqué, played *Horst Wessel* and *Deutschland ueber alles*. Rumours, which are the dangerous daily diet of people in any totalitarian country where news is twisted or kept from them, spread over Berlin like wildfire. In Baarz', a waiter whispered to me, had I heard, Stalin has requested an armistice. At home, the janitor in my apartment house stopped me in the hall to tell me he had it from reliable sources who had good friends high up in the party that Moscow had fallen this noon. The civil population were hanging wreaths of roses on German tanks in joy at being liberated. It would be announced in a special communiqué tonight or tomorrow. In the days that followed, bookshops got in new sets of Russian grammars and simple readers for beginners in the tongue, and displayed shop windows full of them; the eagerness to get a job in the rich, new colony was everywhere. The economics minister of the

Reich, Dr. Walter Funk, sat himself down and wrote a fine speech about Germany's colonial mission in Russia, entitled "The contribution of the East to the New Europe", and next day the papers published it under the heading: "Europe's Economic Future Secured".

The horrible slaughter of Germany's best sons was nearing an end. The boys were being taken out of the Panzers by Christmas. To parched desert-dwellers, the rains had come. Even as God had promised, and his apostles confirmed. And grateful worshippers were wallowing joyously in the coolness of it.

It is hard to realize what this meant to the German people, unless you have lived through those two years of war with them, and watched them suffer. As the core of a strong, steel-willed leadership, they have been remarkably timid and sensitive to trends. They have detested this war from the moment it broke out, and they, the People, have been willing to end it at any juncture. Before it came, they feared it far more than the peoples their leaders and their army threatened with annihilation. On the few oocasions on which the end appeared to be in sight, they have been gleeful as children. Dr. Goebbels has not distinguished himself on the score of telling the truth. But when he said, "The German People did not want this war", he knew, for once, what he was talking about.

The graph of German morale is not a graceful, snaky thing which slithers upwards in long rises and downwards in slow, calm declines like the graph of almost any people living in peace. It is a low, jagged line which leaps spasmodically upwards in one instant and collapses into sharp depressions in the next. The reason for its abrupt contours is the unmitigated fear of this war which afflicts the German people, and their gullible readiness to believe anything, however fantastic, which indicates an early end to it. To understand just what Dr. Dietrich did to Germany, it is necessary to examine the war-graph of German morale as nearly as it can be drawn from impressions.

The graph has never been on a high plane, even in peace-time. From my days of travelling constantly back and forth between England and Germany, I am convinced that, however effective Hitler's nerve-war was against England, really the first victims of the war of nerves were Hitler's own people. The British were worried, extremely worried at the time of Munich; I know because I was there and I was worried too. But when I went to Germany a short while later, the signs of strain there were far greater than any I, personally, had seen in England. A dear friend of mine in Munich told me she fainted from the strain and could not get the family doctor to come because he was visiting two other people who had collapsed from strain. At the pension I usually stayed in when I was in Cologne, I found, after Munich, the manager had given up his lease and moved outside town because he feared living too near the railway station. The general reaction was, I think, best summed up by a German student I knew in Munich who had studied in America. When I asked him how it felt being a young German in Hitler's Reich, he said: "It's like being married to a daring young man on a flying trapeze. There's never a dull moment, but it's disastrous to your nerves".

The morale-graph, from what colleagues told me, dropped and steadied at a new low level when war was first declared. In the second month of the war it suddenly leapt to a record height. The occasion was that amusing day when some miscreant, believed to be a Jew, a Bolshevik or a plutocrat who dropped with a parachute, started the rumour moving through Berlin that Chamberlain had resigned as Prime Minister, and England had agreed to talk peace-terms with Hitler. On that occasion, hundreds of Berliners gathered outside the Fuehrer's chancellery singing *"Wir wollen unseren Fuehrer!"*—We want our Leader!—to thank him for the early peace which had not occurred. In such a mood drops are always more severe than rises, and the discovery that there was no peace induced a fit of depression.

The invasion of Denmark and Norway caused a mild flurry, but no noteworthy change in the progress of morale. The indifference of the populace to this singular, bold leap over water to occupy a mountainous land was registered brutally in the stacks of unsold extra editions by the side of which newsboys stood idly all that afternoon. What little enthusiasm there was, was offset by the knowledge that conquest might be a strategic gain but it did not decide the war, and that is absolutely all the German people were and are interested in. I remember the characteristic reception of this historic event by a couple of old-timers I encountered going into the Berlin zoo that forenoon. One was an old man with turned up moustaches who apparently took his

Dachshund for a walk in the zoo every day, and the other was the
zoo doorman. The latter, taking the ticket of the old man, said:

"*Morgen.* See we invaded Norway this morning?"

"*Ja,*" said the visitor, removing his cigar from his mouth, "and
Denmark too."

"*Ja,*" said the ticket-taker handing back the punched ticket.
"*Auf Wiedersehen.*"

"*Wiedersehen.*" And the old man and his Dachshund went in to
observe the strange manners of the animals, both wild and
domestic.

The opening of the campaign in France, on the other hand,
brought a decided reaction: a severe drop. One of the most dangerous features of the German consciousness is to think in parallels
to the World War. The mention of names of places bloodily fought
over in the last war invariably conjures up images of a similar
outcome. The news of the crossing of the Belgian border on May
10, did this. In a pension on Kurfuerstendamm where I lived at
that time, another pensioner, an ageing Prussian, came to my
room as soon as he had read the headlines on his paper. He sat
down and looked worriedly and intently at me.

"It's begun," he said. I acknowledged it had.

"Now it will really get started," he said, peering again at his
folded newspaper.

"We didn't want this war. We really didn't." Tears welled in
those hard, old eyes as he proceeded to argue the oft-repeated
German case. This was typical of the World War generation: no
faith in German strength, believing more fully than any Englishman or Frenchman in German inferiority, praying for mercy to
the only foreigner within reach. It was a pathetic little show, but it
was hard for me to work up sympathy. Those who cower first also
become the haughtiest and most overbearing when triumph
comes.

The early victories moved the graph upward: the taking of
Eben Emael, Liege, Brussels, Dunkirk. But it is an astounding
record of how little faith the German people had in their army,
that, after Dunkirk, when the German armies, halted temporarily
(one day) to recoil for the final blow at France, most of the Germans I talked to still felt they were licked. Their faith in ultimate
victory had been in no way strengthened. The old vision of
Moltke's drive up to the Marne, the stabilization of the front there

and the long four years misery of a war of attrition was conjured up by the parallel of the sudden halt at the Somme in 1940. The graph rose to a rather high peak when the armistice was signed. Strangely, though this event represented one of the greatest military triumphs of all time, there were no demonstrations on the streets, no open signs of elation anywhere in Berlin. (Shortly before, when Italy chose a safe moment to become involved in the war, the first and only demonstration "march" through the streets of Berlin in the entire war was stupidly gawked at from the kerbstones by a few Germans. The march was organized by the handful of Fascist black-shirts in Berlin and comprised about fifty German students who looked teutonically ill-at-ease at thus parading themselves behind three or four uniformed Italians in black Fascist uniforms.)

About a month later, an extraordinary thing happened. The graph reached its all-time high. It was the only occasion in the better part of six years I have spent in Germany that I saw real, uninhibited enthusiasm, with Germans weeping and laughing from pure, spontaneous joy. It has never happened before and it has never happened since. A division of Berlin infantry had returned from France. It was to march from the East-West axis through the Brandenburg gate of victory down Unter den Linden. Then the whole division was to be demobilized. This was, at last, a real, tangible sign of victory and the end of the war Germans detested and feared. Sons, husbands and fathers, sun-tanned and healthy after long military training, happy as kids after the great triumph, were returning home to their families to stay. The buildings on Unter den Linden were veiled in great red and white pennants forty yards long and ten feet broad. The thoroughfare, and all the streets running into it were jammed with cheering thousands. The soldiers marched past the reviewing stand on Pariser Platz before the American and (ironically) French embassy buildings, where Goebbels and the commander of the local garrison received their salute and returned it. Then they marched on down Unter den Linden in clouds of confetti. Children broke through the police cordon and carried little bouquets of flowers to the marching soldiers, while a dozen military bands, punctuating the ranks of the marchers, played martial music. It was truly a glorious day. And in every happy heart lived the belief that this was the end of it all. Perhaps as symbolic as the fact that the triumphal review stands on the western end of Unter den Linden were erected in front of the old French embassy was the fact that the eastern end of Unter den Linden, the route of march, runs straight into the front portal of Kaiser Wilhelm's palace, from which the first world war was directed. But that escaped notice.

The triumphal review stands remained intact on Pariser Platz, mounted by the eagle of the German army, for another month. Obviously more divisions were coming home to be de-mobilized. Then, from the centre of the stands, the army eagle was removed, and the golden, stylized spread eagle of the Luftwaffe, the air force, was set up in its place. Obviously, there would be a few irresistible blows at England, another victory, and the Berlin Luftwaffe units would be brought home to march in the path of the infantry through the Victory Gate, to freedom from war duty. England would quickly see the sense of the Fuehrer's promise of peace and his desire to "spare the Empire", and the whole thing would be over.

It is no mere newspaperman's creation that Germany, the People and the Leaders, expected Britain to talk peace at this time. From a highly reliable source, I learned at the time that the Propaganda Ministry issued contracts to decorating firms to line the main streets of German cities with Victory Pillars for the triumphal march homeward of all German troops. The source is the director of one of the firms which received a contract and whose firm actually began working on the street decorations in July, 1940. Also, from trustworthy sources, I heard Hitler called to Berlin one of his leading architects to build a new, special Arch of Triumph outside Berlin. The arch was to be slightly bigger than the *Arc de Triomphe* in Paris.

What happened to these hopes is history. Churchill was not having any that season. The gilt on the wings of the stylized eagle tarnished in the first snows of winter, and late one evening when I was walking up Unter den Linden, I stopped to watch a squad of workers knocking the planks of the triumphal stands apart and carting away these tissues of hope, in trucks. They worked swiftly, and next morning Pariser Platz was clean and open again. Morale sank steeply after that. And like the graph of American prosperity after 1929, it never again really rose. The whole show was repeated on smaller scales all over Germany. In villages, crude little triumphal arches were set up over roads at the beginnings of towns. On an automobile trip through South Germany I saw them, neatly frilled with boughs of pine and with little bouquets of flowers hanging by gilded ropes from the centre. The legend across the top read: "Rothenburg (or Nordlingen or Dillingen) Greets its Triumphant Heroes!" I also saw them later when the pine boughs were turning brown and the needles were falling off the branches and the flowers had faded in the rain. It was a cruel blow, no matter what you thought of them. But Mr. Churchill was hardheaded.

Came the Russian war. The much bespoken schedule of the German High Command was actually between six and eight weeks. In an expansive moment after the first week of border victories, a high member of the German High Command assured me of this. Although the censors forbade me using his statement in a radio broadcast, and, later, when things changed, the Nazis vigorously denied it, the fact was confirmed to me several times by persons who had reason to be certain. In an editorial which appeared in the German press on August 23, no less an authority than Dr. Goebbels admitted it was the aim of the German High Command "to place everything on catching the enemy in the frontier region and annihilating him in gigantic battles of destruction". The schedule was, of course, a secret; and like all secrets of this sort in a totalitarian state it became an open one from the first day of battle.

The first weeks of the Russian war were received with no little enthusiasm by the German people, for their visions were bathed in the light of the "schedule". The prospect of an undefeated Britain, strengthened constantly by increasing production and export of American arms, blockading a military superior but continentally hamstrung Germany to slow death had been plaguing Germany since the victory arches had to be torn down, and since the failure of Goering's blitz terror against England. Now, the prospect was better, much better. A few hard, swift blows at Russia, who, it was common knowledge, was tottering with revolution already, would induce civil disorders in towns behind the Russian lines. If this did not result in the overthrow of the government, at least the disorders would hamstring Russian defence, and the *Wehrmacht* would march through the steppes as easily as they had marched down Unter den Linden. This was the dominant conception; I heard it expressed this way dozens of times. And it was invigorating to our graph. One of the most intelligent and well-informed Germans I know, Walter Wilke, a correspondent for the United Press, made a bet with me at the beginning of the campaign that German troops would occupy Moscow within two weeks!

The best evidence that even the German High Command believed in a quick easy triumph is one of its own communiqués. Already on July 13, before the war was a month old, the Supreme Command issued from the Fuehrer's headquarters, a communiqué stating the enemy was "showing signs of dissolution and collapse"! There were reports of whole regiments of the Red Army throwing down their rifles and deserting to the German side. On July 25, the official *Voelkischer Beobachter* announced on its front page Moscow was resorting now to its "last reserves".

But, apparently, Mr. Stalin was not having any this season, either. By this time victory was overdue. There was scratching of heads and wonderment in Berlin. But the matter was far more serious than simply a psychological impatience for the end. This campaign, unlike all the others, was making itself materially felt. Little items, little amenities, were disappearing from the shops and big items were growing scarcer. The number of letters returned to their senders from the front every day, marked "Fallen" in red ink, increased portentously. A queer, new tone crept into the press, a feature which everyone who kept up with correspondence from Berlin in the newspapers in those days must have wondered at. There was more and more emphasis on the "treacherous fighting methods of the Bolsheviks". Goebbels ordered—and his soldier-reporters at the front delivered—hundreds of reports about this feature, to show the German people why things had not gone quite according to schedule. Every day a new story about "inhuman Red methods of warfare" appeared in each newspaper, telling about how the Russians would offer to surrender with their hands high in the air and when the Germans neared, plop! the Russians dropped hand grenades from their hands in the midst of the Germans and blew them all up; how the Bolsheviks lay as if dead in a road, and when a Panzer passed over their bodies, they inserted T.N.T. in its chassis and before it had progressed another twenty yards it was blasted into Valhalla; and how the Russians mined everything including toilet seats in every town they abandoned and caused many a brave Nordic to die an undignified death while engaged in natural elimination. The stories made exceedingly good reading.

But all Goebbels' little propaganda stratagems were not so harmless. A Nazi in embarrassment is a dangerous Nazi, and he will resort to any method to rescue himself. To support his line about the bestiality of the Soviet troops, Goebbels also published in the German press dozens of pictures of dead, tortured bodies of Soviet civilians, killed by the retreating Bolsheviks, the captions said. Jean Graffis, the Berlin representative of the American Acme Newspicture agency, picked several of these out of the files of the Nazi Hoffman picture agency and offered to buy them. But the agent, blushing at the situation he found himself in, told Graffis he was sorry but those were not for sale; they were only for internal consumption. Graffis had wanted to buy them because he read on their backs the date 1920—they were dead bodies from the Russian Civil War! These photographs were being published in German newspapers as snapshots taken by German troops in the war of 1941! Again, a group of foreign correspondents was taken to Lemberg to see a real Soviet torture chamber, in order to reinforce the same line of propaganda in the outside world. The walls of one of the rooms, the "execution chamber", was picked with bullet-holes from the rifles of Soviet firing squads. When the conductor of the tour left the room, one of the correspondents searched the room's contents and found a Russian propaganda poster with Stalin's photograph reproduced on it; it was shot through with holes. He placed it against the wall, and the punctures tallied exactly, hole for hole! Obviously the Germans themselves were responsible for their "atrocity".

But the press stuck to its guns. If victory had not happened, then it was about to happen. On July 29, the official Nazi paper announced: "We can already comfort ourselves and say the knife-sharp pinnacle of the decision has already been crossed". On August 7, the Supreme Command again saw visions of Soviet collapse, declaring in a communiqué that "Extensive information indicates the Soviet leadership no longer has any reliable picture of the situation on its own front". The official sheet echoed, predicting "the end of the rule of the Kremlin is at hand". Elated, this particular editorial finished with the flourish "To be German means to be Invincible!"

The end of the rule of the Kremlin remained obstinately only

"at hand". German morale was slipping badly downhill impelled
to a swifter decline by the sudden worsening of other conditions.
In September, the first month of autumn, the press went on a new
tack, and began publishing those famous "explanatory" editorials,
saying people were silly to have thought the High Command ever
worked according to any particular schedule, that the progress of
the *Wehrmacht* was no surprise to Hitler, for he had planned it
that way. Theodore Seibert, the star correspondent of the *Voelkischer Beobachter*, began the series, and no less a person than Dr.
Goebbels took it up from there in his new weekly *Das Reich*. The
papers announced astronomic Soviet losses and produced figures
aiming to prove German losses were not much more than the
annual death toll in motor car accidents. Nevertheless, on
September 22, notices appeared in the newspapers and on
hoardings calling for fresh volunteers for the *élite* German infantry
regiment *Grossdeutschland*. More and more little independent
shops were shut and on their doors was hung the information:
"Closed because personnel called up."

For purely propagandist purposes the number of "special High
Command communiqués" was increased. A High Command
communiqué has features of Holy Writ which a military communiqué in no other land has. On the radio broadcasting news
from Germany, I was never allowed to say the High Command
communiqué "claimed" any victory; that was sacrilege. I tried to
use "asserted" in the place of "claimed", but the censors ruled
that out too; they said they could not allow even a shadow of
doubt to be cast on any utterance of so indubitably truthful and
authoritative a source as the High Command. Over the radio,
High Command communiqués are repeated each afternoon,
slowly, three words at a time, and school children are required to
write down every word. Now a *Special* High Command communiqué is still more important. It is not simply read out over the
German radio. The announcer interrupts programmes to announce a special communiqué is coming, and repeats this pro-
logue every five minutes until it comes. The *Sondermeldung* is pre-
ceded by a moment of silence, during which all restaurants and
cafés are required by law to turn up the volume of their radio sets
so that people on the streets, too, can hear; waiters are forbidden
to serve during the broadcast, and patrons forbidden to chat until
it is over. It is not an announcement; it is a religious service. After

the silence comes a long drawn out fanfare of trumpets, and the rolling of drums with the strain of *Die Wacht am Rhein* surging up through the clatter. This is repeated three times, then another silence. Then, in the voice of an apostle, the radio announcer sonorously reads: "From the Fuehrer's Headquarters. September the X, 1941. The Supreme Command makes known——" followed by some item of news that is world-quaking in its significance. In the past only such historic moments as the cracking of the world's greatest single fort at Eben Emael by parachute troops, the occupation of Paris, the capture of Athens and Crete, have been honoured by inclusion in *Sondermeldungen*. But in September, suddenly the number was increased, and the contents weakened. Every other day there was a special communiqué; every event, the capture of every single town, was made the occasion for a holy mass. From the point of view of information, the communiqués were pointless, for they were generally issued only an hour before the regular communiqué was published and in the latter the same information was contained. The fact was, people had lost interest and something had to be done to arouse them again. The strategy, of course, failed after the dilution became apparent, and despite law, people in restaurants went right on chatting, and waiters continued serving while the radio blared a *Sondermeldung*.

The graph of German morale struck, in the last days of September, the lowest point it had reached in almost nine years of Nazi domination. It was true that the troops of Hitler in the East were still advancing. But that is not the point, the German people are not interested in military triumph. They have grown callous to the capture of towns, the encirclement of armies, advances of a hundred miles in a few days. As I have already written, the only thing German people were and are interested in is a *decisive* victory which brings the war visibly nearer to an end. The German propaganda ministry had virtually exhausted its psychological stratagems. It became obvious that decisive victory, and not propaganda *Ersatz* was the only remedy, and it was urgently necessary. The situation on the home front had truly grown serious. The campaign's running two months over schedule had caused a serious drain on home supplies. People were dangerously out of sorts. Anti-Nazi slogans were being painted on fences and buildings. Frank, written complaints against too many war sequences in the news-reels, which had been by far the best of Dr. Goebbels' propaganda weapons, were being addressed to the Propaganda Ministry, People were, in a word, sick to death of war and all that savoured of it. That, in a few words, was the situation when Hitler collected his energies for the consummate blow. That was the temper of the times when Hitler told Dr. Dietrich to go to town on the memorable ninth of October—the day the rains came, when my janitor took Moscow single-handed; when Germans began dreaming of cool nights sipping *pivo* on the colonial Black Sea riviera; when God was truly in His heaven, Hitler in his headquarters, and all, absolutely all, was right in this best of all possible worlds.

Hitler had already begun dealing out concessions on Soviet Russian factories to German industrialists. My Hitler Youth friend confided to me his business career would probably be somewhere in the east; great opportunities for development there, you know. The press published photographs of old Russian castles built by ancient Teutonic wanderers and spoke of "Germany's mission of culture in the East". Lest anyone should dream there was anything commercial in Germany's interest in Russia, the *National Socialist Weekly* published a fine, flowery poem called *Ostland* ("Eastern land") every single word of which was wrapped in a separate soft cloud telling how Germans had often consecrated Russian earth with their blood and were called on by a simple sense of duty to bear the blond-haired-man's-burden. An engineer friend whose intellectual appetite was somewhere below the "True Confessions magazine" level, bought a whole set of Tchekov to "dust off my Russian". Everybody was going to be rich. Every Aryan a millionaire.

Those were the balmy days, if I ever saw balmy days. It's almost too bad they did not last longer. But they didn't. The awakening was quick and harsh. Here is a genuine sequence, without a day missing, of frontpage headlines in the *Voelkischer Beobachter* on the days following the Dietrich episode. See if you can feel the draught:

October 10: (commenting Dietrich's speech in big red letters spread all the way across the front page):

"*The Great Hour Has Struck*"
"CAMPAIGN IN EAST DECIDED!"

October 11: (in black letters)
"EASTERN BREAKTHROUGH DEEPENS"

October 12:

"ANNIHILATION OF SOVIET ARMIES ALMOST CONCLUDED"

"Horrible Terror in Odessa; Soviet Deserters being Shot in Back"

October 13:

"The Battlefields of Vyasma Bryansk Far Behind Front"

October 14:

"Operations in East Proceed According to Plan" (!)

October 15:

"Operations in East Proceed as Foreseen"

And on this same day, the main headline read: "Speedboats sink British Freighters from Convoy"! Within two weeks after the greatest military blow in Hitler's history, one week of the Decision being Reached, and four days after Stalin's last armies were in dissolution, the sinking of a couple of British freighters in the English channel had become more important than the biggest military conflict in the world! The very next day the *V.B.* published an editorial on its front page which is relevant. The title of the editorial was "Three Millions" referring to the number of Soviet Russian prisoners the High Command claimed to have made. The author gives the uncomfortable impression of trying to convince himself more than his readers.

"No army", he writes, "even if it does possess an inexhaustible reservoir of man-power such as the Soviet Union has, can withstand such a loss. The Bolshevist army is crushed. What the Soviets may have in the way of questionable reserves can be no obstacle. . . . The war in the East has achieved its objective: the annihilation of the enemy." The editorial concludes: "Stalin's armies have simply disappeared from the face of the earth".

Dr. Dietrich was always a bold spokesman, given to hazarding his reputation, or goodly parts of it, cheaply. He loved to make daring statements and bold predictions; and revelled in superlatives. Once he made the famous declaration to a public gathering that the German press was the freest press in the world, and the German public the best informed of peoples; an utterance which, early in the war, established him as an unconscionable ass with the foreign correspondents' corps. Next to the Labour-front leader,

Dr. Robert Ley, he was the most able of the Nazi leaders at putting his foot in his mouth every time he opened it. On another occasion, he spoke at a dinner in the Foreign Press Club and pointed with pride to the fact there was no censorship of the foreign press and never had been under Hitler. This, he stated, was irrefutable proof that the Nazis had nothing to hide; that the home front was strong as steel. While the atmosphere was still taut with expectation in Berlin after his speech of October 9, a party of foreign reporters made the afore-mentioned trip to the Russian front and, there, took as they had always done, full advantage of this fine privilege. Their stories they sent by special courier to their offices, via the Propaganda Ministry, in Berlin. When the trip was over and they returned to Berlin they made the discovery that only about half their stories had reached their offices, and these were badly sheared. It was censorship! While they were gone, I had confirmed its existence in a telephone conversation with Dr. Froelich. It was one of my seasonal complaints about the growing stupidity of the censorship of radio scripts. Dr. Froelich told me I no longer had grounds for complaint. An open censorship had now been applied to the press as well. I told him I found that interesting, and I would use the fact in my next broadcast to America, for it had never been announced to the public. Dr. Froelich advised against it, and when I included the report in one of my scripts, the radio censors promptly ran their blue pencils through the whole item. It was an "open" censorship, but they did not want it known! Now, the Nazis are certainly entitled to introduce a censorship if they wish to; every other warring nation has one. But the interesting feature is this: if to Dr. Dietrich the absence of censorship meant the Nazis had nothing to hide, and the home front was strong; then, by the same token, the introduction of one, exactly at this stage meant the Nazis did now have something to hide, and the new condition of the home front left much, from their point of view, to be desired. By this time, too, the hangover from Dietrich's last exhibition was setting in with a vengeance. Dr. Dietrich had offered his reputation on a silver platter. He found lots of takers.

For him, however, the disaster lay not in losing it with the foreign press and radio, but in losing it with the German people. The disaster was all the greater, for into his personal *débâcle* the whole reputation of Nazi propaganda was drawn. In the wake of it fol-

Books are poor burners, as oxygen doesn't get to packed pages.
Goebbels achieved this flame by applying more petrol than paper,
then sough cheaper forms of hatefulness.

As war neared, frequent military patrols in Berlin streets
failed to raise cheers. People were worried.

An Austrian contemplates Hitler's easiest victory:
the conquest of Austria by an Austrian.

Back from dress rehearsal for war;
Hitler greets the Condor legion, home from Spain.

1937. Things keep moving Hitler's way. Nazis celebrate
with torchlight parade through Brandenburg Gate.

1938. Nuremberg Rally. Giant parade prior to Hitler's
speech declaring Czechoslovakia's existence insufferable.

1938. Wehrmacht marches freely across the Czech border,
thanks to Munich giveaway.

Students salute inmarching Germans as last peace time
restraint on Germany, Czechoslovakia, is removed.

Governor of Berlin, moulder of Nazi Germany's image,
Reptilian Paul Joseph Goebbels.

June 22, 1942. Biggest clash of armies in history.
Ribbentrop tells sleepy foreign reporters, including author
(circled), Germany has invaded Soviet Union.

lowed a flood of those little *Witze*, those political jokes and three-
or four-line oral *feuilletons* which circulate over Germany by word
of mouth faster and broader than any of Goebbels' newspapers.
In private homes, people took to the little quip of raising their
hands in a clenched fist salute at the mention of the Dietrich
speech, and saying: *Der Bolschewismus ist tot! Es lebe der Bolschewismus!* ("Bolshevism is dead! Long live Bolshevism!") Another
was a crude but clever mimeographed cartoon which was
secretly circulated over Berlin, showing a German propaganda
soldier standing above a trench across the Russian lines and holding up a big placard to the enemy which read: "Russians! You
have ceased to exist!" It was signed "Dr. Dietrich". At the
moment of drawing, however, the said propaganda soldier had
become involved with a Russian shell and his various members
were flying in all directions. Below him in the trench a very
Prussian Lieutenant, who had been looking across through a
periscope, had turned to a quizzical general behind him and was
saying: "Stupid, these Russians; they apparently don't understand
a word of German!"

Less funny, but more incisive was the little observation which
might be called the "Three Climaxes of Hitler", which circulated
at the same time. It has no particular punch-line, but belongs to
the same category of expression for, like them, it was always introduced with the traditional preface: "Do you know what people
are saying? . . ." According to this, the first climax was the climax
of Diplomacy—Munich. After that diplomacy never again played
an important part in Hitler's policies; the rest was guns. The
second was the military climax: the campaign in France, the
perfect application of *Blitzkrieg* with the perfect ending: the total
destruction of a great army. The third was the climax of propaganda: the Dietrich speech. After Hitler's little press chief had
raised the spirits of his people to the skies and then let them fall
again down into the abyss of despair German propaganda could
never again influence to any important degree the morale of the
German people. From now on a wall of distrust separated the
Ministry of Dr. Goebbels from his people. The shepherd-boy had
hollered "Wolf!" too often.

This was more than a cogent little analysis suitable for table
talk. The evidence for its truth is overwhelming. The first sign
was the decline in newspaper sales. To test word-of-mouth reports

that a decline had occurred, I asked my newspaper vendor in a large kiosk on Wittenberg Platz, and was told that sales of newspapers had fallen off in all the kiosks operated by her particular concession-holder. In her kiosk the drop had been greater than forty per cent. As Berliners will, they invented a joke about the German press after that. It concerns a Berlin paper called the "*B.Z.*", meaning *Berliner Zeitung*. You were supposed to ask, to make the joke click, why it was that the only newspaper people read any more was the "B.Z." The answer was: because it lies only from B to Z, while all the others lie from A to Z.

More important still, because it was a positive sign people were seeking news elsewhere, rather than the negative one that they were ceasing to look for information from Nazi sources, was the rapid increase in listening to news broadcasts from foreign capitals —especially London and Moscow. An official of the Propaganda Ministry told me arrests for this "crime" in Germany tripled after the Dietrich speech. In the newspapers it was announced that two individuals were punished with the extreme penalty, death, for listening to London! On October 30, Dr. Goebbels confirmed the increase by publishing in every newspaper in Germany a list of stations to which people might listen, stations in Germany and occupied countries; and he coupled with it a warning not to overstep these limits, which were clearly drawn exactly for this purpose. In November, every citizen in Germany received, with his ration-tickets for the month, a little red card with a hole punched in the middle of it so that it might be hung on the station-dial of a radio set, and on the card was the legend: "Racial Comrades! You are Germans! It is your duty not to listen to foreign stations. Those who do so will be mercilessly punished!" A week later in my neighbourhood houses were visited by local Nazi chiefs to make sure that the cards had been fastened to radios and were still there. People who had no radio sets were told to keep the cards anyhow, and to let them be a reminder not to listen to the conversation of people who did have radios and turned in on foreign stations. The conclusion to be drawn from this is obvious: there had been a tremendous increase in listening to enemy radio stations; people distrusted their own propaganda. So far as I could discover, the main effect of the new wave of propaganda and threats against listening was to make those who had been afraid to do so curious, and to convert them into regular listeners of enemy stations. After all, it is almost impossible to catch a person actually listening to foreign stations; it is so easy for him to switch back to the *Deutschland Sender* the moment the door-bell rings. Almost all those who have been arrested, were apprehended, not while listening but while telling others, in public places, what they had heard.

Captain Sommerfeld is a frog-eyed, congenial hard-drinking Prussian officer who serves the German High Command as their "authorized military spokesman" in the Propaganda Ministry. Captain Sommerfeld is a Prussian and his watchwords are Duty and Discipline. No man could have been a better choice for the job of having to sustain Dr. Dietrich than he. He did it as admirably and obstinately as the Russians have defended Moscow. Each day at five-thirty, sitting in a red-plush chair in the Theatre Hall of the Ministry, under that huge map of Russia on the stage, he struggled to live up to the environment once hallowed by the Fuehrer's special emissary. Each day for months he repeated with a straight face and a stiff back: the Red Army was destroyed. He never let a mere fact phase him. All that was left, *meine Herren*, were a few hastily assembled brigades of starving Russian workers, and a handful of children and women with guns. Moscow would fall, gentlemen, and there is nothing more certain than that!

But the daylight, coming through the red velvet curtains on the windows of the Theatre Hall at five-thirty each day, grew dimmer and one evening, the curtains were drawn and the conference began with the lights on inside. The days were getting shorter. But Captain Sommerfeld, like the stubborn Prussian he was, stood by his guns and his face was straight as his back.

On November 23, the *Voelkischer Beobachter* got out its red-ink pot again to publish a big two-word headline. It was: "ROSTOV TAKEN!" But it didn't raise sales any at all. The people read much more closely an inconspicuous little notice of the High Command which appeared in the *V.B.* two weeks later. Then, it was getting on to Christmas. The shops were empty, except for the toy shops where there were lots of cardboard games, like one called "Bombs on England". There was no liquor for Christmas punch, and there were no geese or rabbits for Christmas dinner. On the streets at dusk, queues before shops were getting longer. The notice in the papers was to the effect that a Russian town named Rostov, and situated at the mouth of the Don river, had been evacuated by the troops of the Fuehrer in order to prepare reprisals against the civil population in view of their inhospitable attitude. It was in black ink.

IV

THE ECONOMICS OF DECLINE

LIKE AN ARMY, a graph of civilian morale moves on its stomach. And the better part of a high national spirit is a well-filled national pantry. These are axioms which cannot be stated unconditionally. For other factors may enter into the complex, such as a growing sense of the righteousness or wrongness of the cause one is fighting for, and destroy the consistent relationship between food and morale. Take Loyalist Spain, Britain and Russia as examples. There, in war, morale actually moved in inverse ratio to supplies of foodstuffs; as food supplies went down morale moved in the opposite direction: upwards. But, regarding Nazi Germany, the axioms fit as snugly as Goering's breast-revealing tunic. In Germany, there has been no disturbing factor such as a clear conscience among the broad masses of the people regarding their leader's acts. I do not mean what Germans *say* about their government's actions. I mean what they feel deep down inside about them. Just as eternal boasting is a sign of some weakness in the make-up of a bully, so constant drum-beating to attest innocence, repeated protestations of guiltlessness are a sign the drum-beater doesn't quite believe his own case, or that he is convincing anyone else of it. Why does each and every one of Hitler's speeches follow the same, monotonous pattern of nine-tenths reviewing the wrongs done to Germany by the world, and one-tenth threats aimed at cowing opponents? The answer is that the nine-tenths are meant for the German people whom the Nazis distrust, and who distrust, deep down inside, the Nazis. The fact that the Fuehrer feels called upon to repeat the same pathetic story with the same pitiful ear-scraping screams of righteous indignation each time he enters the forum is proof of nothing more nor less than that he doesn't quite believe his people believe him. Or why does Ribbentrop lock up a vast staff of office-workers in the upper rooms of the Adlon Hotel before each new act of aggression to prepare mountains of documents proving Germany was not menacing, but menaced, when he knows the outside world does not believe him: obviously, he must try to convince the German people. As loudly and voluminously as possible he must deluge them with paper evidence to convince them that their national conscience is clear. When British troops entered Syria, Iraq and Iran; when American troops joined in the occupation of Iceland, there were no theatrical performances accompanied by car-loads of documents, no incessant tub-thumping for weeks afterwards by a uniform press to drive the conviction in. There were official statements, brief and frank. But Hitler and Ribbentrop cannot let matters rest at that. The characteristic difference between Axis and Allied propaganda is one I have already indicated. The German propagandists are still, after nine years of power, or three of war, pounding the moral tom-tom; still emphasizing Germany's righteousness in fighting the world. Allied propaganda seldom, if ever, touches on this question; it deals only with the technical questions of how this thing we all know is bad can be crushed. Although every allied statesman fears being called on the carpet by his people regarding possible failures in the technical question, none fears being called to account on the moral one. But every German leader does.

In this frame of mind, to Germans Bread—and by this I mean the symbol for food, clothing, shelter; all the things human beings live by and with—is axiomatically the principal constituent of morale. In war, the principal element of the Hitler Myth for me has been, of course, Hitler's phenomenal military triumphs. In peace, the most disturbing element was the success with which Hitler maintained home consumption economics; and this, not even the shocks of war seriously influenced. Despite the inevitable strain on consumption economics his rearmament programme and his campaigns entailed, the home front continued to be enigmatically and disturbingly well provided. Food and clothing were not exciting; they were, like morale, indifferent. But what was surprising in view of the circumstances was that they, again like morale, were not at all bad.

Butter was not abundant, but it was sufficient. A goodly slab of meat, a medium-sized *Schnitzel* or a couple of long, fat sausages were available before the war for almost every meal; and after the beginning of the war for a smaller but not insufficient number of meals. This, garnished with carrots, beans and potatoes, constituted a normal repast; thereto a crock of beer or a bottle of good Moselle wine. For a people engaged in a life-and-death war, in which absolutely everything was in the scales, the German people for two years of war ate amazingly well.

Until the Great Watershed. The quality of things declined perceptibly and automatically from the first day of the Russian campaign. Then quantities of things were cut into. Two months after the outbreak, these two developments seemed to gain speed in a downward direction. And by the time Dr. Dietrich had conquered Timoshenko's armies, a spiral had begun. The old charm had been broken. After nine years of better-than-enough, scarcity, with vengeance slaked by postponement, set in. By the time I left Germany, I could honestly report for the first time that *the German people are undernourished*.

During the long years of apparent Nazi prosperity, accounting for the existence of that visible well-being was difficult, for the Myth discouraged any attempt at reasonable explanation. One simply had to accept it as magic. Now that the mirage of the super-natural has been swept away by one circumstance after another it is not hard, in retrospect, to divine the grounds for it. For two years of war, Germany staved off the diminishing of supplies and the decay of capital equipment which processed supplies, by rapid acquisition of the supplies of her neighbours by quick blows, which because of their speed were relatively painless for the German people. The conquest of France, for instance, yielded a wide-open treasure chest to the German civil popula-tion. The German troops simply pilfered the contents of the rich boulevard shops of Paris and the well-stocked pantries and the wine-cellars of the French countryside. The method was simple. Firstly they exacted exorbitant sums to cover the costs of occupa-tion (which the French could not get out of as easily as the Ger-mans escaped clauses of Versailles, for German troops were on the spot to claim the tribute), which, in the final analysis, was simply exacting the food and clothing of Frenchmen. They set up an arti-ficial rate of exchange between francs and marks by which the small monthly wage of a soldier could be converted into double or triple its value in French goods. It was thus, in Berlin, that the first effects of war were not the traditional ones of decay and scarcity, but a sudden leap upwards in visible prosperity. Berlin charwomen and housemaids, whose legs had never been caressed by silk, began wearing silk stockings from the Boulevard Haussman as an everyday thing—"from my Hans at the 'front'."

Little street corner taverns began displaying rows of Armagnac, Martell and Courvoisier Cognac from the cellars of Maxim's and others. Every little bureaucrat in the capital could produce at dinner a fine, fat bottle of the best French champagne. The first winter after the Norwegian campaign, the streets were filled with luxurious silver-fox fur coats wrapped around gleeful servant girls. A soldier coming home on leave was a fine sight to see. He carried in addition to his war-kit, baskets, big cardboard boxes and cheap suitcases filled to overflowing with all kinds of goodies and luxuries from the "front". I took a trip to France two months after the end of the French campaign, and already, all through Alsace and Lorraine, which the Germans doubtless plundered less recklessly than the other parts of France, food-shops were virtually empty. No objection is meant here to soldiers taking care of families at home as bountifully as possible, nor to housemaids wearing silk stockings; I think it is a good idea, if they like it. I am just pointing out what the horrors of war were like in Berlin. War was almost fun; like a football game except that you got more out of it. Shoes, hams, woollen sweaters, fine gowns, everything removable and some things that were not meant to be removed, were drained out of the serf lands with a careless abandon that might have shocked a Roman tyrant.

Whether the recklessness with which the High Command laid bare these conquered riches to its soldiers, and in more generous measure, to its officers, was moral or not is beside the point. The main consideration is that this was a strategic mistake. It hastened the exhaustion of these resources. A wiser, more gradual exploitation might have made them last twice as long, or longer. But they apparently felt the need to let their people enjoy the fruits of victory in a hurry and a-plenty. At any rate, by the time the Russian war began, Germany was already, actually scraping the bottom of Europe's economic bin (which, doubtless, is one reason why the Russian war began). Too ruthless, too haphazard an exploitation had drained the wrecked losers dry. To prepare his troops for the grand attack, to carry out the *Aufmarsch* of his forces against the Russian border, Hitler no longer had the coffers of food, fuel and textiles of the enslaved nations to draw from. Further, the Russian front was longer and better defended than the border of almost any nation he had saved the world from hitherto; it required far, far more soldiers (it is estimated that the Russian campaign required double the number of soldiers which fought in the West) than any other campaign up until that time.

The later effect on Germany can best be anticipated by marking the effect of the mere preliminaries on Poland. Before the actual campaign began, the mere deployment, lasting several months, of 10,000,000 men who by the nature of their occupation were big eaters and hard on clothing, bled that agonized land white. The German High Command repeatedly refused to let me go to the front (I had been in the dog-house ever since my encounter with Dr. Froelich in the Press Club), so I applied for permission to visit Poland alone, but this, too, was turned down. Unable to go myself, I saw it through the eyes of a German girl I knew who, like so many German misfits in this war, was given a soft secretarial job in colonial Warsaw. Later my room-mate, Jack Fleischer of the U.P., went into Poland and Russia, ten days after the outbreak of hostilities. Their pictures agreed in every common detail. Whole towns had not seen a single loaf of bread for weeks. People were dying by the thousand every day for lack of nourishment and low resistance to illness. Families boiled weeds into a bitter broth to drink in order to keep alive. On the streets haggard women offered their souls for a piece of bread. Like a plague of locusts, Hitler's hordes, sweeping up to the starting line for new conquest without which Germany could not, and cannot live, stripped the land bare of its last pitiful resources. The Nazi governor of Poland, Dr. Hans Frank, at tea in his palatial residence in the *Burg* at Krakow told the correspondents who had been invited there that the hope of reconstructing Poland had been set back half a decade by these mere preliminaries to the Russian war. Since conquest did not occur on schedule, Governor Frank's estimate can safely be multiplied several times.

That Hitler's armies should eventually have to suck at the bung-holes of their last, long-spared reservoir—Germany itself—was inevitable. Take the prime example of meat. Once, when I was writing a feature for one of my broadcasts on how such a gigantic aggregation of men as an army is supplied, the Propaganda Ministry prepared a little hand-out for me in which it was stated that a single army consumes in a single day 100 head of slaughtered livestock. In view of its source and the nature of the information, the figure can be accepted as reliable. Now, a conservative estimate of the number of German armies operating on the eastern front is twenty. There are probably, in reality, half as many more. But even on this estimate this means a drain on livestock supplies as high as 2,000 head each day for the Russian campaign. Thus, at the end of eight weeks, 96,000 head had been drawn away, mainly from Germany's own stock. By the time of Dr. Dietrich's visit to Berlin the number had reached 216,000. And by the day the civilians of Rostov threw the S.S. out of that city and initiated the Great Retreat, the figure had reached almost 350,000 head of good German livestock! That they were mainly German is certain. Innumerable stories written by the soldier-reporters of the Nazi *Propaganda-Kompanie* testified that the Russians were the first of Hitler's opponents who left nothing, absolutely nothing, behind in their retreat.

The effect on supplies for the German home-front was immediate. For the first two years of the war, the German meat ration had been 500 grammes per person per week. That amounts to about five steaks, a little bigger than medium-size, each week. At the beginning of the Russian campaign, the government announced the first cut in German rations since the outbreak of war—a reduction of meat rations to 400 grammes a week.

The war dragged on beyond schedule and another cut became necessary. But an official reduction was never made. From a source in the Nazi food ministry, whose reliability cannot be doubted, I learned that the food ministry had determined to introduce the cut, lopping off another 50 grammes, leaving the total ration at 350 grammes a week. And, if the campaign lasted much longer, this too, was to be reduced by another 50 grammes. The propaganda ministry, which was always in touch with trends in popular sentiment, interceded and protested that another official reduction would have an extremely bad effect on morale and hasten the decline that had already set in. By this time Goebbels was already faced with the decline in morale and had begun those now-famous "explanatory editorials" in *Das Reich*. The squabble that began with meat and then led into other departments of the food problem, eventually cost Walther Darre, the Nazi agricultural minister, the major part of his job. He retained the title, for purposes of front, but Hitler, in anger at the unexpectedly swift drop in all resources, took away from him the administration of one department after another, accusing him of having given false information to the party leadership concerning the abundance of supplies with which Germany began the Russian war.

The solution to the meat problem was eventually settled by compromise—and here we have another typical Nazi "solution" to a given problem. The cut would be made. But it simply would not be announced. Appearances would thus be maintained, and the two parties concerned satisfied; only the people were left out of consideration. So, while there was no official announcement, less meat was delivered to butchers' shops and to restaurants. In restaurants, for a 100-gramme meat coupon, the chef simply dealt out an 80-gramme piece of meat.

But even this could not be maintained. Food supplies were not, to use a figure, walking down a staircase; they were sliding down a chute, and a very slippery one. More reductions were introduced in the same manner, until they passed the limit of imperceptibility; until it became obvious that it was not the chef who was depriving you, but the government. Restaurants not only reduced the quantity of their servings, but in the first days of autumn began to run out of meat altogether before the end of serving time. In order to maintain appearances, the Hotel Kaiserhof began the practice of issuing a menu with two meat dishes on it, when the kitchen actually could serve but one. Just before noon, the hour when law permitted serving to begin, the waiters would simply visit each table and run a pencil mark through the second dish on the menu as though it *had* been available but too many orders had exhausted the supply. The stratagem fooled at least half the clientele, that half which came after one o'clock and thus had no reason to doubt appearances. But I knew one of the waiters, a seventy year-old man who was mad at the Kaiserhof because the management wouldn't pension him off, and he told me. The Kaiserhof can possibly be excused; it has a reputation to uphold. It stands in the shadow of the chancellery, and, before he came to power, Hitler maintained his headquarters there. The poor butchers had no such simple way out; they could only shrug their shoulders and point at empty counters when customers came in after the sell-out. The result of early sell-outs was that the rush hours gradually shifted up to midday and finally to early morning, when housewives gathered outside the shops before opening time.

Just before I left Berlin I had an opportunity to make a statistical measurement of that stage in the progressive reductions. I was sitting with a group of correspondents and petty officials of the Propaganda Ministry in the Press Club on Leipziger Platz, where the healthiest rations in all Berlin were served. The meat course was served and the little officials set up their evening howl at the tiny blobs of meat on their plates. (These infinitesimal twerps who represented Dr. Goebbels to us were by far the worst propagandists he could have chosen. They were *petit bourgeois* to a farcical extreme. Although they ate in the Club at the Ministry's expense and consumed all they could hold, and more, each day, they complained more obstreperously than violated virgins about seasoning and quantity, and, in fact, anything else they could discover to complain about.) The size of the portions was actually a little better than the standard for all Berlin. But the bureaucrats demanded justice and scales. They would weigh the portions. The waiter, noticing me, a foreigner, said there were no scales. But one grouser, who had been down in the kitchen during an air-raid one night had seen scales and could tell him where the scales were. So, reluctantly, the waiter produced the scales and the various portions were weighed. Each was exactly forty grammes. A little simple mathematics yields the result that in five months, the German meat ration of 500 grammes a week, had dropped to 160 grammes a week. I think it is not an exaggeration to say that for the mass of the German people, five months of war in Russia had cost them *four-fifths* of their weekly meat ration!

It is not as easy to measure other foodstuffs. The quality of fats, for instance, is so elastic that its nutritive value can be reduced by dilution to a great extent before the change becomes perceptible—a device which the food ministry took full advantage of regarding cooking fats, lard and oil. In the long run this can only be noticed by its bad effect on the health and strength of the people, which eventually made itself visible. But the fact that dilution was occurring became obvious before this effect set in, for the eastern front drained away already scarce fats so quickly that swift and large reductions had to be made within a very short period, and the stage of perceptibility was entered early after the beginning of the campaign. I experienced it personally twice and had to abandon the relatively good meals of the Press Club on its own doorstep a few minutes after I had eaten them. After the second occasion, I began having my meals in my apartment most of the time, eating meat imported from Switzerland and butter from Denmark. On one occasion a German friend who ate this food at my table grew nauseated and ill because, she said, the fat was too rich and plentiful for her constitution after having survived on German fats for two years. The fact is, that the only decent fats in Germany are shipped off to the East for the troops. What civilian food is prepared with is a weak *Ersatz*, which is made by filtering restaurant rubbish in a special contrivance all restaurants have been forced to install in their kitchens. It is given some sort of flavour by the addition of chemicals.

Most foodstuffs became worse and less in stages. But the main constituent of the German diet, the very staff of German life, potatoes, disappeared with alarming suddenness one day in early autumn. This was the most serious deficiency of all. For potatoes are to Germans what bread is to Americans and spaghetti to Italians. Germans eat twice as many potatoes a year as Britons, and thrice as many as Americans. Throughout the entire war there had been a superabundance of potatoes in Germany. At the beginning of the war all restaurants were required to post little signs on their walls offering second and third helpings of potatoes, without extra charge, to patrons who felt they had not had enough to eat. That patrons took advantage of this arrangement is evinced by an official statement that consumption of potatoes has gone up about twenty per cent since the beginning of the war. Potatoes were, in short, the last and most reliable line of reserve on which the food ministry always knew it could fall back; if all else failed there would always be enough of that item. But one day the unexpected happened, and there was not a single potato in all Berlin.

The potato crisis had but little to do with the Russian war. It was just another one of the many circumstances that "ganged up" against Hitler. The reason for the scarcity was not martial but meteorological. The summer had been brief and unusually wet, and autumn unusually cold. The incessant rains took a heavy toll of the crop, then the early cold made it impossible to remove the potatoes from earth-pits to be transported to cities, for they would freeze before they could be moved, or before the pits could be closed again. The Nazis claim only about five per cent of the crop was lost, but the actual figure, according to my friend in the food ministry, was over thirty per cent.

To housewives who had watched all their other shopping items dwindle, the sudden disappearance of this one thing they thought they could always rely on was a severe shock. For almost two weeks there were no potatoes in Berlin. It was at this time that the government cut passenger schedules on the railways and began using heated third-class railway coaches for transporting potatoes to consumption centres. Even after this, however, supplies were scanty and the quality of the potatoes bad, and ration-cards for potatoes were introduced, something no German would have thought possible! The government also issued an appeal to the people (and an order to restaurants) not to peel potatoes before boiling them, for this wasted fifteen per cent of each potato and served to intensify the scarcity.

Other vegetables came to count as luxuries. Tomatoes were rationed too for a while, then disappeared altogether to canning factories where they could be preserved and sent to the Eastern front. Two-vegetable meals became virtually extinct. Scarcities were made more severe by the prudence of the food ministry which, having had its palms slapped once, began to play safe by preparing more and more canned goods for the troops in the event that the war should last through the winter.

The new situation taxed the ingenuity of housewives. In order to get two different vegetables from the markets on one day, they invented the system of "rotating queues" whereby one woman could stand in two lines at one time. The scheme operated this way: Frau Schmidt reached the market early in the morning and got a place in the potato line, the most important of them all. She immediately set about making friends with Frau Mueller behind her. When relations were cemented and an oral pact made, Frau Mueller agreed to hold Frau Schmidt's place in the potato line while the latter went over to the carrot line and repeating the procedure, succeeding in inducing Frau Hinkel to hold her place while she returned to the potato line in order to hold Frau Mueller's position, while Frau Mueller went over to the carrot line. At length Frau Schmidt's turn for potatoes arrived, and after she had bought her potatoes she rushed over to take her position, by now at the head, in the carrot line. Thus, and thus alone, could one buy two vegetables. Of course, the scheme was eventually prohibited by the police who threatened penalties for its practice.

Lesser amenities of life followed the same pattern of decline: first, dilution of quality, then decreases in quantity, which continued until many commodities disappeared altogether. The little two-by-one-half inch cake of soap one got to keep one's person clean each month yielded perceptibly less lather each distribution period, a development which was registered not only in the qualities of the soap itself, but also by the increasingly bad odour in crowded subways, trams and in theatres. Cosmetics disappeared. Tooth paste was chalk and water with weak peppermint flavouring, and a tube of it hardened into cement unless used rapidly. *Ersatz* foods flourished. Icing for the few remaining pastries tasted like a mixture of saccharine, sand and cheap perfume. White bread was issued after the third month of the campaign only on the ration cards formerly for pastry. A red coloured paste called *Lachs Galantine*, resembling salmon in colour and soggy sawdust in taste, appeared in restaurants on meatless days. Several strange bottled sauces made of incredible combinations of acid-tasting chemicals made their appearance in shops to answer the public's growing demand for something to put a taste of some kind in their unattractive and scanty meals.

Cigarettes suffered the most rapid decline in quality. Perhaps the best cigarettes on sale in Germany were American-length "Johnnies" which I smoked for lack of anything else. Within a year, they have changed flavour three times. As the most marked change occurred after General Rommel's occupation of Cyrenaica, rumour insisted that the main ingredient was camel dung!—the first booty from the latest occupied land. This observation was not so funny when one had to smoke these miserable weeds. My tobacconist told me "Johnnies" were made of the same dry, powdery, inferior tobacco as other cigarettes, but the leaves were sprayed with a chemical to give them a distinctive flavour and kill their original one. The chemical, he said, was severely damaging to the lungs, which I can believe.

The rather sudden decrease in quantitative supplies of tobacco brought Berlin its first substantial queues early in the Russian war. I kept a record of the length of the queues before my tobacco shop by noting every evening at which window or door along the street it began. One could make observations like this for the queues generally remained a fairly consistent length while the tobacco shop had cigarettes and cigars, from the time the door was opened until, about half an hour later, when the door was closed and the "sold-out" sign was hung on it. The queues increased from around twenty yards in length in the second month of the Russian war to ninety yards the evening I left.

The Nazis gave away the fact that a severe shortage was at hand by suddenly publishing propaganda in the press against smoking. Hitler Youth were given lectures on the harm done by smoking to their bodies, which they must preserve for the Fuehrer. Then, the Nazi "corporation" for restaurants and cafés issued an order to the effect that in the future women would not be sold cigarettes in any *Lokal*. The result was a rush on existing supplies. As a consequence, the individual ration of cigarettes dropped from as many as one wanted to buy at the outset of Russian war, to three a day on days when there were any at all, after five months. The recent introduction of "smoking ration cards" is an empty gesture. Rations were three or none and will probably remain three, when available, and none most of the time. The theory of the cards is that they prevent people with lots of time from standing in more than one queue a day. But nobody in Germany has lots of time.

But, certainly the unkindest cut of all to alcohol-loving German *Buerger* was the sudden departure of that commodity from taverns and shops. The troops needed every drop both for drinks and "internal heating", and for medicaments. Beer suffered first, because it had been most abundant and could more easily bear a reduction. By official order, production was lowered twenty per cent in the beginning of the campaign. Then, as in the case of everything else, more reductions were ordered but not announced. Taverns began closing one day a week. Then two days a week. Then they began closing for periods of a month at a time on pretext of undertaking "repairs". Repairs were certainly needed in pubs as everywhere else, but the pretext was false because it was impossible to find anyone to do repairs after the *Aufmarsch* for Russia had drained away every reasonably young man, and many old ones. Actually, there was no law against receiving weekly deliveries of beer whether the pub was open or not. So, in order not to have to close doors after a couple of hours of serving each day, taverns simply accumulated stocks in this manner for a month, and then could stay open a whole week or more. Even with this strategy, after five months of defeating Russia, there were only four places in all Berlin where one could get beer consistently, and their supplies were maintained for sheer propaganda effect, the biggest hotels and the press clubs. Even here, however, "hours" were set outside which beer could not be ordered, and, at least one of these places, the Adlon Hotel, where the foreign office lodges visiting diplomats, began frankly watering its beer!

It was almost pathetic watching these fine old hotels with glorious pasts, and in whose registers had appeared the names of many of the crowned heads and political leaders of Europe struggling to keep up appearances. The Kaiserhof bar, its counter empty, set up a display of bottles of coloured water against its mirror background. It caused visible pain to the old bar-tender to answer an order for a cocktail saying he was dreadfully sorry but today, precisely today, he had run out of ingredients. But perhaps tomorrow. Actually, all he had was some raw liquor the management had been able to squeeze out of a farm-house outside Berlin, *Himbeergeist*, or a fake Vodka that took the roof off your mouth, or wood alcohol with perfume in it which was served under the name of *Sclibovitz*, two fingers to a customer and no more, but tomorrow, *meine Herren*, maybe. The coloured water trick was widely applied after that, but it became embarrassing when thirsty citizens began plaguing the places which displayed flagons of it to sell a bottle or two. One fancy delicatessen on Kurfuerstendamm, eventually placed the frank sign in its window, "These bottles are filled with coloured water and nothing else. They are purely for purposes of decoration. We have no liquor, so please do not bother our sales staff, which is short due to the war." Wine, which had been second only to beer in abundance, disappeared from shops abruptly the last week in November. Wine shops were simply closed by official order and their contents bought at fixed prices for the troops. Thus Germany entered upon the bleakest, dryest Christmas in its history, and in that statement the World War period is included. When I left, there was virtually nothing, almost no alcoholic beverage left to drink. Against its will, Germany had become, perhaps, the most temperate nation on earth. Germany's favourite non-alcoholic beverage was *Apfelsaft*, a good, sweet apple-cider. That too had disappeared. For awhile a juice made of rhubarb was substituted for it, but then the canneries began to claim all German fruit for the troops and not even that was left.

I want to emphasize that all these scarcities and absolute disappearances of things was not spread over two and a half years of war. They came all at once. In five months the face of Germany's supply situation changed with a swiftness that was staggering. The only figure which describes it was one I have used—a dizzy, downward spiral. Clothing offers one of the best examples of this rapid decline. All through the war, clothing was not good, but one had no difficulty in getting one's allotted number of "points" worth, as allowed by the annual ration card. This was still true at the beginning of the Russian war. But by the time the Germans entered Kiev, clothing rationing had become purely theoretical. Clothing simply ceased to exist, to borrow the term the High Command was then applying to the Russian armies. In show-windows all-important appearances were kept up; the windows were full of fine shirts, red pyjamas, striped socks and real woollen sweaters. But the give-away was an inconspicuous little card down in the corner of the window which stated the contents of the window might not be sold until decorations were changed. Decorations simply did not change. In June, I put in a bid at one shop for a pair of those red pyjamas. When I left Germany six months later, decorations—i.e. my pyjamas—still had not changed.

Inside, shops were empty. Shelves were stone-bare. There was nothing, except a lone, worried salesman, who was always sorry but if you would came back next week, perhaps new stocks which had been ordered would have arrived. About shoes, the Nazis were frank. At the very beginning of the campaign, they issued a leaflet to each family in Berlin explaining that civilians could expect no more shoes; all leather was needed for the soldiers. The leaflets did state, however, that "special conditions" might justify the granting of a permit to buy shoes, but nobody in my rather large circle of acquaintances ever discovered what these special conditions were. My charwoman who walked in shoes held together by packing cord whose bottoms were stuffed with cardboard—her only shoes—could not discover the conditions after three applications to the authorities for a new pair. The next blow was to the shoe-repair shops. The authorities stopped delivering leather to most of them and they had to close. The population had to concentrate on the few remaining ones which were soon overworked and began turning down new orders. As their leather allotments from the government were not commensurately increased, the cobblers who remained open eventually had to resort to wood for heels on women's shoes and merely tacking small wedges of old leather on the worn out spots on men's shoes, instead of replacing the whole heel or sole. The Nazi government's "corporation" for leather (a government bureau manned by the biggest shoe industrialists, similar to all the German *Wirtschaftsgruppen*) had already ordered semi-experimental production of shoes made of straw, wood and glass but these materials were in such short supply that shoes produced from them soon became unobtainable, as the materials were needed for more important branches of production. Thanks to long-term hoarding by individuals before the war, and to plunder from the occupied lands, Germans are still shod with relative decency, but, since shoes wear out quicker than any other item of clothing, both on the front and at home, a serious "shoe-crisis" is inevitable.

The third traditional category of things essential to man after food and clothing—shelter—too, has entered a pre-crisis stage. Like the potato shortage the housing shortage, which has now become acute, was not a result of the Russian campaign in particular but a feature, whose appearance had been delayed, of the war in general, and just circumstance. In Berlin the problem was most severe because so many firms from all over Europe have had to set up representations in the new capital of Hitler's Europe; diplomatic corps have been expanded to double and triple peace size, and thousands of rural and foreign workers have been drawn into the city to man the factories. But the problem exists in great degree in every big city in Germany due to the paralysis of the building industry while the birth-rate goes on rising. It is estimated that the population in Berlin has increased by at least twenty-five per cent since the outbreak of war, whilst there has been no corresponding increase in the number of houses. It has become extremely difficult to get a single room and impossible to get an apartment anywhere in the entire city. The leasing of apartments has been taken out of the hands of the rental agencies and put under the supervision of the Nazi party which deals out the few periodic vacancies to families on the basis of their party loyalty and the number of recent children in them. Tex Fisher, a correspondent of the Associated Press, was forced to set up living quarters in the corner of the A.P. office in central Berlin when the lease on his apartment in the residential district ran out; he could not find a room in a pension or anywhere else. Hotels are miserably overcrowded. A German I know, who came to Berlin from Leipzig, had to spend half his first night visiting twenty different hotels before he finally found a room—a bath-room with a cot in the bath-tub! The Crown Prince of Sweden came to Berlin unannounced and was turned down by four big hotels before a fifth managed to vacate a single room for the royal guest. When the anti-American campaign reached its climax—which will be related in detail later —the big hotels issued notices of eviction to the Americans living in them, in order to gain much-needed space for nationals more amicable to the Axis. This, however, was eventually smoothed out and the Americans allowed to stay provided they paid their rent in advance each month. One reason, though not the main one, for the new anti-Jewish campaign last autumn when Jews were thrown out of their homes, was to get *Lebensraum* for Nazi families. Berlin had become with appalling suddenness a city-at-war, and circumstances left not a single feature of the picture incomplete.

Like the "Wonderful One-Hoss Shay", the whole Nazi contrivance seemed to have been precisely so constructed, that it would run along nicely without a single complaint until one fine day the whole thing and all its parts would go to pot at once—the axle would break, the tongue and the bridle, and every screw and spoke decay all at once. Berlin had one of the best municipal transport systems in the world. It is now a crippled shadow of its former self. Buses which had groaned successfully through years of hard labour suddenly stopped running *en masse*. There was nobody to repair them, no parts to repair them with, and petrol was too scarce for their old inefficient highly absorbent motors. Trams jolted to dead stops and had to be hauled off to terminals to wait, like everything else, for the end of the war for repairs. One bus or tram line was discontinued after another. The underground and the electric became shoddy, dirty and worn-out; the number of accidents multiplied due to the decay of cars and tracks and the sudden replacing of thousands of experienced men—who were called to the front—by legions of inexperienced women. The number of taxis has been cut to less than one-fifth the peace-time quota and each taxi driver receives less than half a gallon of petrol a day.

In office buildings lifts have ceased functioning due to super-annuation, banisters on staircases are breaking off and type-writers losing their now irreplaceable keys. In homes plumbing and heating systems get jammed, and it takes weeks to get some-one to repair them; door-locks break and stay broken, door-knobs fall off and have to be reattached with a nail or a match stick. Repair men—radio fixers, locksmiths, cobblers, plumbers—have become a dictatorial *élite*, but an *élite* which on grounds of over-work deserves its new advantages. They are grumpy and can ask any price they wish, and they prefer payment in tangible goods. They are not interested in money. Everybody has enough paper notes and blackened zinc coins; even the poorly paid have more money than they can spend on their needs. As a friend of mine said, after searching vainly in the *Ka-De-We* department stores across Wittenberg Platz for two hours for something useful: "That big barn is empty. It is a feat of skill to get rid of fifty pfennigs on all seven floors". That is only a slight exaggeration, if it is one at all. I, myself, involuntarily saved no less than four-fifths of my salary in the last six months in Germany because there was nothing to spend it on.

The universal superabundance of money is not because things are inexpensive. What is available is exorbitantly dear. Despite measures rigorous as only the Nazis can make them, that most conspicuous element of inflation—rocketing prices—has become painfully evident everywhere in Germany in the past six months, and is causing the government a serious head-ache. By laws, threats and other incentives the Nazis have succeeded in stabiliz-ing rents and the prices of a few staple foodstuffs. But for every-thing else, people are willing to pay any price, and do. For coffee I received regularly from Switzerland, I was offered seventy-five marks (£6) for a single pound by a low-paid German working girl. Suburban farmers around Berlin are being offered from three to ten times peace prices for butter, eggs, meat, or, indeed, any-thing edible, by city dwellers. At Christmas time farmers were get-ting hundred marks each for Christmas geese. Bad, home-fermented liquor brought many times peace-time prices of high grade schnaps. How worried the Nazi government is concerning infringements on any of its newly created laws can always be judged by the severity of the penalties attached to them. Penalties have been rather severe for illegal butchering of livestock for sale on the black market since the beginning of the war. But in September, for the first time, a farmer in Rostock on the Baltic coast was beheaded for slaughtering a single hog without permission.

The economic situation inside the Hitler household has become dismal. All the little things that make life pleasant have disappeared. All the things which are necessary to make physical life continue have deteriorated, and in some cases fallen below the level of fitness for human consumption. The general health condition of the masses has fallen steadily, whatever doctored Nazi figures say. Civilian hospitals are overcrowded and doctors overworked. Environment, which has a great deal to do with mental health and well-being has grown seedy and ugly. Hours are longer and real wages immeasurably lower than they were before the Russian war. Families are losing their youngest and strongest members, or seeing them come home legless and armless. The horizon of the average German is desolate. He may not win the war, and even if he does it will take many years to defeat Russia, England and America. The end is nowhere in sight. Even if he wins, he knows that every day it continues will cost ten days labour at reconstruction afterwards. For every year it goes on, it will taken ten years of work just to bring things back to where they were, not to mention progressing beyond. I borrow that thought from the wife of a German workman I know. She has seen one hard war and suffered through a long, painful reconstruction period and the false prosperity of the Hitler era. Now she is suffering a second, harder war, and before her is another long period of reconstruction, win or lose. She was not given to complaining; she was a mild-mannered, good natured little woman but her spirit was breaking. "What", she asked me, "what have we got to live for? What is there to look forward to"? You would be surprised how often you hear that same desperate question put by Germans. Even loyal Nazis have expressed doubts if victory will be worth it all. Morale has slipped badly.

If these millions were consumers and that were all, Hitler need have little cause for worry. The Gestapo is powerful enough to deal with mere discontent for a long time yet. But these millions also have a social function as producers in Hitler's Reich. They make the cannon, guns and tanks Hitler cannot do without. No Gestapo in the world can make an unhealthy and demoralized man work as efficiently as a healthy, high-spirited one.

The record of the German people as producers has been, technically viewed, an astounding one. Since 1933 the scale of their production has gone up and up and up with never a falter. Every year the yield of armaments has been higher than the year before. One of the main posers the world has been asking since 1938 is how long can it go on; it must reach a peak some time; when will the peak come? In the days of Myth, it seemed that time would never come.

But the incredible Russians who moved so many mountains, moved this one too. In summer, 1941, production in Hitler's arms industries all over occupied Europe began falling steeply. In autumn, the output of German industries, themselves, levelled off and have fallen ever since. I regret I was never able to get figures on this. The Nazis guard arms production figures far more jealously than any other class of military information. I must beg credence only on my word that the source is absolutely trustworthy. I cannot give his name nor the slightest information about his position, for he is highly placed and his identity could be traced on the basis of even the most general hint. The drop in production in the occupied countries, he said, has taken on disastrous proportions. It came first and most pronounced there because the exhaustion of those countries' food supplies, inevitably reducing the efficiency of labourers, coincided with the beginning of the Russian war which revealed a bright flame of hope to workers who had almost resigned themselves to Nazi occupation and Hitler's invincibility. There was outright sabotage from the Communist workers, especially in Northern France; and non-Communist workers joined them in slow-down strikes. He said production has dropped as much as fifty per cent in some industries in the occupied territories! That this is no fable is indicated by known circumstantial evidence. It was only at the beginning of the Russian adventure that Nazi papers began bringing those myriad reports of sabotage, and instituted the brutal shooting of hostages. It was also then that far-reaching sabotage organization in the industrial Bohemian protectorate was discovered and the

Nazi murder of thousands of Czech patriots began. These things are bound to have had a tremendous effect on production.

The drop in production within Germany's own borders, he said, was due in no measure to sabotage, but simply because the delayed effects of bad food and general demoralization at the failure to defeat Russia on schedule were beginning to evince themselves in the lowered efficiency of the workers, and capital equipment had been overworked without sufficiently extensive renewals. For these factors, too, there is much circumstantial support. I have already related the downward course of civilian spirits. German stock-market reports in German newspapers for the past three months, showing increased application of profits to machinery renewals and repairs, supports the other. The diversion of resources to long-needed replacements can mean only that production of arms, themselves, will continue to go down until replacements are completed. My friend maintained there would be a rise in production after that, but his contention is doubtful, for this factor will certainly be offset by the continued drop in personnel efficiency.

To afford some kind of conception of how much replacing the Germans will have to do, here are absolutely reliable figures from a different but equally trustworthy Nazi source, on the situation in the locomotive industry. At the beginning of the Russian war, Germany possessed a total of 11,000 locomotives (the figure does not include between 5,000 and 6,000 switch-engines). Around 4,000 of these were taken from Germany and sent to Poland and Russia for the Russian campaign. As they were destroyed or had to be returned to termini for repairs, the remaining stock of 7,000 had to be largely drawn away from the home front to replace them. My source declared that by the time the winter set in on the Eastern front, a total of 4,000 locomotives—equal to the original total used in the East —had been destroyed beyond hope of repair by the sabotage of partisans and by bombing and artillery fire at the front. An average of 20 locomotives lost per day! If all these have been replaced by drawing from Germany itself, it means that only 3,000 of an original 11,000 locomotives are available for transport of all kinds inside Germany. He said, further, that production of locomotives by all the industries under German control— German, French and Belgian factories—has dropped to 1,400 a year (he refused to give the original production figure, but said this marked a definite and large falling off from the total production of all these factories in past years). This means that three years' production of locomotives was destroyed in about six months of fighting in Russia. Of all the industrial problems facing the Nazis, my source declared, rail transport was by far the most acute.

This is but one industry and similar developments have occurred in all of them. What the loss in this industry alone means to Hitler's future plans should be obvious. Even if Hitler should conquer all Russia, he will have to transport his men and material back to the West if he intends to invade England unless, which is highly possible, he has given up this objective as hopeless. It would take a year or more to make the necessary transference of soldiers and troops from the East to the West, in view of the losses of rolling stock incurred in Russia. But that is an interpretation which is the best of all possible interpretations for Hitler. Actually, the war in Russia is not over. In fact, at the moment of writing, Hitler is even being badly beaten in Russia, and the loss of locomotives and freight cars is continuing.

The fall in production in Hitler's Europe should not be overestimated in importance. It does not mean that German industry has collapsed or that there is a prospect of imminent collapse. Hitler's industry is still dangerously virile, and can still produce plenty of tanks, guns and planes—more than we are producing. But neither should the development be underestimated. Our production figures are still rising and we have lots of slack we can take up. Hitler's have reached their peak and are falling. It is next to impossible to alter either of these trends; our rising production or the fall of Hitler's. The food and clothing of German workers cannot get better, but can only get worse at a faster rate. In America there is not, in the slightest degree, a food problem, or, in fact, any problem of consumption economics. In Germany and Europe, capital equipment has been too much overstrained and is too run down to enjoy a revival for the next five years, even if they were years of total peace instead of total war. Even if Germany occupied all European Russia, the Nazis would find little or nothing they could use for the next three to five years. A German captain told me that when the German troops were in sight of Dnieperstrov, they saw, across the famous, now destroyed dam, on the side of the river the first intact factories they had seen in Russia—a vast colony of plants including an aluminium works and several power plants. When they crossed the river, they discovered every single building was empty; the Russians had removed every machine and nut and bolt to the East!

To replace destroyed Russian machinery or removed Russian factories, the Germans will have to draw still more hundreds of thousands of workers from Germany, itself. The result can only be a further slowing down of production in Germany's own replacement programme. Russia has been, and remains, a total loss to Germany. It is an often misused statement, but it is true in the case of the Russian war, that Germany has been winning herself to death. Every fresh gain of Russian territory has meant a severe economic loss—a loss of valuable man-power from Germany's own factories—to the Nazis. Every military gain inside Russia has been an economic defeat to the most important element of the German home-front: the arms factories. The entrance of Japan into the war certainly benefited the German position; but Japan is suffering severely from the same thing Germany has just begun to suffer from; economic decline. Japan has increased the severity of our problems; but I do not believe ours have increased at anywhere near the rate at which Japan's and Germany's have been increased.

We must certainly avoid false optimism. But there is no reason to be unduly pessimistic. With regard to Japan, despite her overwhelming successes, there are good grounds for optimism. The plenty that she has snatched in Malaya and the Dutch East Indies is more apparent than real, and further, Japan, short of shipping even before the war, has lost at least fifteen per cent of her total tonnage. With regard to Germany, the grounds for optimism are clearly apparent. The phenomenal Cinderella-boy from Braunau-am-Inn has had a swell time. But it would appear to be getting on towards midnight. Even with his expertness at it, it is highly unlikely that he can turn this particular clock back.

V

VALHALLA IN TRANSITION

A FRIEND OF mine who worked in one told me that when you walk through those big German warehouses the propaganda films used to like to show brimming with food supplies of all kinds, the echo of your footsteps frightens you it is so loud and thundery. They're almost empty now. No caravans of trucks and freight cars unload on their platforms for storage any more. The system of food supplying has become much simpler. It is called the "farmhouse-to-mouth" method. What Germans eat today is what was dug right up from the good earth yesterday, so to speak. It didn't go any-where to be stored because it couldn't; else markets would sell out mornings in one hour instead of two and Alois Hitler's little restaurant and hundreds like it would have to cut serving time from two hours to one, or not serve at all, which happens some-times anyhow. Shops are clean and empty, except for a few new bottles of chemical sauces with fancy names nobody has ever seen before. Only the windows outside are full. Full of empty cardboard boxes of *Keks*, which is German for cakes, and wine-bottles filled with water. Willi Loerke's grocery shop next to my house has a big cardboard advertisement for Mumm's champagne in the window, with a pretty girl in a short dress holding up a glass of champagne. Once, before Willi was called up to go East, I asked him why he left that sign in the window when he didn't have any champagne to sell; he said it was because it took up lots of room, the girl was pretty and cheerful, and there wasn't much else to put in windows any more except the sign saying "No more potatoes today", and empty boxes of *Keks*. I like the way Germans try and keep up appearances somehow in spite of every-thing. It reminds me of the way old, aristocratic, southern families in America used to paint the shabby cuffs of their negro butlers' suits with black ink so the lining would not show over their wrists while serving, when friends from the North came to dinner. The little dairy goods shop around the corner from my house has in its window a row of milk bottles which are seven-eighths full with white salt to look like milk. Inside there is three gallons of milk a day, which sometimes lasts two hours when not too many customers come early. Half-pint to a customer while it lasts, and it is so thin it is blue rather than white. Cigarette shops have good windows too, with all kinds of variegated boxes of "Aristons", "Murattis", "Kemals" named after Camels, and a cigarette that used to be called the "Times", but which for patriotic reasons has been changed, at little printing cost, now to the "Timms". The boxes are empty and a sign in the window says they are only for decorations—*Nus Attrapen*. On the shut front door there is a different sign almost every day of the week. The manager, who is a friend of mine, showed me all the signs he keeps under the counter: closed for repairs, or for taking inventory, or for redecoration, or for lunch, or just plain sold-out which he means by all the others, but uses them from time to time "just for variety's sake". On Tauentzienstrasse, one shopkeeper solved the appearances problem by putting no empty boxes at all in the window, but a big profile photograph of Hitler with a gilt swastika above it and below it, in gold letters, "We Thank Our Fuehrer"! The local Nazi party chief thought it was a crack at the leader and made him change his decoration and put some *Attrapen* in the window. The man didn't really mean it to be a gag, he was just trying to be patriotic. But even appearances are beginning to go now. Berlin is really beginning to look the part of a city-at-war. I should like to stroll down Unter den Linden and beyond with my officer friend now. That, however, is impossible because a Bolshevik shot both his legs off east of Kiev. If they hadn't cut off Bus line number one, due to the petrol shortage, we could ride down, or we could take a taxi, if we could find one. It would be mean, but I would like to point out how buildings are getting grey and dirty, and how the paint is peeling, and lots of things. It would be mean, but it is high time somebody broke the Nazi monopoly of being mean.

Do you know Berlin? If you do, maybe you'd like to know what that grand old city looks like now that it has become the capital of all Europe, Valhalla on earth, with—as Dr. Goebbels wrote last autumn—the highest standard of living on the continent. The highest except for the only two countries not yet blessed by being

Newly Ordered—Sweden and Switzerland. That's really not a fair statement, but unfairness is another Nazi monopoly that's begging to be cracked. Take those big, ornate drinking places on the main drag: Café Unter den Linden and Kranzler's. The stuffing is popping out of the upholstery of their overstuffed chairs now. The cigarette girl in one of them, who has nothing else to do now, told me she spent a week recently just sewing up gaps in the upholstery. She couldn't get any thread, but string from wrapping packages will do until the war is over. Not the string from German packages which is made of paper and snaps when you draw it hard with a needle, but string from packages from Switzerland which you can get sometimes. Food there is not appetizing. It is generally a foul-smelling hunk of fish called *Kabeljau* on the menu, covered with a gummy yellow sauce called *Senftunke*. Frankly, it smells like an open garbage pail on Monday morning. Service also is not what it used to be, mainly because there are only three waiters and all are over seventy. They had been retired but, when the young men were called up in June, they had to be called back to work ten hours a day, lumbago or no lumbago. The Café Unter den Linden had a fine, big awning which could be stretched out like a marquee over tables on the sidewalk, in summer time, but the hinges on it got rusty and nobody could be found to fix them, and so rain water was caught in the folds of the awning and ate holes in it. Café Schoen across the street has no troubles about maintaining front. A couple of British fire-bombs solved that seven months ago. The fire-bombs destroyed the upper floors of the building and scaffolding was set up all around it to repair it, but the Russian war came and all the workers were called up so the scaffolding just stays up and hides the whole front of the building. There is lots of scaffolding along Unter den Linden, hiding the fronts of buildings nobody is any longer working on.

All the embassies on that big street, the Russian, the American, and the French, are empty now and closed up. When the Nazis closed the Russian embassy, they put a big white streamer fifty yards long across the face of the building with black skulls and cross-bones on either end of the streamer, and in the middle the words: "Beware! This building is Being Fumigated"! People snickered. The Nazis removed the hammer and sickle on the door, but forgot the one on the top of the building in the centre, and it is still there. Most of the big tourists' agencies on Unter den

Linden are still open but business is not rushing. Tourists these days wear steel helmets and don't buy tickets. Only the Russian agency, Intourist, and the American Express Company were closed. Intourist was later reopened as an "Anti-Komintern" bookshop and in the window is a magic lantern which shows snap-shots of ugly Russian soldiers all day long. Above the screen is a sign saying, "BEASTS are looking at you"! The Russian soldiers are very ugly and might be ugly German soldiers, or ugly British or American soldiers but for their uniforms. Or, did you ever look at your own face in the mirror after you haven't shaved or slept for three days and have just had a fight? In the window of the American Express Company, which has been closed since early autumn, the employees—Germans all—took a last bitter crack at the Nazis for making them lose decent-paying jobs by sticking in a poster saying, "Visit Mediæval Germany". But the Nazis are not subtle, so they didn't get it and left the sign in the otherwise empty window. Even the big florist's shop, Blumen-Schmidt, on the main street, is empty. I went in there once in November to buy some flowers for Jack Fleischer's birthday—a hell present for a man to give a man, but there wasn't any schnaps—and when I saw how it was I told the salesgirl, my God, et tu? She said, yes, she was sorry, but Udet had just been killed and every time there is a state funeral they clean out not only the shop but also the hot-houses. A little later I went back, but it was still empty and the salesgirl was sorry but Moelders had just been killed. I suppose if I had gone back later, she would have said, sorry, but von Reichenau, then sorry, but Todt, and so on. Luck never changes, it continues being good.

Turning off Unter den Linden to the left down the government street, Wilhelmstrasse, you can see the only freshly painted build-ing in Berlin: Ribbentrop's ugly yellow palace, with ugly yellow snakes wrapped symbolically around spheres, that look like the world, on its front pillars, He has just had it remodelled. All the rest of the buildings are getting dirty, even Dr. Goebbels' formerly snow-white propaganda palace. After six o'clock, you can't walk on the side of the street where the Fuehrer's house is located. A cordon of policemen make you cross the street, for they are afraid of bombs after dark, even when the Fuehrer is not at home. The Fuehrer's yellow-brown chancellery is still the same except that the enormous bronze doors on its front have been removed and

melted down for the arms industry and replaced with big, brown
wooden doors. The last building on the street before you turn is
where the New York *Herald-Tribune* office was until the *Tribune*'s
correspondent, Ralph Barnes, was kicked out for saying German-
Russian relations were not so cordial and might lead to an
eventual conflict. Every time I pass the place, I remember that
last night I spent with him in his office before he caught the
train, drinking cognac because he was very sad about being
thrown out; Berlin was a good spot then. Ralph was killed in
Greece. He would have liked seeing Berlin as it is now.

Turning down Leipziger Strasse in the direction of Dr.
Goebbels' fancy, new press club, you pass a whole block filled with
nothing but Wertheims' gigantic department store. There used
to be an enormous animated map of Russia in the big central
show-window, showing the progress of the Germans each day.
After Rostov, it was diplomatically removed and replaced with
Attrapen. Inside, it looks like a rummage depot. It used to be run by
Jews and filled with fine things, but since the Jews were the cause
of all Germany's misfortunes, it is now owned by pure Aryans and
empty except for trash. Half the big cage-like lifts are out of order
until after the war.

At the end of Leipziger Strasse is Potsdamer Platz, a busy,
German Piccadilly Circus; second to the Friedrichstrasse railway
station it is the best place in Berlin to go to if you just want to look
at a lot of people in a big hurry. On Potsdamer Platz is a big
building called the Pschorr Haus, whose state I have always kept a
close watch on because it is *the* typical, average, big *buergerliche*
Berlin restaurant. Inside, it is now dingy and dirty, and so much
bad fish has been served on its white wooden tables that the whole
place smells like bad fish. People from the Potsdamer railway station next door sit at its tables and sip chemical lemonade and
barley coffee between trains, as the Pschorr breweries, which own
the big restaurant, are no longer making very much beer. I have a
menu from the Pschorr Haus somebody gave me dated November,
1916, and on it are nineteen different meat dishes to choose from.
Today, also after two years of war, there are only two meat dishes
on the menu, one of which is struck through with a pencil mark
along the strategy of the Kaiserhof Hotel. The other is generally
two little sausages of uncertain contents, each about the size of a
cigar butt. Before the meat they give you a chalky, red, warm

liquid called tomato soup, but which a good-natured waiter-friend of mine always called: *Ee-gay Farben Nummer zwei null-eex!* all of which means, "Dye trust formula number 20-X". With the meat you get four or five yellow potatoes with black blotches on them. One of the Pschorr Hans' vast windows on the ground floor was broken up by a bomb recently, but since nobody could be found to fix it, the management simply stuck a flattened out cardboard box in the hole, which exudes the odour of bad fish out on the street.

Potsdamer Strasse, which runs from the Pschorr Haus down past the big Sports Palace where Hitler speaks when he comes to Berlin from the front, used to be a busy shopping centre. It is now a row of derelict shops, all closed for different reasons, and their windows dirty and exhibiting pictures which little boys drew in the dirt on the window with their thumbs. The "Fruit Bar" which used to sell fruit drinks is empty because there is no more fruit, and the wood-block letters that form its name on the front are cracking and falling from their white background, leaving dirty stains where the letters were. Many shops are empty because they no longer have things to sell. Some are, as they say, closed for repairs but no repairs are going on. Some are places which had been run for their middle-aged owners who were called up, by wives and daughters who are now also called up into the munitions factories. Farther down the street are the beginnings of a massive structure, behind a big board fence, which was to be the "German Tourists Centre". All tourist agencies in town were to have offices in it. It was being constructed by Professor Albert Speer, Hitler's little dictator for architecture. But Speer's workers had to be called up when the Russian drain on man-power began, and work had to be stopped. Now Speer, too, has been called to the East to take the job of Dr. Todt who died. Thus Potsdamer Strasse is a long monument to the Russian campaign, dead except for the people trudging in thousands down it. It is too bad that the Tourists' Centre could not be finished, for German Tourists deserve a monument of some sort: they've done thorough work this decade.

To the left of Potsdamer Strasse and parallel with it lie the railway tracks from the Potsdamer station. Across them is a huge, long viaduct for the electric, and from it, evenings, you get the best picture of industry and activity in all Berlin, looking down on a maze of criss-crossing railway tracks and a forest of semaphores with engines and trains puffing up and down. It is very smoky and looks good from that height. The reason I mention it is that the three easternmost lines are always filled with long trains and each coach is clearly marked with a red cross on a white circle; hospital trains unloading maimed Germans from the Eastern front to be taken to hospitals in Berlin. One night late, when I was going home on the electric and the train passed over these coaches, a wizened old *buerger*, drunk as a coot, nudged me and pointed to them and said: "From France we got silk stockings. From Russia we got this. Damn Russians must not have any silk stockings, what?" He was lucky he picked on me to say this to, or he would have had his hangover in Alexander Platz prison the next morning. There are other cynical Berliners who say, however, that the coaches are not unloading anybody; that they're just left there on the sidings to discourage the British from dropping bombs on the Potsdamer station. But I've seen them unloading.

If you turn off Potsdamer Strasse to the right just before you get to the Sports Palace and walk about a mile, you run smack into the *elegante Viertel* of Berlin, the West End. They say the Unter den Linden section lives by day, and the West End lives by night. In peace-time it's a gay, brilliantly lighted neighbourhood speckled with dozens of cinemas, theatres and variety houses, and hundreds of little hole-in-the-wall bars. Its geographical and spiritual centre is Kurfuerstendamm, a long boulevard which extends from the big Memorial Church to the Berlin lakes. It is also the Bond Street, with fine shops, of Berlin—in peace-time. In war Kurfuerstendamm reminds me of a beautiful woman who became the mistress of a wealthy man and who, after too much loving and living has now become a jaded, gaudy female who daubs her face with too much artificial colour in order to hide the deepening lines in it. Her jewels are the thousand and one bars and night-spots. They were once neat-looking little places, cubist in decoration and with bright-coloured stucco fronts. Now, the paint is peeling, the stucco is cracking and falling off in blobs, like the polish from paste pearls and the gilt from brass rings. Most of them have closed. The rest of them stay open only certain nights a week. This is all since the Russian war began, since the supplies of French Cognac, Dutch Bols gin, and good Polish Vodka have been exhausted. As they no longer have any of the ingredients for staple cocktails, they have struck these off the menu and instituted a "standard" cocktail. It is called by different names, and by names of varying fantasy, in different bars: "razzle-dazzle", "Hollywood" (pronounced Holy-Voot cuck-tell; this was before America became an out-and-out enemy), or "Extase". But the mixture is always the same, when it is there—a shot of some kind of raw, stomach-searing alcohol with a generous dilution of thick, sweet grenadine syrup. Or, if you are lucky, you can get a bottle of this year's Moselle.

Dancing is strictly forbidden by law everywhere for the duration of the Russian war. Nevertheless, a few joints maintain "hostesses" who sit and drink with Tired Party Men. As the best of their profession have been drawn off eastward for the entertainment of officers, those who remain are a bit on the seedy side. For one thing, gowns are being worn shorter this season; it is impossible to buy new gowns and so the girls simply had to chop off the worn edges of their old ones and put in new hems, higher up. Physical appearance is not so good for the obvious reason that they are remainders of a flock that was never very promising in Germany. Prostitution, itself, is a moribund profession. They tell me there are still a few places, one on Kanonier Strasse near the Wilhelmstrasse and one on Giesebrecht Strasse in the West End, which is said to be run by the foreign office for the comfort of minor visiting diplomats, especially the Japanese. And you can, they say, be approached on the streets if you try very hard, but you must try very hard. But generally, the fact that there are more than twice as many women as men in Berlin, has made inroads into the profession. Regarding the general subject of pornography, those who like to make facile generalizations about the immutability of human nature may find a trace of interesting support in this: one of the first Nazi measures, and one of their best, was the banning of all pornographic picture magazines, in 1933. Since the war, under the heading of "Art", pornographic picture magazines have appeared in legions. Be they called as they may—the "Faith and Beauty" magazine, "The Dance", "Modern Photography"—they all contain nothing but photos of naked women and all boil down to the same old pornographic fare of pre-Nazi days. Sales, I'm told, are terrific.

War seems to have some causal relation with pornography. Through it one old portrait painter, who has roomy studios on Unter den Linden, has gained fame in Berlin. He was once Kaiser Wilhelm's court-artist, by special appointment, but, since the war, and Hitler, he had not been doing so well on sales. So, to make money, he hit on the idea of painting a series of tantalizing nudes and allowing the public in to see them for a fee. On his front door today there hangs a sign advertising for all to see: "Sensation! Vast Canvas of Turkish Harem including eight beautiful nudes, life-sized. Admission: fifty pfennigs". Inside you can see, among natural-size portraits of Bismarck, Hindenburg and Hitler, the Sensation with its swarthy, shapely nudes reclining on velvet-covered divans. The Nazis have never objected, not even on racial grounds. The cheap "art shops" of Friedrichstrasse, just off Unter den Linden, have their windows jammed with fine looking maids in undress and attract a goodly public at all hours of the day.

A handful of truly popular spots are (not my tastes, but those of Germans):

The Golden Horse-shoe. Main attractions: among the hostesses is the only negress in Berlin. A ring in the centre of the floor around which lady customers ride a horse to music and show their legs above the knees in so doing, while male *buerger* shout with glee. The ladies or their men pay fifty pfennigs for a slow trot, seventy-five pfennigs for a good gallop.

St. Pauli's Bar. Here labours a hostess who has lost not only a husband in the war, but two of them! She thinks the war is a personal frame-up against her. The façade of the joint formerly consisted of the porcelain inlaid flags of every nation in the world. One by one the flags had to be painted over for political reasons, and now the façade is a checkerboard half of grey splotches and half of flags.

Walterchen der Seelensorger, which means, Little Walter, the Soul-comforter. This is a small dance-hall near the Stettiner station area in working-class Berlin, where the famous proprietor, "Walterchen", mates middle-aged bachelors and widowers with middle-aged spinsters and widows—a sort of public matrimonial bureau where rheumatic old gentlemen can rejuvenate their chivalry, and women who have forgotten can once again learn to be coy. Very amusing. Walterchen's trade-mark is a red heart with an arrow through it.

Die Neue Welt; the "New World"—a vast multi-roomed beer-hall in the East End of Berlin. Once the most profitable amusement concern in Berlin, the *Neue Welt* is now closed most of the time for lack of beer. It is interesting if you like to see the German proletariat at play; also because the Gestapo keeps close check on the clientele, and you're likely to be arrested if you happen not to have an identification card to show them when they ask you. It is the only place in Berlin where plain-clothes men have ever cornered me and made me show my passport to prove I was not a parachute trooper or a Jew enjoying illegal fun.

The X Bar. This is the liveliest spot in town. That is not its real name, but since I want to tell some of its secrets, I had best not be too specific. It was my favourite spot when the blues got me and I had to go night-lifing or bust, because it has a good orchestra which defies Nazi propriety and plays American music, and also because the manager, who is a friend, still has a secret stock of Scotch whisky. As it is also a favourite spot for big-shot Nazis, the band doesn't play American jazz bluntly; it sandwiches it in between opening and closing chords from some German number, salving the consciences of the Nazi visitors who might otherwise be reminded that what they are listening to was written by a racial inferior. On a Saturday night, after police hours, the manager shoos everybody out except a couple of friends and the policeman on the beat, gets his private bottle of Johnnie Walker from under the kitchen sink, and we take off our coats and smoke cigars he got from someone in the Foreign Office and drink and talk until three or four in the morning. After that, the manager used to wrap up a couple of big bottles of beer in the morning's *Lokal-Anzeiger* and we would go off to my apartment to mellow up on beer, have an early morning breakfast and get the first B.B.C. news. The manager never admitted it, but I think his bar has some special pull with the government, by which he gets pretty good liquor stocks for himself and for friends. The Foreign Office boys often take their foreign guests there. I first saw P. G. Wodehouse there. The place needs a coat of paint badly, but it's a good place when you need a change of atmosphere so much you would pop without it.

Theatres and show-houses out in the West End are packed over-full every night. People haven't anything else to spend their money on, so even the worst show in town is a sell-out every night. The big variety houses, the Scala and the Wintergarten, are having a hard time finding enough talent to fill their bills, as narrowed by a whole sheaf of Nazi decrees since the beginning of the war. Fortune-tellers, crystal gazers and all kinds of stage soothsayers used to be popular with German audiences, but when Hess flew to Scotland, Goebbels banned them all for ever from German show-houses because it was said that one of these affected Hess' decision to go. Another big favourite were funny-men who specialized in shady political jokes, but these too were forbidden by Goebbels after a while. Favourite music was American jazz and blues songs, but the dictator of German *Kultur* unofficially informed producers this well also was poisoned. The Scala used to draw entirely on foreign talent, showing a Spanish bill one month and an American one the next, and so on, but the war has rather rigorously limited the nationalities available or desirable, from the point of view of the authorities. Just about all that is left is acrobatics and juggling, which become tiresome; but they take people's minds off war, and that is what people pay for.

Cinemas are not as popular, principally for the reason that they do not take people's minds off war. Once the Nazi film dictators made the mistake of affording a very visible measure of what the public think of their propaganda films by opening a second-rate comedy called the "Gas Man" at the Gloria-Palast on Kurfuer-stendamm, while fifty yards away at the Ufa-Palast an extra, super-colossal one hundred and fifty per cent war film, "Bomber Wing Luetzov", was playing. The mediocre comedy played to packed houses at every presentation, while the war film showed to a half-empty theatre. Unfortunately, even mediocre comedies have become rarities as war and propaganda films increase in number. The latter can be exhaustively described by a five-letter word. They're lousy. Especially the pure-war films. Take the one called "Stukas". It was a monotonous film about a bunch of obstreperous adoles-cents who dive-bombed things and people. They bombed every-thing and everybody. That was all the whole film was—just one bombing after another. Finally the hero got bored with bombing and lost interest in life. So they took him off to Bayreuth music festival, where he listened to a few lines of Wagnerian music; his soul began to breathe again, he got visions of the Fuehrer and of guns blazing away, so he impolitely left right in the middle of the first act and dashed back and started bombing things again, with the old gusto.

News-reels which last almost as long as feature-films, used to be very popular with Germans, until the Russian war. Since then Germans have developed a bad case of nerves and don't like news-reels any more. Too many of them can visualize sons, fathers and cousins whom they have lost, in those dramatic explosions on the screen. Once they showed a big fat Nazi bomber with white teeth painted on it to make it look like a shark, opening up its belly and issuing a school of bombs, twenty or thirty of them, one after another. All over the audience you could hear women sucking their breath in through their teeth as though cold shivers were running up and down their spines. People began writing letters to the Propaganda Ministry complaining and begging for a change of fare. The bombardment of complaints finally induced the Ministry to allow a sequence of peaceful shots about the home front— harvesting grain, intimate shots of a cement factory at work, a film interview with Franz Lehar, the composer, etc.—before the war films. Then Goebbels began receiving letters expressing thanks, but asking for more home-front sequences and fewer war ones, especially to leave out the shots of dead-bodies on battlefields.

(The Germans do not allow their people to see American films, but the big shots sneak peeps at most of our best while nobody is looking. I tried to creep unnoticed into a showing of "Gone With the Wind" one afternoon in the Propaganda Ministry, but was promptly ordered out because this was a private "study" presentation for German film actors and producers. Some we were allowed to see in private showings, however, "Ninotchka", "Pinocchio" and others.)

In a word, films are trashy just like everything else. The advertisement posters in the subway stations are attractive and full of colour, just like those empty cigarette boxes in my tobacco shop window, but the films themselves are pure trash. I never thought it was possible for a country to go so universally trashy so quickly.

The only things that are not trash are their guns, which are handsome and horrifying. Of these you see many, many more in Berlin now than you used to, on top of buildings and on open fields in the suburbs. The biggest and handsomest ones are within two hundred yards of the Theatre Centre on Kurfuerstendamm, in the big Tiergarten. They are anti-aircraft cannon mounted on a tower which, itself, looks like a fantastic monstrosity from a lost world, or another planet. It is huge and positively frightening just to look at (Nazis like to hear it described this way; they are specialists in fright-propaganda. But the world has now advanced beyond the stage of being frightened in any decisive way by anything the Nazi do or create.) It is an enormous, square clod of cement a hundred feet high, about five or six storeys. It is painted green so as not to be too visible among the trees from above. On each of its corners is a long, powerful gun, pointed at the sky. They are fired by remote control from another, similar tower about a hundred yards farther on in the wood, on which there is a big "ear" resembling a fishing net, big as a big bomb crater. You should hear these monsters in action during an air-raid. In my apartment half a mile away it sounds as though all four guns were levelled right at my window. I had never been in an air-raid cellar in Germany until the night last summer when they were first used in an air-raid (it took two years of incessant day and night work to finish the construction of the towers). For the first time, I confess I got the jitters. My windows rattled as though they would shatter and the floor underneath never stopped quaking as all four guns blasted away at the sky in unison for awhile, then began firing in rotation, an endless barrage which a soldier who fought in France told me was more nerve-racking and harder on the ear-drums than anything he had been in at the front. I didn't mind bombs, I accepted each one as a personal favour from the Tommies. But I couldn't take the guns. Also, I found after ten minutes that I couldn't stay in the cellar, for the neighbours had grown bitter against America and Americans, and made it unpleasant. So I stuffed cotton in my ears and sat in my hall.

They are building more towers like these in other parts of Berlin. They have converted the old Reichstag building into one, reinforcing its top corners and mounting guns on them. The Nazis expect lots of fireworks before the show is over; and they know what effect fireworks have on their people, so they are working night and day to prepare Berlin defences.

They have undertaken the most gigantic camouflage scheme ever known, covering up big spots which are conspicuous from the air all over the city. The most conspicuous thing is the "East-West Axis", a five-miles long, hundred-yards broad street which runs from the Brandenburg Gate in the centre of the town out to Adolf Hitler Platz where my office in the radio studio is situated. Last spring, they began covering the whole street with a vast canopy of wire netting mottled with strips of green gauze to make the thoroughfare indistinguishable from the trees of the Tiergarten alongside it. Lamp-posts were covered with green gauze to look like little trees. The big Victory Pillar, a monument to the Franco-Prussian War, in the middle of the street was covered with netting and the shiny golden angel of Triumph on top which looked like a lighted beacon on a moonlight night was tarnished with dull bronze so that it would not reflect light. At the end of the axis, the radio station was covered in green, too, and straight over the centre of the building a strip of grey netting was laid to look, from the air, like an asphalt street. With Nazi thoroughness they even covered over a whole big lake in West Berlin with green netting and ran another grey, artificial roadway diagonally across it. It was all very nice and very clever. Until the first winds of winter came, straight from the steppes of Russia, like most German misfortunes these days. The first gale ripped yawning holes in the camouflage and blew the false trees off the lamp-posts and hung them, shapeless lumps of gauze and wire, in the branches of the Tiergarten trees. Now the Nazis are having to re-do the whole thing at great expense.

In the past year, Berlin has become probably the best defended city against air-raids in the whole world. I doubt if London can have as many batteries around and in it as Berlin has. I've stood on top of the tall Columbus House on Potsdamer Platz on clear nights and watched the British approaching. As they came closer more and more searchlights fingered the sky, and pin-pricks of light from exploding shells in the air increased from dozens to hundreds. Once, on one small arc of the horizon I counted seventy-five beams of light moving in the sky. Seventy-five searchlights; many, many hundreds of guns on this small sector. There must be many, many thousands of guns all around Berlin. An officer on one of the Flak batteries in the Berlin area once told me that the whole area has been armed far beyond the point of saturation; a real waste of guns has occurred. I asked him the reason for this extravagance, and he said that while the German people were among the worst informed people in the world, the German leadership was certainly the best informed leadership, regarding its own people, in the world. The extravagance is for the sake of morale. The German people simply couldn't take it, and the Nazis were afraid to have them subjected to anything like the London Blitz, he said. I believe him. I have heard it from many Germans, and I've seen enough for myself to confirm it. You can see it in them on the streets today more clearly than ever. They simply could not take it, if it came.

To see Berlin, you take a walk. To see the people you take a subway. You also smell them. There is not enough time nor enough coaches, for coaches to be properly cleaned and ventilated every day, so the odour of stale sweat from bodies that work hard, and have only a cube of soap big as a penny box of matches to wash with for a month, lingers in their interiors and is reinforced quantitatively until it changes for the worse qualitatively as time and war proceed. In summer, it is asphyxiating and this is no figure of speech. Dozens of people, whose stomachs and bodies are not strong anyhow faint in them every day. Sometimes you just have to get out at some station halfway to your destination to take a breath of fresh air between trains.

People's faces are pale, unhealthily white as flour, except for red rings around their tired, lifeless eyes. One would tend to get accustomed to their faces after awhile and think them normal and natural but for the fact that soldiers ride the subway trains too, and one notices the marked contrast between young men who eat food with vitamins in it and live out of doors part of the time, and the ununiformed millions who get no vitamins and work in shops and factories from ten to twelve hours a day. From lack of vitamins in food, teeth are decaying fast and obviously. My dentist said they are decaying all at once almost like cubes of sugar dissolving in water. Dentists are severely overworked as most of them must spend half their time working for the army, and take care of a doubled private practice in the rest of the time. They have raised prices tremendously to discourage the growing number of patients; he said they simply had to do this. This winter there has been the most severe epidemic of colds in Berlin in many winters, and doctors predict it will get worse each year and probably assume dangerous proportions if something cannot be done about food and clothing, especially shoes, which are wearing out fast.

Weary, and not good in health, Berliners are also, and consequently, ill-humoured. That is an understatement; they have become downright "ornery". All lines in faces point downwards. I can recommend no more effective remedy for a chance fit of good humour than a ten-station ride on a Berlin tube train. If the packed train suddenly lurches forward and pushes your elbow against the back of the man standing in front of you, it is the occasion for a violent, ten-minute battle of words, in which the whole coach-load of humanity feels called upon to take part zealously as if their lives hung on the outcome. They never fight; they just threaten (*Ich zeige dich an, junger Mann!*"—That's the magic phrase these days: "I'll have you arrested, you imprudent young man", that and "I have a friend who's high up in the Party and *he* will tell you a thing or two!" They're like children threatening to call my Dad, who's bigger'n yours). Berliners have always been notorious grousers. They always complained about anything and everything. But it was a good-natured kind of grousing you could laugh at. What has happened in the past year is something new and different. It is not funny; it is downright morbid, the way people with pale, weary, dead-pan faces which a moment ago were in expressionless stupor can flash in an instant into flaming, apoplectic fury, and scream insults at one another over some triviality or an imaginary wrong. You could watch people's natures change as the war proceeded; you could clearly watch bitterness grow as the end of the war appeared to recede from sight just as you watch a weed grow. It has been depressing to watch and it leaves a bad taste in your mouth. Partly it's the jitters and partly it's a national inferiority complex. But mostly, it is because people are sick; just plain sick in body and mind.

It may be just an impression, but it seems to me that the sickness has hit the little middle-classes hardest. Take those little family parties I've been to time and again where middle-class people, bred on middle-class Respectability, used to play *Skat* all evening and maybe open up a bottle or two of cool wine for refreshment. Recently, I've been to several, and the whole atmosphere has changed. They do not play *Skat* any more at all. They round up all the old half-filled bottles of anything alcoholic they can find (this was before the December Drouth set in with a vengeance), and just drink. They do not drink for the mild pleasure of drinking, not to enjoy the flavour of what they drink nor its subtle effects. They drink to get soused, completely and unmitigatedly; to get rollicking, loud and obstreperous, pouring down wine, beer, sweet liqueur and raw *Ersatz* cognac all in an evening. The general atmosphere is that of a cheap, dock-side dive. I'm not trying to make a moral judgment, but there are grounds for making a social one. The atmosphere is one of decay. And that atmosphere seems thickest among just those strata of Germany's population which have always formed the basis of German society, the *Kleinbuergertum* (lower middle classes). Any type or form of society exists because broad sections of the people have an interest in it existing. In Germany, the petty middle-classes are the ones who have always had an interest in *Bourgeois* society being maintained. They brought Hitler to power in the hope of maintaining their society against the air-tight caste of privilege maintained by the classes above them. Now, it seems to me that the little middle-classes are losing interest, and drowning their disappointment in alcoholic lethe, or lethe of any other sort. Superstition has grown apace. There has been a wave of morbid interest in all sorts of quack sciences and plain superstitions, phrenology, astrology, all kinds of fortune-telling. I am sure one reason Goebbels banned all soothsayers from the German stage was that they were becoming too influential among the people. I am always inevitably reminded by these things of another society where a man named Rasputin gained influence and power in a higher circle but for the same reason, shortly before that society collapsed. People who are either unwilling to admit they know what is wrong with them, or are unable to do anything about it—i.e. get rid of Hitler—are seeking escape in *Ersatz* directions. That is psychological, but it has its physical complement. People who are suffering from nothing else but the inevitable effects of bad nourishment, are inventing fancy names for their ailments and buying the patent-medicine houses out of wares. Outside the armaments industry, the only business which is making big money in Germany is the patent-medicine industry. Every woman carries a full pill-box of some kind along with her almost empty vanity compact, and no man's meal is complete without some sort of coloured lozenge for the belly. A substance known as *Okasa* for sexual potency has become almost a German national institution. Young girls welch boxes of *Pervitin* from air-force officers to reinforce energy that should be natural. The general atmosphere smells strangely like that of an opium dive I once visited in New Orleans many years ago.

If I had to describe Hitler's Reich in one figure, I would compare it with a fine looking fat apple with a tight, red, shiny

skin, which was rotten in the core. The strong, polished
hull is the army and the Gestapo, which has become the main
constituent of the Nazi Party. It is a strong, very strong cover.
The rotten inside is *the whole fabric of Nazi society.*

This is a serious statement to make. I sincerely believe that a
journalist who consciously misinforms his people and allies about
the state of the enemy in time of war for the sake of sensation
is the second lowest type of criminal (the lowest type being anyone who makes profits out of arms production). I have always
sought to avoid underestimating the strength of the Nazis. I
refer to the internal strength of the Nazi system, which this book
concerns itself with alone, not the military strength. But, with
these self-imposed restrictions in mind, I am sure of what I say:
Nazi society is rotten from top to bottom and in all its tissues, save
the strong hermetically closed hull. The people are sick of it. The
general theory of society denoted by the name *Fascism*, of which
Nazism is a form, has had its flare of popularity in Europe, and
so far as popular following is concerned, its day is over. It will
never again be an attracting force as it was before the world discovered its meaning.

In Denmark, the Nazis are opposed to parliamentary elections
being held because they know that elections would result, as certainly
as sunrise, in the Danish people throwing out the three measly
Danish Nazis who are in Parliament. In Norway and Holland,
the Nazis do not dare even to support a planned "plebiscite" for
fear of the evidence it would give of how dead their philosophy
truly is. As an idea, Nazism is dead as a door-nail. As for the German people, they are attached to the Nazis like the man who
unexpectedly found himself holding on to a lion's tail, and kept
right on holding on, not because he enjoyed the lion's proximity,
but because he was scared speechless at what might happen
if he let go. Or like the little boys who were having a fine ride on
a toboggan until it hit a slippery place and started zipping down
curves on one runner; they were scared to jump off and it got
more impossible every second. Don't get me wrong. I don't
mean only that the German people are afraid of the Gestapo
and that all they are waiting for is for someone to weaken the
Gestapo, and then they will revolt. Though the Gestapo is certainly a big element in the fear complex, it is not the biggest.
The main reason the Germans cling to the lion's tail is that they

are terrorized by the nightmare of what will happen to them if they fail to win the war, of what their long-suffering enemies will do to them; of what the tortured people of their enslaved nations, Czechoslovakia, Poland, France, will do when there is no longer a Gestapo to hold them down. The German people are not convinced Nazis, not five per cent of them; they are a people frightened stiff at what fate will befall them if they do not win the mess the Nazis have got them into. Take note of the new tone of Nazi propaganda of late. For two years Goebbels blew the shiny, gilded horn of how beautiful Victory was going to be, in order to urge his people on to battle. Suddenly in autumn, the tone changed to that of what will happen to Germany if Germany *fails* to win. If you read the dispatches from Berlin by American correspondents at that time, you will recall that famous editorial written by Goebbels and published in *Das Reich* entitled, "When, or How?" In that leader, for the first time, Goebbels admitted to Germany and the world that conditions had grown extremely bad inside Germany, and he ended by warning his people that however miserable things might be now, they would pale beside what would happen to Germany if Germany lost the war. This tune is now being played long and much in the German press. In all its forms, the incitement of Fear in the hearts of Germans, is the only strong weapon in Goebbels' armoury since Dr. Dietrich played hell with the others.

People in the outside world who know the Nazi system only from photographs and films; from dramatic shots of its fine military machine and the steely, resolute faces of its leaders, would be amazed at what a queer, creaky makeshift it is behind its handsome, uniform exterior. It is not only that the people who support those stony-faced leaders are timid, frightened and low-spirited. It is also, the government, the administration of those people and their affairs. In *The House that Hitler Built*, Stephen Roberts drew as nearly perfect a picture of that strange complicated mechanism as it was in peace time, as it is possible for a human to draw. But even that capable author would be bluffed by the thousand queer, ill-shaped accretions that have been added illogically to it and the contraptions that have been subtracted illogically from it since the beginning of the war. It looks roughly like a Rube Goldberg invention, inspired by a nightmare, but it is more complicated and less logical. And there are no A, B, C directions under it to show how it works. The men who work it have no idea how it works, themselves. The old, experienced, semi-intelligent bureaucrats who made the old contraption function wheezingly in peace, have been drained off to the war machine where their experience can be used more valuably. The new, screwier contraption is operated haltingly by inexperienced little men who do not like their jobs and know nothing about them. The I.Q. of the personnel in the whole civil administration machine has dropped from an average of a fifteen-year-old to that of a ten-year-old.

For example, it is strictly against the law for any foreigner to remain in Germany more than a month without a stamp in his passport called by the formidable name of *Aufenthaltserlaubnis*, a residence permit. But nowadays, between the time you apply for one and the time you get it, a year generally passes; you break the law for eleven months because nobody knows what to do with your application once you've filled it out. Most foreigners never get one at all. But that is one of the more efficient departments. My charwoman's sister, who worked in a hospital, disappeared once. Together my charwoman and I tried every police and Gestapo agency in town to find out about her, but nobody knew anything, or what to do to find out anything. Thirteen months later, it was discovered she was killed in a motor car accident in central Berlin, and the record of it had simply got stalled in the bureau drawer of some little official who didn't know which of eleven different departments he should have passed it on to. He tried three of six possible departments, but they didn't know what to do with it.

Nobody knows who is *zustaendig* (responsible) for anything. When I complained to the Propaganda Ministry about being refused trips to the war-front, I was told the Ministry had nothing to do with the matter, that I should see the radio people. I went to the radio people who were not *zustaendig* for such matters and who sent me to the censors. The Foreign Office censor knew nothing about it and told me to see the High Command censor who told me to see the Propaganda Ministry censor, who told me to go back to the Propaganda Ministry itself and complain there. Ultimately, Dr. Froelich, in the Ministry, showed an uncommon sense of the state of affairs and shrugged his shoulders and told me neither he, nor anybody else, had the least idea who the responsible official was, or which the responsible department. I was simply banned from trips to the front by nobody for no reason, but no one could do anything about it. When I was finally banned from the air, I went to the American embassy and asked the proper officer to protest to the Nazi authorities. He smiled and said: "It has become hopeless to protest to the Nazis about anything. Not only because of their ill-will towards Americans, but also because they frankly do not know which department any particular protest should be delivered to." He told me the whole Nazi civil government is in a state of unbelievable chaos. Hitler no longer pays the slightest attention to the civil side of German life, and his underlings have followed the transition of his interests to the purely military side of things. Nobody of any consequence has any interest in the government of the German people, and it has become hopelessly confused and chaotic, and, in its innards, irremediably constipated. It is, in short, going to hell in a hurry.

For a land ridden by laws, Germany has become the most lawless land on earth. Law means nothing; the password today is *Beziehungen*, which means good relations with a party big-shot, influence, pull, jerk. You can threaten someone on the subway with getting the law on him, but when you threaten a bureaucrat or a grocer who doesn't give you full rations, you must threaten that you have *Beziehungen* who will fix him. If you have no pull you can get no goods or service, no matter how strong the law is on your side. If you have got *Beziehungen* you can get anything, any commodity which has disappeared from the shops, or any service, no matter how many laws there are against it—and there are hundreds, against everything—written down in the law books. Law has lost all meaning. We know cheap, corrupt, court-house politics in localities in America all too well. But Germany is one great big nation of nothing but cheap, corrupt, court-house politics, ruled by a single party whose leaders are mostly fanatical ascetics, but whose several million underlings are as buyable as postcards. For a half-pound of coffee I have rewritten whole German law books in my favour.

In the field of economics Germany is corrupt and rotten too. The state is allegedly national "Socialist", but for a socialist state it maintains the finest, fattest crop of unadulterated plutocrats you ever dreamed of. Half of them are the old plutocracy, the old families who grew rich on guns and chemicals; half of them are the new plutocracy of higher up Nazis who had not a pfennig ten years ago, but who got in the elevator of financial success on the ground floor in 1933, after its shaft was greased by Nazi victory, and shot straight up to the top, like Ley the contraceptive king, and Goering the steel king. The German people are not as conscious of their moneyed classes as other people are, for the Nazis shrewdly do not allow their newspapers to publish society pages, which make American and British people conscious of their plutocracies. Dividends are, of course, limited to six per cent. But there is no law against watering stock; against giving two six per cents to a shareholder instead of one six per cent, when business is good, as it is today.

The big red apple is rotten and worm-eaten. If and when it is ever pierced, it will stink to high heaven. But the hull is very red and shiny. And it is very strong. And the worms inside who thrive and grow fat on the fruit, like it that way. And the people of Germany are afraid that no matter how rotten it is inside, it is better than being gobbled up by the birds outside.

Only one element has been left out of the picture. It is one of the most important elements of the German population. It, alone of the civil population is not demoralized; it is enthusiastic and keeps crying for more of the same. It remains, due to the many favours shown it, the most enthusiastic supporter of Adolf Hitler. I mean the German Youth; the little boys and girls. I neglected it, because one no longer sees much of it in Berlin. Most of the little boys and girls have been shipped off to nice boys' and girls' towns in Eastern Germany to get out of the air-raid areas. Hitler is very particular about them.

They are not disappointed with Nazism. Hitler has done well by them, materially and psychologically. His colourful, shallow civilization appeals to them. They enjoy, as children will, its dramatic brutality. Too little attention has been given to the little boys and girls who are growing to maturity in Germany now. For nine years now, their malleable little minds have been systematically warped. They are growing up in a mental plaster-cast, and they like it with its accompaniment of drums, trumpets and uniforms and flags. They are enthusiastic; the biggest hauls in the Winter Relief collections are always made by the Hitler Youth and the *Bund Deutscher Maedel*, the League of German Girls. I have never seen so completely military a German as the little seven-year-old boy who knocked on my door one day and, when I had opened it, snapped to rigid attention, shot his arm high and shouted at me a falsetto "Heil Hitler!" after which he asked me in the clipped sentences of a military command would I donate twenty pfennigs to "support the Fuehrer and the Fatherland in this, our life-and-death struggle".

Of all the Germans, they have been most closely guarded in their camps in Eastern Germany against the effects of the Transition. The Fuehrer is still struggling to keep the other side of war a secret from them. With the exception of the soldiers, if it comes to starving, the Youth will be the last to suffer. For Hitler has plans for them, the *Herrenvolk*-in-being.

The little creatures in their brown shirts and short black trousers could be amusing if they were not so dangerous. They are dangerous; more so than a cholera epidemic. There is, so far as I know, no demoralization in their favoured ranks. They love the whole show, and are just aching to get big enough to get into the fight themselves. Frankly, I am more afraid, more terrorized, at watching a squad of these little boys, their tender faces screwed in frowns to ape their idolized leaders, on the streets of Berlin, than I am at seeing a panzer brigade of grown-up fighters speeding across the city. The grown-ups we only have to fight; but we shall have to live under the children who are being trained for their role. They are being trained every day and every hour of the day in their little barracks in Eastern Germany right now. What children of other nations read about, and thrill at, as a record of the past—feudal knighthood—they are reading about and thrilling at in the communiqués of their own High Command every day, embellished by specially trained authors-for-children. Their toys for seven years before the war have been miniature tanks, aeroplanes and guns that actually shoot, and though latest developments have robbed them of their more realistic toys, the insidious training, with cardboard war-games, has continued. Hitler Youth training, drilling and study used to be something which took place after school, extra curricula activities. Now Hitler has decreed it shall be a part of the curriculum: mornings must be given to studying the Nazi version of history and other subjects, and afternoons to Hitler Youth activity. If a boy is a good Hitler Youth, he passes, no matter what he knows about anything else. If he has not been a good, vigorous Hitler Youth, he cannot even enter a secondary school, regardless of how intelligent he is or what talent he has. That is another decree of that year of progress, 1941.

These are the elements of Germany who have not been affected by the Transition. They bear watching. If Hitler wins, they will become the gods, not only of Valhalla but of the rest of the world. They will be worse than the present gods. Hitler got most of his present Gestapo while it was on the verge of becoming adult, or after it became adult. These he has had from birth. If you think the present Gestapo is brutal, just wait until these little tykes—bred on insolence and on their innate superiority to all else in the world, and inspired by the great deeds of the "War of German Liberation", as it will be called—grow up and become the rulers of Victorious Germany and the World. In a sense, this is a war to stop little twelve-year-old Hans and Fritz. We are fighting not so much for the present as for the future. If they win, woe betide, not us so much as our children!

VI

THE ETERNAL JEW

WHEN PEOPLE become discontented, they can get angry at one of two things: at conditions, or at people. The one reaction is generally that of maturity; the other, of immaturity. The capacity for getting sore at conditions denotes the presence of a certain amount of intelligence, while getting mad purely at individuals indicates a lack of it. The rule is not hard and fast, but it is, I think, valid. A child always personalizes his misfortunes, and works up ephemeral grudges against the school-teacher, or a playmate who beats him at marbles, or Dad, after a licking. It is the mark of adulthood to be able to look behind and beyond individuals to see if the core of a difficulty is not something in the way in which things are done, in conditions as they are. The distinction is an important one and deserves emphasis. It is the difference between *Nick Carter* in *Dead Man's Gulch* and *Strange Interlude*. In *Dead Man's Gulch*, the hurdle between page one and a happy ending is bad Jim Dustan, who wears a moustache to mark him for the wretch he is, and is just plain "ornery" by birth and got to be shot up and that's all there is to it. A simple concept for simple minds. No dillying around with the possibility that Jim might have *become* bad due to conditions that are left unchanged and will create many more Jim Dustans after bad Jim has been shot up. It's easy to get mad that way, and it is downright fun, just as it is relieving to spit a string of oaths at a hammer which has banged your thumb blue, although the hammer was a passive accomplice and in no way responsible for the crime. But try and find the villain with a moustache in *Strange Interlude*. There isn't any at all. No character in the piece caused the misfortunes; it was just circumstances or may be human nature, or conditions; and small minds cannot appreciate that. I choose this play for the comparison, because it so happens that once I loaned a copy of it, with high recommendation, to a farm-hand I knew, and his reaction makes the point clearer than a bookful of words: "It's writ purty", he said, handing it back, "but somehow it ain't satisfyin'."

The urge to personalize hate is a quirk of human nature which is important, for it is strong in the best of men—everybody likes a good, juicy personal-hate session now and then, for it sometimes purges and relieves like the oaths at the hammer. It is socially important because it can be used to divert social discontent from conditions, where it belongs more often than not, to individuals or to a group, preferably to a minority group which bears clearly visible marks of distinction like the moustache on a Nick Carter villain. Privileged castes and governments have often in the course of history made use of it in this way. For purely personal hate has the social characteristic of being assistant to conditions-as-they-are, while the other attitude implies reform, or in extreme cases, revolution. (It might be objected here that also the revolutionary Socialists hate people—the owning classes. That is true, but no Socialist worth his oats believes the owning classes are the basic cause of the trouble; the trouble is traditionally "The System". In fact on the basis of socialist theory, persons are neither good nor bad, but conditions make them so.) In the southern States of America, the notorious Ku Klux Klan of hooded white-riders was used to steer the hate and misery of small farmers and small-town shopkeepers against the Negroes, clearly marked by their colour, and defenceless, and, oh, so easy to hate. If you had suggested to anyone of those white-cloaked night-raiders that the basis of their misery was a national economic development whereby their farms were being gobbled up by banks and their shops made to run at a loss due to interstate chain-stores, you would have been tarred-and-feathered for a nigger-lover or an anarchist. The Russian Tsarist government applied the same method with the Jews as the metal rod to divert the lightning of mass discontent. But the world's past masters at the technique have been the Nazis in our own day. So effective were they at it, in fact, that Mussolini belatedly wondered why he had not thought of it, and later he did take it up. But with his people it did not work so well because the Jewish minority was not so clearly distinguished from the Italian majority in appearance. Clear, unmistakable distinction is a *sine qua non*.

The theory of the Jewish problem, as outlined here, is well known. I repeat it, and in this particular form, because it has, seen in this light, undergone a new development during the Nazi mutation.

Since the great pogrom of 1938, when Jewish shops all over Germany were smashed by Storm Troopers in plain clothes as a "spontaneous" demonstration against the shooting of a Nazi consular official in Paris by the Jewish youth, Herschel Grynszpan, the Jews in Germany have led a quiet, miserable existence. It has been passively miserable. The Nazis have pilfered their possessions and withdrawn every right from them, but have not, since that time, actively and physically molested them. When the war began they were made outright helots. They were drafted into factories and made to do all forms of manual labour from twelve to fifteen hours a day regardless of age or sex. Seventeen-year old Jewish girls and sixty-year old men alike were forced to labour over dirty jobs for ninety hours a week at a wage which, when taxes and "contributions" had been subtracted, amounted to twenty marks a week. A Jewish curfew began at nine o'clock, and Jews caught on the streets after that time were subjected to heavy money fines and prison sentences. They were allowed small rations of a few staple foodstuffs, but forbidden luxuries such as fruit, or tomatoes or cheese or tobacco or alcohol. They were allowed to do their shopping only between the hours of four and five o'clock in the afternoon, when shops were so crowded that a Jew could seldom visit more than two stores a day; their ration cards were spotted with little purple "J"s for Jew to prevent them buying outside this time, and even within the single shopping-hour shopkeepers were expected to serve Aryan customers first, no matter how long the Jews had been waiting in queues outside the door. They were not allowed to buy clothing during the war, but, if they could prove they were unable to continue working without it, they were granted a permit every six months to buy twenty pfennigs worth (about three pennyworth) of cheap yarn for mending purposes. The existence was a vegetable one—vegetable in a hard winter and on a stony soil. Every amenity was strictly forbidden! No cinemas, no theatres, no taverns, no wireless sets, no telephones. Actually, they did not require means of recreation, for they were given no time for it. The few hours of freedom they enjoyed between the end and beginning of their workdays, they used in trying to restore fitful sleep in the tissues that were overworked and undernourished beyond restoration. On Sundays, they were not allowed to use the trams or buses or the underground to go outside Berlin for fresh air and a walk (eventually, they were forbidden to leave their districts of the city for any purpose at any time), and were not permitted to walk in parks inside the city. Near the Zoo underground station, the Nazis permitted them to establish a *centrale* where they might meet and talk together on Sundays, but most of the Jews I knew in Berlin shunned this dubious privilege for it became too depressing to listen, on the only day free of work in the week to the thousand woes of their racial fellows who, after eight years, knew of nothing else to talk about.

Their life was miserable, but it was still just bearable. The first two years of war were actually dog-days for the poor old creatures; they were an off-season on active torture and persecution. The Nazis were winning. The national Aryan cupboard was being constantly replenished by conquest. The Aryan middle classes, for whom the Jewish Question had been created in the first place, were not discontented, but could see a brilliant, easy triumph just ahead. The old lightning rod was allowed to rust in the rain, for there was no lightning.

And there was actually little reason why they should be molested. They were quiet and inconspicuous. The strong, aggressive Jews had been either executed or imprisoned long ago. The wealthy and influential, who had friends in the outside world and might thus be construed to be "conspirators in the international Jewish plot against Germany" had long since escaped to safer climes. The young had mostly escaped or been imprisoned. Those who remained were old, decrepit, pathetic creatures whose spirit of resistance had been broken long ago, and whose bodies were almost broken. The Bernsteins—Frau Bernstein about fifty, and her aged mother-in-law—who lived in the apartment next to mine, were typical examples. The husband and son, respectively, was arrested in 1938 and was still in prison. The daughter of Frau Bernstein, the younger, had escaped to Czechoslovakia early in the Nazi regime, and had not been heard from since. For the first two years of the war, the old couple lived unobtrusively in their three-room apartment on Wittenberg Platz. I knew them and spoke to them daily, but our familiarity never overstepped a smile and a casual greeting, for it was obvious that they preferred it that way. They did not want to attract attention by having too close a friendship with me, a foreigner and—through no fault or virtue of mine—an "Aryan".

They seemed as content as they could be with their meagre lot; they were being left alone, and that, after eight hectic years, is all those broken souls still in Germany could demand of Fate—to be left alone until a quiet, merciful death overtook them.

No Nazi read with greater horror last autumn than these poor, helpless people the omens between the lines of Nazi communiqués from the East. The Germans had already liquidated their sterner brethren who would have enjoyed the news. Those who remain were faced with the awful dilemma of not wanting the Germans to win, but fearing the consequences of a German defeat. The Nazis were no longer winning in the East; it was obvious to Jews as it was to Aryans. The home cupboard was approaching bareness with alarming speed. The people were growing obviously ill-tempered. The feeling among the people resembled that of 1918 as closely as Berlin's greying streets and buildings did the Berlin of the revolution. And the Jews in Berlin have never allowed themselves to be deceived about what these developments would mean, when and if they came; it haunted every moment of their lives. The Nazis would never lose, or even approach defeat, while there was a Jew within the reach of Hitler's armies still alive. They were the last pawn, the most horrible hostage of all the hostages created by Hitler's horrible Inquisition.

In mid-September came the harbinger, as clearly indicative of something to come as wild geese against an autumn sky. The *Reichsgesetzblatt*, the German law journal, published an announcement that, from September 19, every Jew in Germany and Bohemia would be required to wear a yellow star over his left-breast, the six-pointed Star of David marked in black hebraic characters: *Jude* for Jew. The *Voelkischer Beobachter*, explaining the new measure, was transparent: "The German soldier," it wrote, "has met in the Eastern Campaign the Jew in his most disgusting, most gruesome form. This experience forces the German soldier and the German people to deprive the Jews of every means of camouflage at home". The logic of the justification leaves much to be desired, but its transparency nothing. With typical subtlety, the *V.B.* thus gave away the fact that it was not the Jews, but conditions—i.e. the failure of the blitz to destroy Russia—that were at fault. The people were discontented at the slaughter of German men in a campaign that seemed never to approach an end, and the Nazis were scraping the rust off the old lightning-rod. The villain's moustache was being painted bigger and blacker that he might more easily be hated.

At the end of September, when depression in the German people reached its lowest point before Dietrich's famous speech, the Propaganda Ministry, apparently not cognizant of the plans of Hitler and the High Command in Russia—just two days more and the big offensive would be unleashed—pulled a ghost, a very scrawny ghost, out of its idea-cabinet. It was a book which many people have certainly heard of, but only few have read: *Germany Must Perish*, by an American Jew named Nathan Kaufmann. In this obscure volume, Mr. Kaufmann revealed himself to be a despicable mental case, afflicted by a psychopathic disease removed exactly no stages at all from Nazism if only the terms "Jew" and "German" were exchanged for one another. He recommended the wholesale sterilization of Germans, and inevitably forced an intelligent reader to the conclusion that, though it would not solve the problem, at least a solution might be approached if Mr. Kaufmann himself were sterilized as painfully as possible and very slowly drawn and quartered. No man has ever done so irresponsible a disservice to the cause his nation is fighting and suffering for than Nathan Kaufmann. His half-baked brochure provided the Nazis with one of the best light artillery pieces they have, for, used as the Nazis used it, it served to bolster up that terror which forces Germans who dislike the Nazis to support, fight and die to keep Nazism alive, to delay the Nazi decomposition for, perhaps, years in which millions of good people from every country will be killed and nations will suffer destruction and starvation.

And did the Nazis use it! Discovering it in a moment of deepening despair, the Propaganda Ministry ordered every newspaper in Germany to publish long, belated, powerful reviews of *Germany Must Perish*. Its contents became better known than those of any Nazi book that has appeared since *Mein Kampf*. The *Voelkischer Beobachter* gave its review the front-page banner-line: "JEWS WANT COMPLETE ANNIHILATION OF GERMAN PEOPLE".

The inspiration, Goebbels discovered by dubious logic and on evidence still unrevealed, was right in the White House.

"In the Jewish literary circles of New York, it is an open secret," his official organ wrote, "that Roosevelt himself inspired and personally dictated the most important parts of this work of shame . . . it is the political credo of the President of the United States."

"On the grounds of the close relations between this author and the White House, one can accept this monstrous programme as the policy of Roosevelt, himself".

Striking while the iron was hot, the Nazi printing houses in Berlin published several million pamphlets, titled with white-hot words on a flaming red cover: "The War-Aims of World Plutocracy"! Inside was the most baffling mixture of fiery passion (fifty parts), quotations from Kaufmann's delirium (forty-nine parts) and fact (one part, or less) that even Nazis have ever compounded into a propaganda philippic.

The pamphlet closed with the revealing words:

"German People! You know now what your eternal enemy has prepared for you. There is but one means of frustrating these plans for our annihilation: Win! The reading of this Jewish murder-plan will steel your strength and make mighty your will to win. Now, go back to the gun, to the plough, and the lathe and the desk. The parole is: Fight, Work, Win!"

Thank Wotan for Nathan Kaufmann! If he had not existed, the Nazis would have had to create him! The pamphlets went on sale at news-stands for fifteen pfennigs a piece. Sales were good at first, but much of the interest was withdrawn from them when Dr. Dietrich came to Berlin the following week. The following month, the Nazis began giving the pamphlets away, one to each family in Germany along with monthly ration cards. Since then the Nazis have used in the press the "War-Aims of World Plutocracy" a source book on their oft-used propaganda principle of issuing dubious evidence about some point that must be made, then referring forever afterwards to the said point as something now indubitably proven and about which, therefore, it is no longer necessary to give evidence (like the time the Propaganda Ministry "proved" President Roosevelt was a blood-Jew; the evidence, such as it was, was never repeated, but the assertion was for ever afterwards mentioned in German newspapers as "the well-known established fact").

In the outside world the Kaufmann episode was hardly noticed; those who did take notice regarded it as just one more inanity of German propaganda, disgusting and amusing at once. To people who like to observe social psychology, it was another beautiful application of the lightning rod technique. In both cases it was little better than academic in interest. But to the helpless Jewish derelicts in Germany, it was a storm-cloud, real, all too real, and horrifying. The Berlin paper, *Boersen Zeitung*, published an editorial reinforcing their fears, frankly stating that, in these times of distress, the "German people must naturally expect their leaders to take further measures against the death-enemy of the German people within Germany's borders". All Germany's anti-Jewish campaigns began this way—the Gestapo always allowed itself to be "prevailed upon" by the *vox populi*, as registered in the German press, before it did its duty against the racial enemy.

Late one night in October, the first showers of the storm came. A Jewish friend, Fritz Heppler, came to my house at two o'clock in the morning, when I had just returned from a broadcast, and told me the Gestapo were raiding Jewish households all over town. The grounds given were that Jews were hoarding foodstuffs and intensifying the shortage, especially of vegetables. They had just been to his room. They found nothing and did not molest him.

Fritz (this is not his name) was a tall, stringy powerful young man, one of the few young members of his race who had neither escaped nor been held in prison, though he had been arrested twice. I met him a year before in an underground train parked under Potsdamer Platz during an air-raid. He had spotted me for an American, and showed me his identification-card, marked *Staatenloss* for stateless, with his name "Friedrich Israel Heppler" (the *Israel* was a Nazi contribution to his name. For Jewish women it is *Sara*), and with a great blue "J" for Jew stamped on every page. I liked him, for he was approximately my own age and maintained an unusual spirit of resistance, nourished on a hate that was truly beautiful. Out of sheer bravado, he broke every Jewish Law in Hitler's voluminous Law books. He never wore the Yellow Star, and averaged a fist fight a month with Nazis. When I first met him his face was bruised from a bar-room scuffle with a uniformed party member, in the course of which he had knocked his racial superior cold and afterwards escaped in the blackout. After that, he visited me at least once a week and was an invaluable source of news about Jews in Berlin.

Fritz was tough, to the point of being overbearingly so, but on this night, fear was written in every line of his swarthy, very Jewish, face. He punctuated his account of the Gestapo raid saying, "It's come. I knew it would come, as soon as they started losing". What he meant was transportation to occupied Russia, which would be nothing more nor less than banishment to sheer mediæval slavery and to certain death. He had talked about it to me more and more often as the Russian campaign proceeded.

At two o'clock in the morning, and weary after a long, fruitless battle with three increasingly stubborn censors at the radio station, I was in no mood for dramatics, and the only pity I could muster was for myself. I gave Fritz a cigarette, a couple of drinks of *Korn*, and told him peremptorily: (*a*) the Germans were not losing (Fritz had been a Communist and was convinced from the first day of the Russian campaign that the Russians would eventually beat the stuffing out of the Germans); (*b*) he was letting his imagination expand a trivial night-raid into a personal Nemesis; (*c*) if it were as serious as all that, which it wasn't, he was a damned fool to come out on the streets just after his room had been raided; and (*d*) to go home and sleep it off, and to drop in to see me next day. He went, but only after he had made me promise I would go to the American Embassy the first thing in the morning to ask about the possiblity of his getting a visa for the United States. He said he was ashamed to admit it, but his spirit was cracking fast; he did not any longer want to wait and "see the revolution"; he was scared. He wanted to get out of Germany as quickly as possible. I promised desultorily, and shoved him out of the door.

For people living outside Germany, and more so for people who have never been inside Germany even on a brief tour, it is hard to conceive, to the full sympathetic extent, of the fear with which utterly helpless Jews—completely at the mercy of heartless brutes who do not even consider them as entitled to as much consideration as stray curs on the streets—watched every little indication of events inside Germany that might bear on their fate. It is hard to feel with them the paralyzing fear that gripped their hearts even at something so trivial as an unconscious stare at them from some uniformed Nazi on the streets. They lived in the terror of expectancy, which is always more horrible than actual persecution itself. I have lived in Germany for the better part of half a decade. My callousness on this occasion can hardly be justified. I did not go to the

American Embassy the next morning to help Fritz. I simply forgot about it. Not that it would have helped him; but it would have helped soothe my own conscience at the manner in which I said good-bye to long-suffering, hard-fighting Fritz. For I never saw him again after that night.

He did not come back the next day nor the next. I could not go to his room, for I did not know where it was. He had never told me, because it would have been dangerous for him had his land-lady ever seen a Gentile entering his room. Two nights later, when I returned home after a broadcast, I discovered the reason why Fritz had not come back. The door of the Bernsteins' apartment next to mine was sealed to the doorpost with six little white stamps, and another little white stamp covered the keyhole. On each little stamp was a spread eagle, gripping a swastika in its claws and around it in a circle, the words: "closed by the *Geheime Staatspolizei*". Fritz, and the Bernsteins, and thousands of others had gone colonizing in the East.

The Nazis thus opened one of the vilest little chapters in the Nazi decade's record of unblemished vileness. Their case was so utterly transparent and guileless, that it stank even in the dulled nostrils of their own people. To steer a tide of discontent from them-selves and conditions they had created more systematically than ever a ruling clique which actually created conditions with its own hands, they pounced upon a handful of enervated, helpless human beings and assigned them to death by slavery, while their press screamed that these hopeless wretches were involved in a plot to destroy Germany, the most powerful military nation in history. These were not the mentally ill whom the Naizs have slaughtered in modern hecatombs; they were old people, raw from much suffer-ing, and able to feel, with double sensitivity, each blow. They were not a vigorous opposition; their fondest hope was to die quietly and from natural causes; not torture. To have executed them would have been almost humanitarian, too much so for Nazi taste.

In the dead of night, when the old people had either gone to bed or were undressing, the Gestapo fell upon them. Generally, there was no warning; just a sudden pounding on the door. They were given from a quarter of an hour to an hour to pack, to settle the affairs of a life-time and leave homes they had lived in since child-hood. The time was sufficient, though, for they could take only what they could pack and carry with them—a bag of shabby clothing. What they could not carry with them in their own hands and on their backs, automatically became the possession of the German state: their furniture, worn bits of linen, heirlooms, meagre possessions, but all they had in the world. The haul, was not very good; not nearly as good as in 1938, for Goering had left them little of any value.

They were then led to depots by the Gestapo, places where they were sorted out and given tags on which they could read, for the first time, their various fates—which town in Poland or Russia they were being transported to. One of the "depots" was said to be the vast, ruined synagogue in Fasanen Strasse, a stone's throw from Ribbentrop's club for foreign correspondents on one side and the Kurfuerstendamm on the other. It had been burned out inside, the windows broken and the apertures were licked with soot. The Nazis burned it in the pogrom of 1938, and while flames had leapt from its three great domes and its windows, the party men had ordered the jazz band next door in the Wiener Grinzing café to play louder so that music might be heard by people watching the fire from the streets: an almost orgiastic performance. Due to the same Nazi love for rubbing it in hard, no doubt, the old people were made to spend their last morning in Germany standing on the rubble and stones of the old synagogue receiving their little tags with the names of their new "homes" on them.

Then, they were marched in the darkness to suburban railway stations, for the exodus. Morning after morning at half-a-dozen stations, long trains of dilapidated unheated coaches waited for them. The Jews were packed inside to more than double the normal capacity of a railway coach, and most of them had to stand in cramped corridors without sleep and without food for the long exodus to the East lasting, over rails congested with military traffic, forty-eight to seventy-two hours. Toilets in the filthy, ancient coaches were clogged and most natural urges had to be answered out of windows, for the odour of the toilets was stifling, and the corridors were too jammed for passengers to elbow their way to them.

Some were lucky, and were stuffed, after a trip of two days, in disease-ridden ghettos of Eastern Poland. Starvation was almost certain for the weakest of them, but they had a fighting chance. The others were shipped into Russia to work themselves to death, more quickly and more painfully. They were settled in towns wrecked by war, where there was no plumbing, no heating, and houses were skeletons of wood left precariously standing by *Blitz-krieg*. Together with Soviet civilians they worked on roads twelve, fourteen, fifteen hours a day. Their weak, thinning bodies were nourished on thin watery gruel, with no bread or anything solid, thrice a day. Many of them died soon; many more must have died in the bitter eastern winter that followed, which they suffered in their skimpy clothing, made for the western cities they had lived in all their lives. If any old fool dreamed of escape, well, the yellow star was over his heart and easy to spot for a gunner. But escape was purposeless, anyhow, for the land was bare of food. It was only in the Nazi road camps that there was anything to eat at all. Many did try to escape, just to invite the blessing of a merciful bullet. Others committed suicide on the way. The greatest number of suicides, however, occurred among Jews still in Berlin when the transportation first began. The pitiful little Jewish weekly newspaper which the Nazis allowed the Jews in Germany to pub-lish, became filled with death notices each week after the raids began. It was death one way or another, and the sensible ones chose it the sooner and easier, rather than the later and harder.

At home in Germany, their pitiful belongings were sold at public auctions, and good Aryans fought like jackals over a car-case to buy shabby objects the Russian war had made scarce. The government got good prices for the rubbish because the auc-tioneers were ordered to work in conjunction with plain clothes men who stood in the background at each auction to bid prices up. The auctions were carried out in the abandoned homes them-selves. The doors were unsealed for the first time after the mid-night raid, and the auctioneers, accompanied by policemen, elbowed their way through little crowds, called together by news-paper announcements of the auctions, outside the former Jewish homes. When the auctioneer opened the Bernsteins' door, next to mine, one could see on the table inside two tea-cups still half-filled with brownish water. The two old women had been having a night-cap of *Ersatz* tea when the Gestapo had arrived, and were not given time to finish it. The auctions were ugly spectacles, with ill-tempered citizens crying curses at one another and at the auc-tioneer, threatening with all the standard threats to have one another arrested and to call friends "high in the party" into their squabbles. One woman was arrested for calling the official bid-up man a "lousy white-Jew". Another woman was taken to the police station for saying, as she went out of the door after an auction, "Thank God, this mess is over. They've sucked the last measly penny out of the Jews now; they can do nothing more". She was expressing a view held by more people than herself.

The ideology of Nazism may be compared with a Christmas tree highly decorated with yards of sparkly tinsel and hundreds of bright, shiny, empty baubles. Just because of this sparkly brightness it appealed immediately to the child-minds of the German middle classes, just as a bright, red, cheap toy attracts a three-year-old. Nazism meant colourful uniforms, brand new salutes, a new distinctive flag, fresh if empty ideas—a new lease of life for simple people sick of years of misery and sameness.

But an Idea is only as good as its real Content. That adage, a good one, I borrow from Dr. Goebbels. He made it early in the war in reference to the ideas with which Britain was fighting the war. With justice, he said the British and the French were still operating on the military side of the war-of-positions, an idea which had no more content in the day of *Blitzkrieg*. In the field of propaganda, Britain was using slogans and methods which could no longer make men's hearts beat faster and make them willing to fight and die for the fulfilment of these slogans. That was certainly true at the beginning of the war. But today it is far more true of Germany than of Britain. I am convinced this war has been transformed in its course into a true People's War for Britain. It is no longer a "private affair", but a revolutionary struggle of the British people and their allies against the Anti-culture of Fascism. It is the Nazi slogans that have no content. No Nazi slogan or idea can any longer speed up the dull, uninterested beat of a German heart, except the idea of fear, which is almost the only one of real content the Nazis possess.

No Nazi idea has ever existed on its own innate worth. They have all prospered on their newness. But Dr. Goebbels' adage has the inevitability of physical law. An idea which is novel and nothing more must inevitably lose its effect with time. People given to shallow and quick enthusiasm also lose enthusiasm quickly and fall easily into depression. The Nazis have tried to keep one step ahead of the fulfilment of their own adage by discarding old ideas and taking up new ones periodically. In their

propaganda for their foreign policy, they have been alert and in-
genious. If you remember, Hitler's first declaration of foreign policy
was "Liberation from Versailles". All he wanted of the world was
Germany's old borders back again. This he discarded for "One
People, One Reich, One Leader", at the time of the invasion of
Austria. He now wanted to unite all Germans, regardless of earlier
national boundaries, into one German family; an idea with
obvious appeal. But events, created by Hitler, began to dull the
shine on this bauble and make it transparent, so the war-slogan
of the "New Order of Europe", another idea with obvious attrac-
tiveness, though a far more ambitious slogan than that of liberation from Versailles, was created to replace it. When it became
apparent to the world and to his own people, that Hitler's ambitions extended even wider than this, the latest slogan, and the
truest yet created, was introduced: the war is a "War Between
Two Worlds". What began as a liberation of Germany thus has
developed into a struggle in which the stake is the whole world.
The development has been clever and interesting.

But in their internal propaganda policy, the Nazis have not been
so alert. They have never altered the basic slogan of the Racial
Idea—"The Jews are Our Misfortune". It really never seemed
necessary. It made every shopkeeper a social scientist, and gave
every *Hausfrau* the Open Sesame to causality in world politics.
The answer to everything, the World War, the German Revolution, the Spanish war, this War, rising prices, falling quality, was
always—the Eternal Jew.

In the *débâcle* of Nazi propaganda, initiated by Dr. Dietrich,
perhaps the most eminent eventual victim was the Racial Idea.
After making almost ten years of history and news, the Racial
Idea was dealt a blow which has crippled it beyond repair with
those people it was created for, the German middle-class. Its
decline and fall has formed one of the most interesting and meaningful developments of the sweeping mutation inside Germany.
Doubt was spread immediately at the beginning of the war in
1939, when the German people, bred for years on *Rassenkunde*,
found themselves, the vanguard of Nordicism, friendly only with
"inferiors", the Italians, the Spaniards, the Russians and the Japanese. The little Nordic brothers, Holland and the Scandinavians,
remained cold and the Anglo-Saxon kin were outright enemies.
People began to scratch their heads, and doubt was so widely whis-

pered, that the organ of Himmler's Gestapo, *Das Schwarze Corps*, felt
called upon to publish an answer of sorts on its front page, in the
first winter of the war. The answer was no answer at all, for Racialism is a stupid doctrine and can provide no answers to the hundreds of obvious objections to it. The filtrate of the newspaper's
response served merely to brand people who questioned the theory
on the basis of Germany's alliances and enemies as dumb oxen.

In the second winter of the war, when at least three little
Nordic brothers had been taken over by Germany, the Nazis
set about repairing, in part, this academic inconsistency. Alfred
Rosenberg called the foreign press together to announce in
his own roundabout language of fake profundity that a brother-
hood of Nordic nations was in process of creation; put in plain
language, Germany was going to annex Holland and Norway,
and possibly Denmark. This was the first successful approach
to doing what the Nazis had always hoped to do—turn the
war to some extent into a racial war, bringing foreign policy
into line with domestic policy. The Nazi press gleefully supported the project with articles on the natural affinities of the
Nordic nations. But the Russian war nipped this symmetrical plan
in the bud. Among the Nordics, no less than among the Latins
and Slavs, the Russian war set a spark of hope aglowing, and the
little Germanic brethren began expressing the real extent of their
affinity to Germany by planting T.N.T. under German railway
trains and playfully snipping the Luftwaffe's cables by which the
air force learned of the approach of the Jewish British fliers. The
plan of the Nordic Union has never been heard of since. The press
has never again mentioned it, and has ceased to discover any
more "affinities".

The Race Idea bauble had actually lost most of its gloss before
the Nazis instituted the new anti-Jewish campaign. It was one of
Dr. Goebbels' ideas without content, an idea as transparent to
most Germans as it is to foreigners. Under these circumstances, it
was a fatal strategic error of Goebbels to resurrect it precisely at
the time he did.

The new campaign was a monumental flop from the day of its
birth. The day the Yellow Star was introduced, people all over
Berlin were asking one another, why, in God's name, was a
manoeuvre like that necessary. It was too obvious that the
poor wretched Jews living in Germany had nothing to do with the

disappearance of foodstuffs, and the failure of the High Command to conquer Russia in time. When Germans passed Jews wearing their vivid stars on the streets they bowed their heads—the unanimity of the reaction was remarkable—partly in shame and partly to spare the Jews the humiliation of feeling stared at. Since that day there has not been one single case on record in which Jews were molested in any way by non-party Germans, who form ninety-five per cent of the German population. Not by any organized plan, but from individual sympathy, Germans began showing little courtesies to the branded minority. "Aryans" shopping during the only hour the Jews, too, were allowed to shop, began taking their places quietly in line with the Jews and waiting their turns, instead of entering shops and taking advantage of their Aryan privilege of making their purchases while the Jews waited. Giving up one's seat on a tram to a Jew was too conspicuous and an unpardonable racial crime, but German men did allow Jewish women to enter trams before them, and to climb down from the tram platforms first. Once I saw a big, fat, ill-tempered *Buerger* block with conspicuous intent the path of two S.S. men in uniform while an aged Jewess got out of a subway train first. One of the young S.S. men bitterly whispered something in the fat man's ear, but the man did not answer, and left them looking angrily at one another in the coach. I thought I saw a trace of a smile on the plump *Buerger's* face as he left the station.

The star was called by Germans, outside the earshot of a hundred and fifty per cent Nazis, the "yellow badge of honour". *Witze* about it flourished. The star was called a new decoration, *pour le sémite*, a take-off on the world war decoration won by many Jewish Germans, *pour le mérite*. In another gag, you were supposed to ask who is going to win the war in order to hear the answer, "it is written clearly in the Stars". Still another maintained that the letters written on the Yellow Star to form the word "Jude" meant *Italiens Untergang; Deutschlands Ende* (J and I are the same character in the German alphabet)—Italy's decline; Germany's Fall.

Even Nazis, dyed-in-the-wool party-members, were disgusted. One of them told me he thought it a cowardly act and his opinion was shared by his fellow party-members. A young member of the Propaganda Ministry, who had to defend the campaign in public, told me in private it was suffering a severe setback from highly placed persons. Especially the old Prussian military caste considered it a major strategic error of propaganda, he said. All over Germany, an anonymous leaflet was circulated, branding the campaign as an act of "treason to the German people", and accusing the Propaganda Ministry and the Gestapo of playing into the hands of enemy propagandists. The leaflet, which every foreign correspondent in Berlin received in his mail, begged for understanding that the campaign was undertaken without authorization from Hitler, which is unbelievable, and requested that it be discounted as an irresponsible act of a few leaders whose actions could not be properly supervised by Germany's real leaders: the officers at the front. The leaflet was widely believed to have emanated from circles of the military caste, and to represent the first overt sign of a rift between the officers and the party.

Whether or not this is true, Goebbels apparently had his fingers rapped by someone, for his propaganda, in connection with the Jewish campaign, dropped after that into the purely explanatory category. The Kaufmann pamphlet was issued as a partial explanation of the new anti-Jewish campaign. And, although it certainly found an echo of fear in the German people, its value as an explanation of the attack on the impoverished, decrepit Jews inside Germany was nil. It sold well in the first weeks, but after the Dietrich affair sales dropped to an average of one copy per day per kiosk.

When the real set-back came, Goebbels had thirty million vivid leaflets printed and one distributed free to every family in Germany, along with the monthly ration cards. The leaflet was jet-black, with a bright yellow star on the cover and under it the words: "Racial Comrades! When you see this emblem, you see your Death enemy"! The pamphlet explained the campaign in simple terms and few words, aimed at the minds of children aged about six. The war was simply a Jewish plot against Germany. Jews were spiritually involved in the plot no matter where they were. Therefore the German Jews were involved in the plot, and must be destroyed. A housewife in my apartment house, who had been an ardent Nazi, told me, unconsciously quoting a now dead American humorist, that it was too bad the pamphlet was printed on such expensive, slick paper, or she could have found a use for it.

To save a dying cause, Goebbels threw his personal weight into the scales writing a signed editorial in *Das Reich* explaining, on a slightly higher intellectual level, the same grounds for the campaign, and incidentally scolding people who were led by a "false sentimentality" into feeling sorry for the German Jews. Not satisfied with the publicity his own paper gave to his essay, he had it printed in pamphlet form and issued, like the black leaflet, to every household in Germany along with the ration cards for the following month. He enlisted the services of his most eminent editorial assistant, Dr. Theo. Seibert, in the *Voelkischer Beobachter*, and Dr. Seibert took on a more appeasing tone. "It was," Seibert wrote, "somewhat pardonable that many of us have lost interest in the Jewish problem in the past few years—the German Jew has profited from the old German proverb, 'Out of sight; out of mind'. It is only in the past few months, when the Yellow Star made impossible even the most clever camouflage, that we have learned with amazement how many examples of this unholy race still live among us. But," Seibert went on, struggling hard to link the German Jews to Germany's contemporary misfortune, "out there on the other side of our borders Judaism has done everything humanly possible to prevent us from forgetting its existence, and most recently [the Great Retreat began two weeks after the editorial was published] more than ever"! In the course of his editorial, Seibert declared, "the battle against the Jewish International is a struggle for Life and Death, which must be waged absolutely unscrupulously to the end".

By this time popular faith in German propaganda had suffered severely. Newspaper sales had fallen off badly, and Germans were resorting to British news broadcasts for their information. So Goebbels turned to a stratagem justly famed, and ill-famed, in the annals of back-alley politics: the old whispering campaign. At this time, a rumour, unsupported by written evidence, could enjoy far more credibility than a written fact. It is the mark of the German Propaganda Minister's cleverness, that he recognized this weakness in the very nature of his own state and attempted, with no little success, to make a virtue of it. The whispering campaign was directed in the first instance against America, but offered at the same time an extremely clever justification for the Yellow Star policy. It was that the American Government had secretly adopted a law requiring all Germans—there are upward of 30,000,000 people of German origin in

America—to wear black swastikas on the left-breasts of their
clothing. I was speechless when my charwoman presented me
with this "established fact". I asked where she had heard it and
she told me the janitor had "revealed" this to her, and that the
Nazis were trying to keep it quiet in order to prevent demonstrations on the streets against America and a fresh pogrom of Jews
in Berlin! I immediately visited the janitor and he assured me it
was true; he had heard it straight from the local *Blockleiter* of the
Nazi party, who had been told it at a meeting of all *Blockleiters* of
the district that very day. He said, the Yellow Star campaign had
been initiated, reluctantly, by the Nazis as a sort of reprisal as
an attempt to force the Jews in America to leave off their persecution of Germans! I heard the same report later from a dozen other
sources, and in each case it had been put in circulation by some
petty Nazi official, at approximately the same time. Its official
inspiration was indubitable. Such an obviously inane report
could be believed nowhere else but in Germany. It was so
clever it was almost admirable. It lived a brief life, but it gave, at
least to a few smaller Nazis, the balm they needed for consciences
grown sensitive through much wear.

At the same time, an article appeared in the provincial press—
not in the Berlin press; the Nazis often made use of the tactic of
publishing fantastic information in the provinces which they
dared not publish in Berlin for fear the foreign correspondents
would find and make use of it—purporting to be an exhaustive
report on the condition of *Volksdeutscher* in America. I saw it in the
Stuttgarter Zeitung, but later learned it was published in six or seven
other provincial newspapers. The article declared people of German origin in America were being persecuted systematically,
according to a plan prepared by the Jews who slept in the White
House, and dictated each day the activities of the American President. The article recommended as the only solution to this unbearable situation, a new repatriation scheme to bring every
German from America back into the Reich, just as the Fuehrer
had brought Germans from all over non-German Europe *heim ins
Reich*. I ran across the article while preparing a script for one of
my broadcasts. It was an excellent story, but I knew from long
experience it would be impossible to get a single quotation from it
through the rigorous censorship, so I simply earmarked it for
future reference and use, if I should ever get out of Germany.

While I was clipping it, however, I noticed the author's name. It was one Dr. Lessing—an acquaintance of mine, who had lived for a long time in America and taught German at a mid-western American university. The most interesting feature was that Dr. Lessing was one of the censors who slaughtered my scripts each day. I took the article to the censors immediately—unfortunately Dr. Lessing was not there that day—and made known my intention to use it in my next broadcast. The military censor informed me that I was wise in seeing him before I wrote it, for I saved myself the trouble of doing so. He said he would never allow a word of the article to be used in my script! I pointed out to him the fact that the article was written by one of his colleagues on the censorship board, and that, theoretically, we correspondents might use any item which appeared in an official publication, or a publication authorized by the government. He merely shook his head and said I should know by now the difference between propaganda for internal consumption and propaganda for external purposes. I told him undiplomatically I could only interpret his judgment to mean the story was a shameful lie, created to deceive the German people, but which had to be kept from the outside world in order not to reveal how dishonest Nazi propaganda could be. He told me I could interpret it for myself as I wished, but I still could not use a single word of the article, and that was that. This was about three weeks before I was banned from the air in Berlin for good, and the incident was certainly one reason why the Nazis refused to grant me a permit to leave the country until the Columbia Broadcasting System had offered the Nazi government a substitute correspondent as a hostage. The occasion was the bluntest, most artless confession of the bankruptcy of German propaganda-for-Germans I have ever experienced.

The last and hardest blow to their own anti-Jewish propaganda was crudely delivered by the Nazis themselves. They aimed it secretly against that particular little group which enjoys perhaps more independence than any small clique in Germany—the *Artistenwelt*, the film studios, where a few hard-working, energetic actors and actresses have been waging a losing, but none the less inspired battle against the shackles of propaganda for years. The story involves Joachim Gottschalk, one of Germany's most intelligent and hardest working actors. Gottschalk, a sort of German Fredric March, was a born picture-stealer, and made his way to fame strictly against the will of the Propaganda Ministry, which deprived him of all publicity in film magazines and newspapers. The reason the handsome young actor was disliked by the authorities was the fact that he was married, and happily married, to a full-blooded Jewess, and repeatedly refused suggestions from the Nazis to divorce his wife and enjoy a smoother rise to fame. As the war proceeded, Gottschalk's popularity grew in Germany, for he seemed to have a knack of getting good roles in strictly non-propaganda films, which irked the Nazis all the more. With Paula Wessely he made the biggest box-office hit of the first year of the war, *Ein Leben lang*. The film was truly excellent and with it, Gottschalk first won fame in countries outside the German sphere of influence to which the film was exported. With Brigitte Horney he made another truly good film, *Das Maedchen von Fanoe*, then played the role of Hans Christian Andersen in *Die Schwedische Nachtigall*, which made him perhaps the most popular actor in Germany. When the anti-Jewish campaign was begun, Goebbels presented Gottschalk with an ultimatum; he was becoming a German institution, he had qualified inadvertently as good propaganda, and he must divorce his wife, or he would be banned from his profession for evermore. Gottschalk promptly refused to leave his wife, and the half-Jewish child she had borne him. So he was informed that, regardless of his decision, he could no longer live with his polluted family; the Gestapo gave his wife and child one day to pack and join the Jewish exodus to the East. Gottschalk was not to be permitted to go with them.

On the appointed evening, the Gestapo invaded the Gottschalk home to put an end to this unbearable *Rassenschande*. They found the family there waiting, but it was dead. Ten minutes before they came, Gottschalk had killed his child, his wife and himself. The incident was a hideous one, and the story spread over Berlin like wildfire. The *Artistenwelt* was incensed and it was said that there was nearly a revolt in the film studios. German women who, in legions of millions, had cried their eyes dry at Gottschalk playing a war-cripple in *Ein Leben lang*, were horrified. Dr. Goebbels and Herr Himmler had under-estimated the fibre of their film-hero, if they had not under-estimated the breadth of his popularity. People said, in one of those little quips that circulate faster than newspapers, Gottschalk killed himself, but he was not the only eminent suicide that day; the other was Goebbels. Goebbels doesn't know it, and I do not believe the rest of the world realizes it, but he is quite dead. He is not even a lascivious joke in Germany any more. He died last autumn, but he hasn't been buried yet.

As a means of influencing his own people in favour of National Socialism, Goebbels has crippled the Racial Idea for all time. The circulation of Germany's most famous anti-Jewish newspaper, the notorious *Der Stuermer*, has dropped more than eighty per cent since the beginning of the war. The whereabouts of that pornographic sheet's publisher, Julius Streicher, the erstwhile *Gauleiter* of Nuremberg, are not known. It is generally believed that he has been placed in an insane asylum, which, in any case, was his spiritual home. Other reports say he has been shot. In any event, not a word about him, nor his picture, has appeared in the German press since the beginning of the war. It is symbolic of the fall of Streicher's idea, that those little red show-cases which used to be screwed to buildings all over Germany in order to contain, behind glass covers, each week's issue of *Der Stuermer* for public inspection, have almost disappeared. Those which remain are never looked at, nor regularly cared for by the local Nazi officials who are supposed to change their contents each week. Their red paint is fading, and the glass covers are mostly broken. Propaganda Ministry officials are downright ashamed of *Der Stuermer*, and tell correspondents to disregard it as a part of German propaganda for the issues of this little paper are numbered in small integers. It is only an expensive concession to the sensibilities of a few members of the old Nazi guard who still believe in the Jewish Question and would be indignant if the principal organ of anti-semitism were dropped.

If he crippled the dogma inside Germany, Goebbels has annihilated it outside Germany. The string of anti-Jewish films which the Nazi studios have been turning out lately, including *The Rothschilds* and *Jew Suss*, have been boycotted by the public in the countries outside Germany to which they have been exported. In Sweden, a Nazi book-dealer who placed in his window the sign, "Jews not allowed to enter", was almost mobbed by the populace, and the police forced him to remove the sign so that order might be maintained. In Czechoslovakia, when all other means of expression of their discontent was withdrawn from them, people, last autumn, began showing such conspicuous courtesy to Jews on the streets, that the Gestapo had to issue a whole sheaf of decrees setting penalties for such crimes as the tipping of hats to Jews, standing in queues behind Jews, and giving Jewish women seats on trams. In Alsace and Lorraine, German soldiers destroyed Jewish shops and set fire to synagogues. Later when I went there, propaganda authorities pointed out the destroyed houses as indications of how strongly anti-semitic the Alsatians and their neighbours were; but civilians with whom I talked denied emphatically that anyone but German soldiers had taken part in the demonstrations. Similar incidents, indicative of a general trend of feeling against the threadbare theory of Racialism come from almost every country in Europe. The Racial Idea has died a painful death all over Europe, and, even if there were no other gain, this alone almost justifies our war against Hitler.

VII

THE WHITE PERIL

WITH BUT one conspicuous exception the Nazis have been not so
very good at hate-making since the Racial Idea first began to lose
its lustre more than two years ago. The atrocity campaign against
the Poles, which served as a preface to Hitler's war, enjoyed but
little success outside the immediate eastern German border districts. People were too frightened about the prospective consequences of the anti-Polish campaign to be able to hate effectively
at that time of tension. There has never been, and there is not yet,
any large degree of intense hate for England among the broad
masses of the German people, for in their heart of hearts Germans
are convinced, despite years of propaganda to the contrary, that
not England, but their own leaders systematically prepared and
began this war. When Churchill refused to capitulate after the
fall of France, disappointment was great, and this might well have
turned into hate had not Hitler, himself, forestalled the transformation by initiating the blitz on England. Oddly, it was the
lurid accounts of the blitz, day after day, in their own newspapers
that made Germans secretly, and surprisingly often overtly, express admiration for the British people. This admiration was, in
fact, so often expressed, that one big Berlin newspaper, the *Lokal-
Anzeiger*, issued an editorial reprimand to Germans at the time for
believing the resistance of the British people signified the presence
of some national virtue. Actually, the newspaper explained, it was
lack of spirit, which made the British people subject themselves
to constant day and night bombardment; they had been enslaved
by Jews so long that they had lost all spirit of revolt. This editorial,
and others like it, had, however, little effect, and the few English
people caught by war in Berlin and not interned enjoyed singular
hospitality from Germans everywhere they went. The English
language was not only endured, but actually favoured in restaurants in the cosmopolitan West End of Berlin. One could speak it
anywhere, in a café or in buses and trams, without the slightest
fear of those unpleasant little incidents that are often induced in
belligerent nations when people are heard speaking the language
of the enemy.

Each of the campaigns found a complement of fear among Germans that it would not turn out favourably, but, excepting the Russian war, they all ended long before any vindictiveness against their victims could be aroused. Even Russia, perhaps potentially the most hatable candidate of all the national candidates, failed to earn any direct bitterness from the German people. Certainly Russia might have become the first truly successful target of German national hate; but before the Russian campaign began, something else intervened, and on the basis of one fire burning out another's brightness, fended off a reaction that might otherwise have been inescapable.

What intervened was—Roosevelt. Before the Russian campaign began, Roosevelt had already displaced Churchill as the Nazis' "World-Enemy Number One"; Stalin himself never had a chance for a high place in the Nazi hate-scale. After the beginning of the Russian war, German bitterness against the "White Peril from the Ghettos of Washington" began surpassing itself on each successive day, which, if you know the Nazis, is no small achievement. It is odd that the target at which Goebbels ultimately succeeded in directing anger in his eternal pursuit of steering popular hate, should be precisely that nationality which before the war was indisputably the most popular among Germans, but it is certainly true that this target eventually absorbed more unmitigated bitterness than the German people have been able to generate since the French occupation of the Ruhr, twenty years ago.

The grounds for the white hot intensity which Nazi and German hate for America attained are not hard to divine. Somewhere in *Mein Kampf*, Hitler gives the clue in a passage asserting that the effectiveness of a politician or a statesman can be gauged by the bitterness of the denunciations his enemies pour on him. By this token, President Roosevelt became the most effective single opponent to Nazism in its history.

If one wants to understand the German abhorrence of Roosevelt, all illusions regarding that incredible national leader must be cast aside. It must be admitted—nay vigorously upheld as a feature that is praiseworthy—that President Roosevelt is a cool, collected, clever calculator. His idealism is certainly great, but it is alloyed with an uncommon sense of practical, hard-headed politics in the meaning of that term with which men who wear bowlers and smoke cigars and talk hard politics in saloons use the word politics. People who like to forget we live in a world of tough reality and power politics, and that our enemies are unscrupulous men on horseback could accuse this verdict of being in bad taste. For them I can only recommend a re-reading of history without tears. It is exactly this alloy which has distinguished the men who have led us from feudalism to democracy, in the long course of history. Pericles had it, as did William Pitt and Abraham Lincoln. Or, think of the men who did not have it. President Wilson had the idealism without the sense of politics. Huey Long had the sense of politics without the idealism. One was duped, and the other duping, but neither, if the truth may be spoken, actually contributed anything to the advance of democracy. The opponents of Fascism are luckier than most people realize in having in these critical years three leaders of the same unusual fibre: Churchill, Stalin and Roosevelt—all hard men, tough men, and, with it, idealists. Churchill, unfortunately, did not become chief of his government until the error of appeasement had been committed and he was forced to apply the pound of cure rather than the ounce of prevention. Stalin played an exceedingly clever game of power politics with Hitler, but allowed himself to be outsmarted, perhaps only by hours, when the crucial period approached. Both represented nations which had yielded a certain amount of appeasement to the Nazis regardless of the qualities of their leaders. But the record of Roosevelt's government was clean and unblemished. Years before, the American President had laid his cards down on the table for all to see. While Chamberlain appeased, and the German-Russian friendship agreement was a mere prospect, Roosevelt had sworn opposition to Hitlerism, and begun, in his own way, to act upon it. If there was one man in the world who directed foreign policy with the same consciousness and purposefulness as Hitler, but against Hitler, it was the American President; and he did not swerve from his course until events he rightly predicted changed it from an outlook shared only by a few intelligent liberals in America, to a national one.

This the Nazis hated; this they could not stand. The strength of Nazi foreign policy is expressed in the slogan: Divide and Conquer; dope one nation with a promise of security, and crush its neighbour; then promise a third neighbour safety and crush the second, and so on, *ad infinitum et ad nauseum*. But President Roosevelt proved immune to opiate. Against strong internal opposition, he branded each false promise for what it was, and proceeded to gird America's loins as well as possible in view of the difficulties in his path. Another Nazi tactic has been to drive the thin edge of a wedge very subtly between a nation and its independence, in trade, on the seas, or otherwise, and when the nation yielded, to drive the wedge in further and further, until the appointed victim was too weak and dependent to resist the final blow which robbed it of all possibility of self-defence, making it finally a Nazi colony. This, too, Roosevelt rejected. Each petty challenge the Nazis issued he paid back, with interest. When they approached American ships, he ordered battle patrols to go into the Atlantic. When they fired on his ships, he armed them. And when they sank American vessels, he ordered American warships to answer the fire, and then to fire on sight.

This was *unerhoert;* it was unheard of, something unique in Nazi annals. But Roosevelt not only parried every thrust, but adopted the offensive himself. He revealed to the world the Nazi plan to carve South America into units fitting German political and economic expediency, and the Nazi plan to establish a universal Nordic "religion". Before the President made these revelations, the documents supporting them were circulating secretly in Berlin. Both plans sound, on the surface, fantastic, and it required unusual boldness on the part of a national leader to present them to the world not as fantasies, but as prospective facts. But there is little doubt of their genuineness. The South American map which I saw in Berlin bore the stamp of a geo-political institute in Munich, apparently a product of Alfred Rosenberg's. The constitution of the new church, which was kept on file in the *New York Times* office, corresponded in its general outlines to schemes I have heard expressed many times by highly placed Nazis, and in every detail to Roosevelt's description of it.

The hate which Roosevelt's "impertinence" generated among governing Nazis was not like the hatred of the Jews; it was no fake, but the real thing. Day after day, in the two main press conferences, and in a third, which was instituted at that time, Nazi spokesmen grew apoplectic with rage at the mention of the name Roosevelt. The various Berlin papers began in October, like hounds unleashed, to outbid one another to find new, more vicious expletives. In a single editorial, one morning newspaper one day found space to call the American President a "gangster", a "butcher", a "cannibal in a white collar", a "negroid maniac", and a "depraved Jewish scoundrel"!

Ribbentrop's go-between with the foreign press and radio, Dr. Paul Schmidt, a fat, repulsive ambitious individual, took over the leadership of the Nazi choir, and struggled hard to build himself up a reputation as the German Specialist-on-questions-involving-Roosevelt. Like a good holy-roller preacher, Schmidt was capable of working into an alarming fury and actually slobbering at the mouth with rage. His attacks grew filthier day by day, until on one occasion, when he was unable to find more relevant features of the American President to pour vitriol on, he spat forth a long, vile essay on the President's physical affliction. The American press corps promptly agreed to boycott his commentary, and not a word on it was sent from Berlin to America by the press. Schmidt, who cherishes ambitions of becoming Foreign Minister one day, was unusually sensitive to the treatment his commentaries received at the hands of the American press and radio at whom he levelled all his essays. Vain as a peacock, and a guileless lover of personal publicity, Schmidt once suggested to the American correspondents that they quote him directly by name in their newspapers hence-forth—a practice which had been strictly forbidden by both the Propaganda Ministry and the Foreign Office. The result was that all American reporters held a conference in secret and agreed never to publish Schmidt's name in any connection. After his last Roosevelt attack was boycotted by the American corps, Schmidt considerably tempered his language in reference to the President and America.

The Propaganda Ministry linked the President with its new campaign against the Jews in the obvious hope of buoying up and justifying the latter by the former. One evening, the Ministry ceremoniously produced a learned geneologist at the Propaganda Ministry press conference who, in a long speech, purported to prove that somewhere way out on an indistinct limb of the President's family tree there had existed a relative with a name unmistakably Jewish. The press unanimously lapped up this un-diluted and irrelevant eye-wash and declared the case for the Jewish ancestry of Roosevelt was clinched by the fact that his mother's first name was Sara! Dr. Robert Ley's yellow sheet, der Angriff, published a special section on the President, including a

THE WHITE PERIL 157

half-page photograph of him in the company of three Jews. The official Nazi party newspaper reproduced an anonymous leaflet said to have been distributed in the streets of Washington itself, showing a six-pointed star of David, with the name of an influential Jew at the tip of each point and Roosevelt's name in the centre —aimed to prove Roosevelt and America were directed by Jews and that the American populace was so incensed that people risked their lives distributing "underground" propaganda under the President's very nose. The propaganda was "underground" in the same sense that a worm is. The Ministry attained a zenith of inanity with a "sensational document" which German soldiers "discovered" in a Norwegian Freemason lodge. I was telephoned on the evening of the Great Find by an official in the Propaganda Ministry and, in the whisper of important mystery, tipped off to get the early edition of the *Voelkischer Beobachter* as soon as it appeared that day; it would contain something of sensational character, and very, very interesting to an American correspondent. The discovery which was supposed to rip the world apart, up and down and sideways, was a half-page reproduction of a photograph of President Roosevelt wearing a masonic apron in a group of eminent New York Freemasons, proving beyond all human doubt that Roosevelt was, despite any denial he might make, a Freemason! A little Balkan correspondent telephoned me that night to get my reaction. (The Balkanesers always telephoned American correspondents to ask for comments on events, and the next day their newspapers published whatever we said as "authoritative comment from high American sources in the German capital.") We exchanged comments. His was: "A bombshell"! Mine was Nuts. The only thing the newspaper's text under the enormous cut neglected to say was that any German child could have discovered the same world-quaking fact by looking up, at any time, the President's record in *Who's Who* in the Berlin municipal library.

The only significance these examples of ideological bankruptcy have is that they were, on the basis of Hitler's precept in *Mein Kampf*, a remarkable compliment to the leader, by clearly expressed choice, of the American people. He was effective, too damned effective. But certainly the best compliment was delivered by the creator of the precept himself—Adolf Hitler, in the speech in which he declared war on America. The Fuehrer, if you heard the speech and recall the part, had reviewed the sins committed against Germany with uncommon restraint of voice. For exactly three-quarters of an hour, he had worked his way through Greek, Roman and German history, through the World War and up to the contemporary phase of this one. Then he asked the rhetorical question: *Who* was responsible for this bloody conflict; who was the biggest war-monger of all? Then, taking a deep breath, the Fuehrer screamed at a pitch he has never before or since attained—his voice cracked after the first syllable—*Roosevelt!* If you recall, the Leader did not resume for more than sixty seconds (seventy-two seconds to be precise; reporters notice things like that). The fact is, if I may trust a German friend who was there in the Berlin Sports Palace while I listened on the wireless, Hitler overstrained his voice, and coughed twice to recover it! Throughout the rest of his speech his tone of voice was unusually moderate. The question was rhetorical, but certainly the bisyllabic answer came from the bottom of his unusual heart. Whatever may be said against the Fuehrer, he is capable of a profound sincerity. He hates the Jews sincerely, and the Russians. But he never approached breaking a vocal cord over a Jew or a Russian.

The anti-American campaign caught on quickly with the German people. One reason was that they were still thinking in parallels with the world war and dreaded Roosevelt's growing belligerency and the ever more real prospect of America actively entering the war. But the more important reason was that Roosevelt was actually doing just what the Propaganda Ministry accused him of. He was actually lengthening the war, and putting easy victory at a distance which the German nation might not be strong enough to cover. The success of this particular propaganda campaign was but little to the credit of Goebbels. It was due more to actual facts which Goebbels could not have hidden from his people had he wanted to. The anti-American idea was quite definitely an idea with real content.

While the Propaganda Minister was still pondering whether it might not be a good idea to keep the whole thing quiet from his people and perhaps appease just a wee bit if it could keep America out of the war, Germans already knew, by word of mouth, how far things had progressed. Little Herr Simon, the door-keeper of the Foreign Press Club, who used to visit each table when an air-raid was brewing to tell patrons "The Tommies are coming", surprised the same patrons on a similar occasion late one evening by whispering to them that, not the Tommies, but "the Yanks are coming".

When the Propaganda Ministry no longer tried to hide the uncomfortable situation, but played it up and even exaggerated it, bitterness against Americans became serious. The change in sentiment was so swift that by last autumn it had become perilous for an American to speak English on the streets of Berlin. I myself was ordered out of two restaurants in the Kurfuerstendamm area for committing the crime of speaking my own language. A preposterous feature was that in one case, in the *Tusculum* restaurant, I had addressed the waiters in German but they had insisted on answering me in English, until the manager, on the suggestion of people at tables near mine, scolded them and told them to direct me to leave the premises immediately and, please, not to come back again! It was a fantastic incident. By the time I had paid my bill (I insisted on paying; God knows why), men at the tables around mine were standing up and crying plain and fancy curses at me. One old fool, wearing a Nazi party button, insisted on meeting me outside. I waited outside for twenty minutes, then tried to go back for him, but the doorman forbade me entrance and a waiter later came down and told me the silly old hysteric had left, with his wife, through the back entrance. My room-mate, Jack Fleischer, came home one night bruised from having been beaten up on Wittenberg Platz by three German officers for addressing in English a German girl we both knew in a restaurant near our place. For the same crime, three members of the staff of the American Embassy were set upon in *Horcher's*, Berlin's best restaurant, by three Italian patrons and two German waiters. One of the Americans suffered a broken hand after a fifteen-minute fight, but he did not discover it until all five of the enemy were on their backs cold and policemen had been called into the restaurant to arrest the victors. They were, of course, released after they showed their diplomatic passports. Berlin had become a not very pleasant assignment for Americans.

When the pinch came to Nazism, American correspondents suffered at first more acutely than the few other Americans in Germany, due to the very nature of their vocation. They were the eyes and ears of the hated America inside Germany. What 130,000,000 Americans knew about contemporary Germany was bottlenecked through fifteen or twenty reporters on the spot. They were cast in the egregious role of being spectators who wrote and spoke what they saw in a country that was virtually at war with their own nation, and in which they were thus enemies by nationality, no less than by personal conviction. The role was not a comfortable one, you may be sure.

All the old liberties, the futile rose-coloured glasses, disappeared with the introduction of the Lend and Lease bill in Congress. Hotels requested American correspondents to vacate their rooms. The Nazis placed every conceivable obstacle in the way of their leaving the country, however. My former boss, Harry W. Flannery, was flatly refused a permit to leave Germany until he made a vigorous protest to the German Foreign Office. All our telephone conversations were obviously tapped, and our houses were watched by not very subtly disguised plain clothes detectives. These little features, combined with the growing belligerency of Germans on the streets and in restaurants, made life for us in Berlin more than unpleasant. Anxious to prevent reports of what was happening in Berlin from reaching enemy ears, the Propaganda Ministry several times warned the American corps to mind its ways of reporting, for misdemeanours—and there was no fixed guide as to what was a misdemeanour and what a comprehensive, conscientiously written dispatch—would be considered military and political espionage, and that we knew what the penalty for espionage was. It was a ticklish situation; the whole resembled what people talk about when they refer to a Reign of Terror. That is not an exaggeration, it is quite serious. The Nazis were not fooling or making empty threats; they meant it and they proved it.

The most convincing proof came quite a while before the Russian war began. At the time, I was still working for the United Press. The proof touched me all too personally. It came while I was on overnight duty in the U.P. offices on Unter den Linden.

I was completely alone in an office suite of eight or nine rooms, half dozing over an empty copy desk and hoping to hell my relief, Walter Wilke, would come on time this morning for once. Precisely at five o'clock in the morning, the door to the hall outside clicked open; doubtless it was Frau Muekov, our *Putzfrau*. But the door did not click closed, so I rose and went into the main editorial room, to go out into the hall and see what was wrong. When I got there, the door from the hall into the editorial room was blocked by a short, thick-set man in a heavy brown overcoat. I asked him what he wanted, but he did not answer; nor did he look at me, but surveyed the vast room from one end to the other with the air of a very important fire-insurance inspector. I asked him again, and, still not looking at me, he pulled a small metal disc attached to a brass chain, from his pocket and flipped it at me. It was stamped *Geheim Staatspolizei* — long for Gestapo. Apparently satisfied that he would not be ambushed from any corner of the room, he looked back over his shoulder, nodded a come-on nod, the way they do it in films, and walked in. He had acted as a sort of stopper, and when he ceased to block the entrance, men, all of one pattern—big, hard-faced men, wearing gum-boots and thick, heavy overcoats—flooded into the room; five, ten, fifteen, twenty of them. The foreman told me to sit down; which I did, at the copy desk where the telephones were. No, not there, he said, and one of his men moved a straight chair up against a blank wall, far from any desk where I might pull a revolver out of a drawer or find a paper-weight to throw (!), and told me to sit there, and sit still. The big men, their faces screwed in important frowns, worked meanwhile, silently and swiftly, going through each desk and every file as if according to a plan carefully laid down before. They apparently knew just where everything was, to whom each desk belonged and just what they were going to find in it. I sat and smoked cigarettes chain-wise. Once I asked what was up, but none of the bruisers answered, nor did they talk to one another. Complete quiet, except for the shuffling of thick rubber soles on the plank floor, reigned for an hour.

Frankly I was plenty scared. In Germany, life is that complicated by decrees and laws that, no matter how conscientious you may be, you can't help breaking at least a dozen regulations you've never even heard of. Furthermore, in my drawer in the copy desk I had a sheaf of notes a foot high, of facts, mostly economic, and quotations from interviews, filled with names and details, in addition to exhaustive information on several air-raids, the locations of anti-aircraft guns, and a lot of unpublished material on the German army. I had gathered them over two years principally for journalistic purposes, but they could very easily be construed to represent political and military espionage in a state where everybody is potentially guilty of treason or espionage whether he can prove himself innocent or not.

My heart bobbed up and down in the pit of my stomach while I watched the little foreman of the group diddling unconsciously with the knob to my drawer, and looking out blankly into space. But he never opened it. Once the foreman came over and attempted to throw the fear of God into me with a series of short clipped questions about me, my parents, grandparents, race, religion, and a dozen other topics. Later he tried (he not only tried; he succeeded) to impress me with how complete his information on me was by saying, it was too bad, Mr. Smith, that I had been unable to finish my studies at Oxford due to the war. He also casually asked me once how long I had belonged to the British Labour Party when I was in England. Again, he asked me how high the salaries of American reporters with the United Press in Berlin were. Knowing full well that one of the laws every foreigner in Germany broke was that requiring all residents in the Third Reich to keep their entire incomes inside Germany; and that every American kept half his income in New York, I told him my own salary, but refused to give information about the other correspondents' salaries on the ground that I was authorized to answer only personal questions. He was satisfied and returned to his armchair.

Frau Muekov came in at length, filling the air in her wake, as she waddled down the dark hall, with her matutinal kicks about how on earth could people be expected to get up early and work all day if they weren't fed decent food, her rheumatism and how dirty newspaper offices can become in a single day. When she entered the editorial room and spotted the visitors, the voluble old woman clasped her hands to her head and began waddling around in circles shouting, *Ach, Du lieber Gott!* The little foreman took her by the arm and sat her down in a chair next to mine with the paternal warning that if she kept on shouting he would bounce one off her chin.

Frau Muekov relieved the atmosphere. She kept right on talking like a gramophone, breaking, I thanked God, the chill silence, and even loosening up the tongues of the ponderous visitors, who were now sifting through piles of literature on top of desks. Then a couple of German employees came in, and a messenger boy, and all were lined up beside us. Sides were evening up, so I, as the senior member of my team, grew bolder, went over to the foreman and asked with simulated indignation what, in God's name, this outrage meant, that I was an American citizen, and if I did not receive an explanation immediately I would report this affair to the American—— He interrupted me and told me I wouldn't report anything to nobody.

It was a raid, and it was none of my damned business what for. To reinforce his authority, he put his feet up on the desk, drew out a long cigar and lighted it and told me to go and sit down.

Later, the Chief arrived. He had apparently been out taking care of a more important phase of the raid somewhere. I could tell he was the Chief, for he burst into the room with the gusto of somebody very busy and in a hurry. He was tall and thin and handsome and did not wear gum-boots. He was the personification of the word Gestapo. All the heavy men stopped talking, and the strained frowns slipped off their faces and they watched him. Even Frau Muekov held her tongue. The foreman met him half way across the room and made a quick whispered report on the general situation. He gave the foreman a few, snappy, inaudible orders, turned on his heels and hurried out of the room.

The appearance of the Chief lessened the tension all over the room. Detectives have as much romance in their fat-plated souls as anybody else. They had obviously enjoyed the thrill of a dawn raid. They had tried hard to live up to their roles in the eyes of me, the original, one-man audience. They were a wee bit disappointed at being shown up as mere underlings when the Chief came in, but they were also obviously relieved, for the facial strain had, it was easy to see, been great. The material they were sifting consisted mainly of stock hand-outs from their own Propaganda Ministry. They had found a few manuscripts written in English and had tried hard to scan them with a studious air although they understood not a word of that mysterious language. Now, the veil was down, and they got just plain bored. So one by one they gave it up and relaxed in their chairs and twiddled their thumbs. Frau Muekov raised the black-out curtains and the light of early morning streamed in, washing away all illusions. The little foreman told one of them to get the facts about me. This was just to take time until the Chief should come again and call things to an end, for the Gestapo headquarters certainly possessed folders of facts on me and all my colleagues which contained more than enough information

for any purpose they might have. The man who was assigned to
this task was sweeter than saccharine. He almost bowled me over
when he began: "May I have your honourable name, please, Sir?
—*Darf ich um Ihren werten Namen bitten?*"

The foreman, also much softened by the advance of dawn
through the windows, told me I might sit at the copy desk now.
He asked me, would I answer all telephone calls, but, please, speak
German, not English, as he did not want anyone to know a raid
was in progress. I told him that was silly, for if an American
phoned and I talked to him in German he would know something
was wrong. But the foreman was adamant; those were his orders.
As telephones will do, one of ours rang. It was Dorothy Oechsner,
Fred Oechsner's wife. The conversation:

"Good morning, Howard."

"*Guten Morgen.*"

"I wanted to ask you . . . what did you say?"

"*Ich sagte bloss, Guten Morgen.*"

"Guten Morgen, yourself. I . . . Why don't you speak English?"

"*Das darf ich nicht, gnae' Frau.*" The little foreman was leaning
over my shoulder.

"Why, in heaven's name, not?"

"*Auch das darf ich nicht sagen.*"

"Oh-h-h. I think I see!"

She hung up. What did she say, the foreman wanted to know.
She said she could hear your breath over the telephone, I said,
and she was calling up the American Embassy which would take
this matter straight to the American state department in Washington; and Oechsner would be down in a minute. The foreman appeared to bite his lip, and I got the impression he was not very
pleased with me and the way I had handled things. He left the
room and came back five minutes later and said, all right, go
ahead and answer the telephones in English, dammit! He had
apparently gone downstairs to call headquarters and ask what the
handbook said should be done in a case like this.

Meanwhile, the detectives, quite human creatures but still a
little chary about admitting it after their dramatic entrance, got
hungry. They yawned casually at one another and looked self-
consciously about the room. One of them leaned over and whispered something in his neighbour's eye, and the other nodded
back, yes. In unison they scratched their heads, indicating casual-

ness, then, when the space between their little conference and the mutually agreed course of action was properly bridged over with the head-scratching, they abruptly dug their hands into their coat pockets and produced dainty square packages in oil-paper, undid them and brought to light neatly cut sausage sandwiches, which they began devouring in big gobbles. The others looked around relieved, scratched their heads and dug into their own coat pockets for sandwiches. They were like country kinfolk at a rich city cousin's dinner table watching one another to see which spoon to pick up first. After the meal the boldest scratched his head, pulled out a long, black cigar and lighted it. His neighbour scratched his head and followed suit; then all the others scratched their heads in succession and did the same. For the first time they began to look quite comfortable, now that bellies were appeased, and everybody's hair was down.

One of them, a tall Goon with a prominent Adam's Apple, got curious and started asking me questions about everything, why we had so many telephones, and, we must use up a world of typewriting paper every day, mustn't we? About that time Walter Wilke came in to relieve me. The Goon was gobbling a sandwich near the desk and Walter, after he realized the place was being raided, recalled he kept a revolver in the copy-desk drawer, and became afraid he might be taken in as a hoarder of arms for revolutionary purposes. I had, by that time, correctly gauged the I.Q. of our unwanted callers and consoled him that they would never look in the obvious place. But Walter was not so sure, and was especially afraid of the Goon (the gentleman acquired this appellation in our bull-session about the raid later), who couldn't seem to keep his big, bony hands off things on the desk. Walter ultimately enticed the interloper over to the teletype machine, where Walter plopped into a chair, expertly flipped on the red light and began writing Nowisthetimeforallgoodmen. . . . The Goon was fascinated and his Adam's Apple bobbed up and down as he swallowed what was left of his sandwich and wiped his hands on his coat. He asked if he could play. Walter yielded his chair and the Goon pecked away for hours, remarking from time to time *Donnerwetter!* the words he was writing could go all the way to New York two thousand miles away in a second, just the way he had written them, couldn't they? The Goon never approached the desk again.

Able to guard personally my drawer in the copy-desk I felt re-lieved. But we were all still worried about the raid. The detectives had taken nothing away; in fact, they had even, after the thawing out, put every little piece of paper back in its proper place and tidied things up. I asked several times what was up, but the detec-tives said they couldn't tell me. Later one confessed they did not know themselves. The reason became quite clear an hour before they left us.

The old D.N.B. ticker machine next to my desk began function-ing late that morning, wheezing, groaning, grinding then reeling out its morning greeting in hazy blue letters on a thin white strip of paper tape. The first message was "B-e-r-l-i-n dash dash D-N-B dash dash Because dash of dash serious dash suspicion dash of dash espionage dash in dash favour dash of dash the dash enemy dash—then a few white spaces—the dash american dash citizen dash and dash correspondent dash in dash berlin dash for dash the dash united dash press dash of dash america dash Richard dash C. dash Hottelet dash has dash been dash arrested dash and dash imprisoned dash dash white space cross cross cross."

I had relieved Hottelet nine hours before. He had then gone home to bed and at dawn, his home had been raided, and he taken away, by the young, stone-faced Chief, to the Alexander Platz prison. God knows what Dick Hottelet had done. He never found out. No evidence was ever produced. There was no trial. For months he lived in the grey dungeon walls of Alexander Platz. He was questioned for hours each day with no apparent purpose but to exhaust him physically and drive him mad. None of us was allowed to see him. The affair was a warning to the rest of us. It was not a comfortable way to work, with a dagger over your head all the time. That is what I mean by a Reign of Terror. To the men who had to live under it, that is in no way an exaggeration.

Dick Hottelet had a bad, very bad case of Berlin blues. He was suffocating inside Germany. He had lived there too long for his own safety. He had reached the point, which most correspondents eventually reached, where he could no longer hide his nausea and bob his head stupidly at the inane dinner-table propaganda essays of the little Propaganda Ministry bureaucrats in the Press club restaurants. To use Dick's own expressive language: he hated their goddam guts. He began expressing his own opinions all too openly—you get that way after a while. His situation was getting dangerous and a well-meaning Wilhelmstrasse tipster told him as much. Dick applied a rather expressive four-letter word to tell the tipster what the Wilhelmstrasse could do itself. Though an unusually talented observer and writer, he was a little on the loud-mouthed side anyhow. He also had the unpleasant habit of going on his own post-air-raid tours of mornings after the Propaganda Ministry ceased taking us in army cars. That is why Dick was chosen to make an example of.

Had he been a spy, the Gestapo would have known it. They knew everything about each of us; every single move we made. They maintained agents in the two press clubs, vile little fellows who tried to appear chummy, but who could be trusted to knife you in the back at the first opportunity, just to get another piece of gold braid on the uniforms they wore on official occasions. They kept agents in the hotels, the Adlon and the Kaiserhof, and in the restaurants and bars, the Taverne and the Jockey bar, which Americans frequented. If Hottelet had been a spy, the Nazis would have been all too happy to prove this new plot of Roosevelt's. They would have loved to put on a gaudy, theatrical trial, invite all correspondents to watch the case against a "Roosevelt puppet" tried, and see the defendant condemned to death. But they had no information of this sort. They questioned their victim for months to try and break him down without success. They allowed the American consul to pay him but one fifteen-minute visit all the time he was held in prison. No one else was allowed to see him. I tried three times, once taking some cigarettes to him, and twice on the pretext of fetching his laundry, but was denied entrance each time. After several months of mental torture, he was released and sent to America in exchange for a German who had been imprisoned in New York.

The incident was meant purely and certainly to intimidate the Americans in Berlin. The Nazis had begun the war without a censorship and boasted about it. The American reporters had taken full advantage of the luxury and succeeded in keeping the world surprisingly well informed about Germany. The day was approaching when the Nazis could no longer afford this luxury. They hoped they would not have to institute a censorship and back down on their boast. Thus they tried to make fear do what a censorship could do, without having to introduce censorship.

There is no doubt about the validity of this interpretation. Only on this interpretation can the comic-opera raid on the United Press office be clarified. The big, dumb detectives were not smart enough to carry out a serious raid. They got no information of any import, nor did they seriously try to get any. The raid was a show, meant purely to intimidate. It was not entirely unexpected. Two weeks before it occurred, Fred Oechsner had ordered the files to be cleaned out thoroughly as a precaution against the present menacing attitude of the Propaganda Ministry and the Gestapo. Oddly, he assigned Hottelet, the man who was eventually chosen for the stiffest blow, to weed out all material that might be considered suspicious from our files and morgue.

Little Nazi bureaucrats undiplomatically hinted this was the only reason for the whole affair. And one night in the Foreign Club bar on Leipziger Platz, Dr. Karl Boehmer, the Propaganda Ministry's counterpart to Dr. Schmidt in the Foreign Office, stated it quite openly. Dr. Boehmer was a brilliant young man and, like all young and clever Nazis, was an ambitious opportunist. On this occasion he was in his cups, and told Jean Graffis, the representative of Newspaper Enterprise Association in Berlin, that the German government intended "to fix Americans. You have had it too good. Hottelet is only the beginning; we'll get some more of you soon". Dr. Boehmer was given to speaking too much and too loud when he was in his cups, which was often. But he generally told the truth in that condition, which he seldom did in his official capacity as leader of the foreign press section of Goebbels' ministry. Once, later, at a reception in the Bulgarian legation, Boehmer got drunk and told the Bulgarians Germany was going to fix that false ally, Russia, too. This was before the Russian war, and Boehmer boldly declared, within earshot of several officials of the German Foreign Office, who despised and envied him, and had been "gunning" for him, that the German army would one day wipe Russia right off the map. Dr. Boehmer disappeared from the Wilhelmstrasse a short while later. Dr. Rascha, of the Foreign Office press section, told his superior Dr. Schmidt about the indiscretion, and Schmidt, overjoyed to get something on his counterpart, called in the Gestapo. A month later, when the Russian war had begun, Boehmer was sentenced to two years' imprisonment.

The old fogey, Dr. Brauweiler, a much safer and more sober party wheel-horse, got his job. There was a sort of divine justice in Boehmer's liquidation. But his prediction that the Americans, too, were in for some more fixing turned out to be well-founded—perhaps better founded than he himself imagined.

An understandable epidemic of jitters among the Americans left in Berlin followed on the heels of the Hottelet case and Dr. Boehmer's dire drunken prediction travelled over the journalists' corps with the speed of light. It was at this time that Fred Oechsner applied to his New York office for a necessary breathing spell in America. The *Chicago Daily News* took matters into its own hands and ordered its correspondent, Dave Nichol, to close up the *News* office in Berlin and go to Switzerland. At the same time, *Time* magazine ordered its representatives, Steve and Lael Laird, who were my closest friends in Berlin, to close up and return to America. Those who remained conferred together with the object of requesting their home offices to recall all American reporters as a common protest against the threatening attitude of the German government. The project was rightly frustrated by a few men who were governed by the old journalistic adage that an assignment is an assignment no matter what difficulties it presents and whether it is in Nazi Germany or anywhere else.

It was uncomfortable to feel that you might be suddenly picked up by a little band of Gestapo men one morning and, if you were not as lucky as Hottelet, never be heard of again. But the feeling was quite real. The two American agencies instituted the practice of having each of their correspondents "phone in" to their offices every eight hours to have their names checked off as present and accounted for. If any man failed to telephone, the fact was reported to the American Embassy immediately for investigation. I was surprised one evening when a secretary in the American Consulate telephoned me at home and asked regarding my condition. I answered I was slightly underfed, but otherwise all right, and why? The voice responded that there was a rumour about town that I had been arrested and the call was only a check on the rumour.

A wholesale note-burning period ensued. Both agencies ordered their men, for their own personal safety, to get rid of every unessential scrap of paper, all notes and diaries. It was heart-breaking, but I burned my great stack of notes, gathered with many pains over two years, which might have made this book more detailed, and, in any case, would have been of immense value

to me for reference later. We burned all our notes, no matter how
harmless, for had any of us been picked up, the Gestapo would
have read what it wished to read in the most innocuous scrap of
paper written in our own handwritings.

The jitters epidemic found its justification only a short while
later. One evening in late summer, Alex Small, of the *Chicago
Tribune*, telephoned me to ask if I had seen John Paul Dickson,
the correspondent for Mutual Broadcasting System, that day;
Dickson was supposed to have met him in the *Tribune* office but
had not shown up. I told him I had not, but I would check to see
if anything had happened. Brooks Peters, of the *Times*, then
phoned and told me he had heard Dickson had been picked up by
the Gestapo. I called the Propaganda Ministry and got in touch
with a good acquaintance and learned that there was talk of four
Americans having been arrested that evening. The American
Embassy raised the number to six. Then, from the agencies I
learned, and it was later confirmed, that not six but eight
Americans had been taken from their homes that evening, including Dickson, three students who had been caught in Berlin by
the war, and the secretary of the American Chamber of Com-
merce! The report was confirmed by the Embassy in a second
telephone call.

The situation was fantastic. The Nazis never announced the
arrests. They did not even inform the American Embassy of
them, as was customary. No one was told. The eight men might
simply have disappeared from the surface of the earth but
for the efforts of a few conscientious reporters who checked with
landladies, janitors and well-informed friends, and reported the
facts to the American Embassy. The Embassy was utterly helpless.
The Germans told them nothing, and when they protested, the
authorities only shrugged their shoulders and said they had heard
nothing of the matter!

Seven of the eight men arrested were released the next day.
Dickson later related that he had simply been picked up by the
police, not allowed to inform anyone of his arrest, taken to the
Alexander Platz prison by the underground with enough clothing
for a week and held there overnight. He was never questioned,
and though he repeatedly asked what he was charged with he was
never told. The next day he was, also without explanation, released and told to go home. One of the men, a student, was held

for three months in the dingy Alexander Platz, and all efforts by American diplomatic representatives to see him were rejected by the Gestapo. He was never charged, no evidence was ever produced against him, but he was questioned for hours on end each day until he nearly collapsed after each period of questioning. One day, he told me later, a gaol attendant came to his cell, unlocked it and simply told him to go. No explanation, no apology, nothing; just discharge!

It is true to say that Americans in Berlin after that were entirely at the precarious mercies of the Germans. Theoretically, America still maintained diplomatic relations with Germany; actually, relations did not exist. Every representation the American government made to the Reich government was ignored with purposive insolence. It was one of the strangest little epochs of international relations in history. To protect its nationals in Germany, America was actually as helpless as England, which was at war with the Reich! Journalists, though they were insulted on every hand, and co-operation was gradually withdrawn from them, still enjoyed some mite of respect due to their vocation. But commercial representatives and students who had been caught by war inside Germany were thrown around like so many sofa pillows. British women, nationals of a country at war with Germany, were allowed far more freedom than private Americans. They were not interned and were at least helped by neighbouring Nazi party officials to find rooms to live in. One private, non-journalist American I knew spent at least one night on the streets of Berlin because he had been thrown out of his apartment and could not find another in that overcrowded city. Another lived in a motor-car garage on a straw pallet. A British girl I knew was once called down for speaking English in a café; but when the complainant learned she was belligerent English and not American and at peace with Germany, the gentleman took off his hat and apologized! Private Americans were nothing less than prisoners inside Germany. They were flatly refused permits to leave Germany and every obstacle to their comfort, or even to their continued existence, was placed in their paths. As one little Nazi party member told one American just before his jaw was broken in two places, according to a story which circulated in Berlin at that time, there was only one thing worse than a Jew and that was Negroid American, and the only thing worse than a Negro American was a white one. In a period

which covered not more than a single year, Germany learned to
hate Americans with a hate that was the most sincere emotion a
German could stir—next to the paralyzing fear that America could
wreck every chance Germany had of winning the war.

The question is near: why on earth did the few Americans, the
reporters, who could, with some difficulty, leave Germany, not
do so? In my own case, it was always the insidious urge to stay a
little longer and see just a little bit more. Though the Berlin blues
recurred at briefer intervals as time wore on, I was always impelled to hang on, with the argument that I had suffered it this
long, so I must be able to stay just a while longer. It was only when
my usefulness as an informant to my company and my country
was utterly eliminated by the censorship and direct pressure to
lie had been exercised that I took decisive steps to be withdrawn.
Certainly none of us remained because we liked it. What influenced all of us most was the spirit expressed by one New York
editor, when his Berlin correspondent pleaded with him by trans-
atlantic telephone to withdraw him; the editor said, "I'm sorry,
fellow, but Berlin is your assignment. And if I assign you to cover
a Mississippi flood, it's not my business if you get your feet wet".
The principle was hard, but it is also journalism.

This spirit, which kept a dwindling colony of reporters in Berlin
under circumstances that were almost unendurable, has often been
misinterpreted with injustice by people in the outside world,
totally ignorant of the conditions under which Americans in Berlin
worked. Quentin Reynolds, working in London with only Nazi
bombs to disturb him—much easier to take than Nazi atmosphere
and insolence—once intimated that the American reporters in
Berlin had sold out to Nazism. Sections of the British press once
attacked Alvin Steinkopf, of the Associated Press, as being under
the charm of the Propaganda Ministry because he had once reported, after a tour of Hamburg, that a certain British raid had
had little visible effect, and later that Smolensk was actually in
the hands of the Germans not the Russians. As a matter of fact,
Steinkopf was one of the most outspoken and adamant opponents of
the Nazis in the American correspondents' corps; I once applauded Al as he poured fire on Goebbels' chargé for American
affairs, Dr. Froelich, whom he called a hypocrite and, using Bill
Shirer's perfectly suited term—an oaf.

With the shadow of the ruthless Gestapo, and the prospect of sudden, unannounced arrest, hanging over them constantly, the American correspondents in Berlin fought a singular battle for the maintenance of their freedom of expression. The raids of intimidation did not influence them in the slightest degree, and that is why Goebbels eventually was forced to instal a censorship, when threats had miserably failed. When the Nazis issued an order to one of my competitors, an American radio correspondent, to use an invective against President Roosevelt prepared by Lord Haw-Haw in one of his scripts for broadcast, the correspondent flatly refused. And when the censors, indignant at his refusal, began chopping out whole sections of his script to "make room" for the commanded insertion, the correspondent told them they need not waste their blue pencil, for he would not broadcast that day or any day when they issued him orders as to what he must say. Alex Small, of the *Chicago Tribune*, was forbidden entrance to press conferences for telling Dr. Sallett, the foreign office chargé for the American Press, quite frankly and in so many words that he could go to Hell, when Sallett reprimanded him for publishing a factual story regarding the Russian war. In a democratic nation there is nothing in getting tough with a government official; you are his equal before the law, but according to the degree of your servility to the Nazis it takes more than a little nerve. Consider the case of Joe Grigg, who later became chief of the United Press Berlin bureau. Joe had been reared in England and loved England. His family still lived in England and suffered the full impact of the blitz. But Joe, covering Berlin, probably suffered it far more than they; Berlin was for him pure unadulterated torture, and, due to his background he was under constant suspicion by the Nazis. But it was to him, also, an assignment and he handled the assignment admirably. In the period of extreme disaffection among the Americans just before the Russian war, Joe and I had a bitter squabble which, along with the increasingly depressing atmosphere of Berlin, resulted in my resigning from the United Press. Neither of us was to blame, and later, when the Dawn came, we became again the best of friends.

The best tribute that can be paid to the unjustly criticized American corps in Germany is, however, to recount the incident of the *Verein* elections. The story was not reported to the outside world at the time, and I do not believe it has been reported since. This is it.

It happened long before the Russian war. The Foreign Press
Association, *Der Verein der auslaendischen Presse,* was a unique
institution inside Nazi Germany. In eight years of power, the Nazis
had carried out a *Gleichschaltung* of all other organizations in
Germany; every organization of every kind had been either placed
under control of Nazis, or disbanded and then refounded as a
purely Nazi organization, with the one exception of the Foreign
Press Association. Last year, after almost a dozen nations had been
conquered by Germany, the German Foreign Office and the
Propaganda Ministry, launched their long delayed campaign to
crush the independence of the Foreign Press and bring it under
control of the Nazi government to the same extent as the German
press was. The method was by dilution; by flooding the ranks of
the Foreign Press corps with a sort of Axis fifth column. Each
conquered or quislinged nation was invited by the German government to withdraw its former correspondents (if these had not
listened to Nazi reason and changed their ways) and replace them
with an increased number of carefully chosen hacks who could be
depended on to take orders. An amazing, motley crew of fake
newspapermen began to show up in press conferences. Old
friends, able friends from Holland, Norway and Belgium disappeared and their places were filled by local Nazis, some of them
barely able to write their own names! All, by virtue of being
accredited journalists, were allowed to join the Foreign Press
Association. It was a considerably increased burden to the expense account of the Propaganda Ministry, but Goebbels was expansive and invited especially the little Balkaneers by the dozen
to the big city. They were noisy and exuded odours clearly indicative of their unaccustomedness to soap and water. At first, the
Nazis gave them free run of facilities, but eventually even the Nazi
journalists began complaining about the plague, and both press
clubs, Goebbels' and Ribbentrop's, ultimately forbade most of
their invited newcomers entrance, refusing to issue them guest
cards! The Propaganda Ministry used to maintain a service whereby all journalists could telephone in at a certain time of evening
and be told whether or not there was likelihood of an air-raid that
night. The service was suddenly discontinued one evening. The
reason was that all the little quisling newspapermen took advantage of the service by arranging with restaurant owners to tell
them when an air-raid was coming, so that the restaurant might

1944, Annecy in the French Alps in occupied France. Having crossed the border from Switzerland, I was taken by my hosts, the Forces Francaises de l'Interieure, on a tour of their local triumphs. The scene here is a German prison, the subjects Gestapo jailers. I begged to interview them; the FFI agreed but insisted that the Germans respond in a kneeling position. I like to believe there was no comparable coup by a journalist in the war.

November 1941, HKS and bride-to-be Benedicte Traberg in Berlin Tiergarten, before it was turned into a moonscape by allies.

THE EXECUTIONER.

In my last year in Oxford, 1938–39, I wrote and drew for the Labour Club's periodical. This is an editorial cartoon I drew in that service, exaggerated beyond belief as is customary in the craft.

1944, HKS as war correspondent with
US 9th Army in western Germany.

Benedicte, (Bennie for short),
at the time of our wedding.

1942. HS at time of wedding in Berne.

Field Marshal Wilhelm Keitel, Hitler's chief of staff, at Templhof Airport on May 9, 1945, being led by Red Army officers to Marshal Georgi Zhukov's H.Q. in the Karlshorst suburb of Berlin to sign unconditional surrender. In the rear, and to Keitel's left, my unworthy person, bespectacled and with beard. What a nice way to end a war.

TV tour of burned-out Reichstag in Berlin 1950 by Mayor Ernst Reuter of Berlin who had been socialist deputy in that Reichstag.

Publicity photos, HS as anchorman,
Evening News.

warn its patrons; this in exchange for free meals for the informers every evening! The dignity of the new Foreign Press corps in Berlin left considerably much to be desired. The first considerable black market for Balkan currencies in Berlin was instituted by the new employees of Dr. Goebbels. But, like it or not, these individuals were poured in to the *Verein*, even as German "tourists" were poured into nations marked for conquest.

Wallace Deuel, of the *Chicago Daily News*, was the president of the *Verein*, and he was retiring and going home to America. Elections to fill the vacancy were called. The Americans, anxious to save a ship that appeared to be sinking, appealed to Fred Oechsner to run for the office. Oechsner's answer was: Not in a thousand Sundays! He wanted nothing to do with it. He had no time for the job, and furthermore he did not like the government officials with whom he would have to deal. The remaining independent journalists, from all countries, begged him, but Oechsner's answer remained a flat No.

However, the Nazi Foreign Minister, von Ribbentrop, had heard of the little underground movement to induce Oechsner to run for the presidency of the *Verein*. But he had not heard that Oechsner had refused. Ribbentrop ordered Dr. Schmidt, of the foreign press section of the Foreign Office, to frustrate the movement. So, bright and early one morning, Oechsner was visited by one of the Wilhelmstrasse tipsters. Behind closed doors, the tipster informed Oechsner that the Foreign Minister had heard Oechsner was being approached to run for office, and that he, the tipster, was delegated to tell Oechsner that the Foreign Minister himself would "look with disapproval" on any such action; that Oechsner was a citizen of a country whose relations with Germany were severely strained, and the German government did not want to deal with the foreign press through an American national. It took Oechsner, an unreconstructed Southern rebel, just about three and a half seconds to answer the tipster that he might tell the Foreign Minister, with the compliments of the American press, that Oechsner had refused the request of the foreign press to run, but in view of the distinguished attentions his Excellency had given the matter, Oechsner had now changed his mind and would run for the presidency of the *Verein!*

Now, you can do things like that in democratic countries. You can tell a municipal or even a federal official to go suck his thumb.

And you can get your picture in the papers that way, But you can't do things like that in Nazi Germany. It's something that just isn't done. It never has been done, and it never will be done. Dr. Schmidt and Ribbentrop knew it wasn't the thing to do, and when the tipster presented them with Oechsner's message, they were at a loss for an answer or even a comment. They hadn't calculated with a revolt. They were bluffed; they were speechless. But they had absolutely no answer. It was as though the Duchess of Luxembourg should rise up one morning, call Hitler on the telephone and tell him to get his confounded troops out of Luxembourg within ten minutes or she, the Duchess of Luxembourg, would throw them out. The Duchess of Luxembourg would never do a thing like that, because it just isn't done.

But, sure enough, on the morning of the elections, Fred Oechsner, cocky as a little red rooster, marched into the Assembly Hall of the Esplanade Hotel, his flanks covered by a phalanx of American reporters, and took his seat in the audience. The independent correspondents from the independent nations, and even many from occupied lands, rubbed their hands in glee. The Italians, bluffed at Oechsner's appearance, turned red with discomfort. They and their Axis brothers withdrew disconsolately from the election and later rose as one man and marched out of the room, uttering oaths under their breath. (Later, I was told by an Italian, their gesture was against the will of their majority, but they had been ordered to do this, should Oechsner appear, by Braun von Stumm, Dr. Schmidt's assistant, in a special meeting of Italians called just before the election occurred.)

The Chairman, an Italian, uncomfortably called for nominations. Sigrid Schultz, of the *Chicago Tribune*, was on her feet, before he stopped speaking, to nominate Oechsner, and before she could sit down a Swede had seconded the nomination. The Chairman called for other nominations, but the quislings were taken as if by storm. Their orders had not covered this unbelievable eventuality. The Chairman called again for nominations, this time weakly, but there was no response from any quarter, so a Jap rose and moved that nominations be closed. Oechsner marched up to the rostrum to take over the gavel, grinning like a Cheshire cat, while Americans and friends applauded and a deep gloom settled over the Axis and its comrades.

At a time when Americans were disappearing from their homes

just for being Americans, it required uncommon spunk to do something like this. Aside from the personal peril, Oechsner was also head of a large news agency in a totalitarian country; and the Propaganda Ministry, through which most news is bottle-necked, has a million different little methods of taking revenge on recalcitrants. But it is also true that in Germany, as nowhere else, the best way to fight fire is with fire. The Nazis do not understand kindness; their language is impudence, bluff, the strong arm tactic. By every calculation, save this one, Oechsner should have been discovered by the Gestapo to be a spy, and arrested; his agency ruined in Germany. Actually, several of his German employees were called on the carpet by the Nazis and threatened with imprisonment. But no German authority ever went near Oechsner after that. He was like the bestial Russians; he hit back. Mr. Winchell, please note.

VIII

THE END OF THE NAZI REVOLUTION

THE NATIONAL SOCIALIST Revolution in Germany came to an end, after eight eventful years, in August and September, 1941. Of all the elements combining to create the German metamorphosis, this one is far and away the most significant. Unlike the Dietrich affair, its relation to the present war is of secondary importance; and its influence on the eventual outcome of the war, though it will have a big one, is only indirect. But its inevitable effect on the revolution to come inside Germany, and perhaps all over Europe, is of primary and immediate importance.

All that was revolutionary in Nazism collapsed last autumn. I was surprised, on coming out of Germany for the first time in two years, to learn that the fact was virtually unknown in the outside world. Apparently not a word about it seeped out, and good friends, well-informed friends, were struck with amazement at hearing of it. Briefly, what happened in August and September of last year was the decline and fall of what had once been Hitler's mightiest political weapon—the glorious brown army of the *Sturm-Abteilung*, the thunderous Storm-troops, the fighting vanguard of the National Socialist Revolution. They were progressively weakened, then struck down by the man they had deified and carried to power—Adolf Hitler. For every practical purpose, the Storm-troops have been disbanded, forbidden to meet, and their every means of expression has been withdrawn. This is true, and I have irrefutable proof that it is true.

The event has a tremendous significance. In the Social history of Germany it deserves to be ranked with the Napoleonic conquest of Prussia, which swept Feudalism out of western Europe for ever. In American history a parallel is the War between the States—Charles and Mary Beard's *Second American Revolution*—and in English history, the crushing of the last feudal Scottish clans. For, like these events, Hitler's moves against his own party had the effect of sweeping a whole Social Class out of existence. An entire, important stratum of German society was, so far as its ever again possessing any political or economic influence is concerned, per-

emptorily liquidated, And its consequence will be, almost un-
avoidably, that Hitler has created a new force amongst his own
people which will play a major part in destroying him.

Whoever thinks these are exaggerations has not followed the
History of National Socialism closely enough, or properly understood the meaning of National Socialism. Those-who suffer from
misconceptions are many. Of all the volumes that have been
written on Nazi Germany, I know of but a very few which have
properly interpreted that political phenomenon. The best, in
my opinion, is Frederic L. Schumann's *The Nazi Dictatorship*, published long before the present war. Most of the others have
accepted the very name of the present German State, National
Socialism, the most ridiculous and devoid of content of all the
concepts of Nazi ideology—as a real representation of what
Hitlerism is. They have accepted Nazism as a form of Socialism.
They have also accepted the Nazi revolution as a *bona fide* Revolution. In actual fact, Nazism is the most reactionary and vicious
form of capitalism that has ever existed, and Hitler has destroyed
systematically every element in his state which was, in any degree,
revolutionary.

A revolution, as that term has customarily been used in history,
is something which, however horrible and destructive it may be in
practice, is progressive in idea. Hitlerism has been retrogressive.
Hitler has truly turned the clock of social history backwards; his
ship of state has ridden the wave, not of the future, but of the
blackest past.

Revolution means nothing if it does not mean the overthrow of
existing rulers of a society by the ruled-over elements of that
society. The existence of those two social factors in that particular
relation has characterized every revolution to which history has
given the name: the French Revolution, the American, Russian
and Mexican Revolutions. Revolution also means a vast, sweeping
change of a whole system of society. Nazism possesses neither of
those two requisite features.

The rulers of German society not only did not struggle against
the Nazi rise to power in the early 1930's; they suborned, abetted
and aided Hitler to gain power with all their vast resources of
money and influence—a strange manner of revolution, indeed!
And, contrary to the views of the majority of observers, Nazism
w s not a vast social change. Superficially, things appeared to be

altered: people were put in gay uniforms; there were new salutes and a new flag, and new, but empty ideas—empty baubles on a highly and cheaply decorated Christmas tree meant to hide, by its brightness, the basis of corrupt German society which Hitler left intact. The only actual change that occurred with the rise of Hitlerism consisted in this: the old, corrupt system of acquisition was dying, and Hitler was called upon—and he and his followers were ready to accept their historical assignment—to save that moribund society by reinforcing its most unsalutary features and crushing all opposition to unlimited militarism, by which, alone, his system could be preserved for any period of time. The only new feature the Nazis introduced was a set of measures to make permanent the existing basis of society; to freeze solid the little fluidity German society possessed before 1933. To use a simile applied by one acute observer, Hitler locked himself and the German ruling classes in the top storey of society and threw the key out of the window.

Compare the Russian with the so-called Hitler Revolution. The Bolsheviks never called on the Tsarist rulers for aid; and never got anything from them save opposition as ruthless as their own. Hitler not only called on Germany's wealthiest families, but received generous gifts of millions of marks. The whole propaganda weight of the Scherl newspaper and news agency combine, controlled by Ruhr industrialists, was thrown into the political scales in Hitler's favour. Dr. Dietrich in his little volume *Mit Hitler an die Macht*, relates how the Fuehrer, addressing a luncheon meeting of Germany's biggest capitalists in Duesseldorf before the *Machtuebernahme*, outlined to them the danger to their society, told them what he could do to save it and melted their solid gold hearts into a flow of funds for the Nazi party. Dr. Dietrich tells, with surprise, that these hard-fisted men whose hearts, one would have thought, were in their pocket-books, mellowed and softened under the Leader's words, and, at the end, applauded thunderously.

Whether one likes it or not, the Bolsheviks came to power on the shoulders of the working classes of Russia. When foreign nations intervened and occupied Vladivostock and, after arresting all active reds and banning the Communists from the polls, held a "free" election to allow the people of that city to choose its own government, the results showed a Communist majority over

the combined votes of all the legal parties which participated!
Also, whether one likes it or not, the Nazis came to power against
the will and violent opposition of the German working class
which acted with singular unity at the last, late moment. Too
many observers have allowed themselves to be fooled by the fact
that, for reasons of expediency, Hitler chose to call his party the
National Socialist German *Workers* Party. In the last partially free
elections to the Reichstag in Germany in 1933, the two working
class parties presented a solid phalanx and balloted 40 per cent
of the votes, *against* Hitler. One of the two working class parties,
the *Kommunistische Partei Deutschlands* achieved the highest representation in the Reichstag it had ever enjoyed—one hundred
deputies. And this was after the Brown Terror had begun; when
a working man took his life in his hands by voting against the new
dictator! Hitler did not, and—I am convinced of it after living in
Germany for two war years—has not yet won the German workers
to his cause. In the year 1940, after eight years of Nazi rule, a
German S.S. man I knew told me there was but one dull element
in National ·Socialism's bright, triumphant perspective at that
moment (this was just after France had fallen and Nazism was
enjoying its happiest period). That, he said, was the German
workers. They were following, but reluctantly. They do not believe it can last, he said, and if we ever slip badly they've got
"their damned red flag hanging over our heads".

When the Bolsheviks achieved power they did so by the ruthless
suppression of every agency supporting the old order. They
destroyed all capitalist institutions. They placed all factories in
the hands of the state and forbade the issue of dividends to
private individuals. They made the Trade Unions the almighty
dictators over the Russian economic state. When Hitler came to
power, he destroyed the Trade Unions and the workers' political
parties; confiscated their funds and shot or imprisoned their
leaders. The funds he confiscated were used, indirectly, to buy
armaments and to pay profits to his wealthy supporters. The
economic history of Nazism ever since has been, in plain language,
the systematic confiscation of workers' incomes to pay profits to
the owners of material Germany. As for the principal institutions
supporting the old order, the industrialists' associations, which
were formed long ago to keep prices up, he either maintained
them as they were or allowed *them* to reform *themselves* into more

powerful capitalists' combines—indeed, the most powerful capitalists' combines that have ever existed in any nation in history. What elements of Socialism existed before Hitler assumed power, he abolished. The few shares of private industry which the former Social Democratic government had bought up in the hope of gradual socialization, Hitler actually sold back to their former owners at dirt-cheap prices. The total effect of the Social Democratic government's weak attempt at socialization was a monetary gain, good business for the industrialists who had been the target of the Socialist attack.

Many people who maintain Hitlerism is a form of Socialism are willing to admit that Hitler came to power with the aid of the wealthy, and favoured them at first; but, they say, digging themselves in in the traditional last ditch, Hitler has, since that time, duped them. He deceived his wealthy supporters, and instituted something entirely new, neither Capitalism nor Imperialism, but an oppressive form of state which is oppressive to capital and labour alike. In truth, what Hitler has instituted is just about as new as the Old Army Game. Hitler's government is shot through with the representatives of wealth. Goering dictates to the economic state, but Goering, himself, has become an economic royalist in the bountiful Nazi decade and receives his advice as to what measures must be adopted from several dozen boards, representing each big industry, and each board is made up of the men who live on profits from those industries. Walther Funk dictates financial policy, and because Walther Funk wears a brown coat and a military cap, rather than the traditional civilian array of the plutocrat, people are inclined to think of him as a party functionary rather than, what he is first and above all, a man born and bred in the atmosphere of profit making and ownership.

The only basis on which to judge the relative oppression of the two social classes by National Socialism is the manner in which German national wealth has been, and is, distributed between the two said classes, one of which lives by its labour, and the other by its ownership. The individual incomes of workers have fallen each year of Hitler's rule, and fallen severely. Nazi statistics on this matter are faked, but even on the grounds of Nazi statistics the real wages of workers have fallen. Money wages have been frozen or lowered, since 1933, and the prices of the goods workers can buy with them have risen without interruption. A better way of determining the same development is simply to ask Germans. In the course of the past two years in Germany I have, inevitably, talked to thousands of German workers in taverns, in tubes, trams and in offices, and without a single exception, I have never heard of a case in which a worker's real income has risen. They all agree, even a few workers who claim to be Nazis, that what they get to eat and wear with their wages is less and worse than before 1933. Even the little bureaucrats in Dr. Goebbels' propaganda ministry testify to the same fact; they are all miserably under-paid. Dr. Froehlich, who bears the high-sounding title of *Referant* for the American Press and Radio in the Propaganda Ministry, was paid a salary lower than that of an office-boy in the editorial office of the United Press—an American concern. There cannot be the slightest doubt about it that the wages of German workers have fallen each year of Hitler's rule, and are now unbelievably low.

The Nazi indices for the earnings of capital, on the other hand, show a steady rise since 1933. Both, the figures for total net profits for major industries as published in the magazine of Reichsmarshal Goering, *Der Vierjahresplan*, and the index for the average value of all German stocks and shares as published in the industrial periodical *Der Deutsche Volkswirt* show falling profits and share-values from 1929 until 1933, when Hitler came to power, and from then on an unbroken rise. If Hitler has duped his benefactors, it has been for them, indeed, a pleasant manner of deception. It is a strange form of oppressing wealth which allows the oppressed owners of mills, mines and factories to earn more and more each year, and even, as in the case of the Krupp works, to reach and break records for annual profits, while the standard of living of the other ninety-eight per cent of the population falls precipitately. Of course there is always the argument which admits that German capitalists make egregious profits, but maintains all these profits are taken away in taxes. Since the people who determine the tax scale are the representatives of the fattest, richest banks in Germany, which in turn, are owned body and soul by the arms-makers, this is obviously false on the surface. Did you ever hear of a man granted the power of making out his own tax returns gypping himself? Anyhow, the above facts are based on statistics of *Reingewinn:* pure profits after taxes have been extracted from profits; and nevertheless the munitions factories break records! Of course, after the pure profits are turned into dividends and made the private funds of individuals they are taxed as private incomes. But a member of the American embassy once worked out a schedule for me to show conclusively that plutocratic American capitalists pay more taxes per unit of income than German capitalists who are supposed to be fighting plutocracy. Furthermore, those funds which are taken from the German industrialists in taxes go to pay the same industrialists for more arms. Germany·is good business—for millionaires.

There is no denial of the fact that Nazism was and is a retro-gression, not a revolution; it is not socialism, but a form of capitalism that is virtually feudalistic in the safeguards granted to and preserved for the wealthy, as well as in the total servitude it demands of those who possess nothing but their hands and brains to work with. These great "warriors against plutocracy" have established one of the best protected plutocracies any nation or civilization has ever known. I am not, here, exploiting the theory that Hitler is a will-less puppet of the German capitalists. It is not nearly so simple as that. That is an over-simplification and it is untrue. Hitler rules, and there is no doubt about it. But no man can govern alone, for it is humanly impossible for a single man to run a whole state. He governs with the aid of governors and bureaucrats who agree heartily with him, and they are the wealthy families of Germany. Hitler is president of a board of directors which runs Germany, and each member of the board is, by birth, as Krupp and von Borsig, or by party influence, as Goering and Ley, a member of that class of German society which has a stake in the game of Profit-making, and stands to lose by higher wages and labour costs.

If the point can be considered established, then a concession can safely be made: though the net effect of Hitlerism has been retrogressive rather than revolutionary, there was indubitably one revolutionary feature in the rise of National Socialism. That feature was the rise of the German petty bourgeoisie; the irrepres-sible *Kleinbuergertum*, the middle classes of little shopkeepers, white-collar clerks and bureaucrats and a goodly portion of the unpros-perous professional classes.

Lodged uncomfortably between the upper and nether mill-stones of society, the great middle-classes were being painfully ground in the depressed years from 1929 to 1933. They were crying for organized leadership; they were God's gift to a clever, unscrupulous demagogue. They were begging for leadership, for a little colour to brighten their dull lives, and for rescue from extinction, and History gave them a Man and a Platform. Hitler promised death to the proletarian left wing with its trade unions which kept wages and labour costs above the head of the pinched independent shopkeeper, and made prices for their goods higher. He promised to bridle the wealthy right-wing of privilege, to break the *Zinsknechtschaft*, the slavery of interest, and make capital flow more easily to the small shops and stores. And he promised death to the Jew, who was, to the German middle-classes, the symbol of the prosperity they envied.

Nazism was *Spiessbuergertum* in Revolt, the Timid Soul in shining armour. There had been revolutions for Capitalists, and Revolutions of the Proletariat, but there has never been a Revolution of the middle classes, and the attraction of the idea was overwhelming to Germany's millions of Little Men. Those were the days when Hitler was still called the Apotheosis of the Little Man. It was their Revolution, and they carried their Leader—who in his very personal appearance was another prosaic, ordinary exemplar of each of them—to power on a wave of middle-class enthusiasm.

The financial basis of the Nazi ascension was the rich privileged class. Its main basis, and its revolutionary impetus, however, came from the middle classes. The little men also furnished it with its Army—proudest element in Hitler's little state within a state, the colourful, exciting Storm Troops, who beat up the Jews and the Communists and "freed the streets" in German cities, in outright armed political warfare. The generals of the Brown Army of the shopkeepers and clerks were Hitler's war comrades, young men who grew up in World War, whose minds were warped by war, and who were utterly worthless for anything else. They were the neurotic lost generation who suffered torture worse than death when the only element of excitement in their lives, the Army, was taken away from them by Versailles, and the trend of German opinion, after the revolution, turned against militarism. Ernst Roehm, their psychopathic, homosexual commander-in-chief was leader and prototype at once. To this uniformed body flocked the sons of the middle classes, bored, suffering from personal and national inferiority complexes, thirsty for colour and excitement, and they learned well the precepts of their warped generals and idols. It was organized Rowdyism, it was tough and ruthless, but it was truly the vanguard of the middle-class revolution, the Army of the Middle Class state.

When Hitler won, they were content with the world, and sat back to watch the realization of their hopes, the materialization of the first State founded on a Dictatorship of the "small" *Buerger*. Results were swift in coming, satisfactory beyond expectations. The Fuehrer eliminated the proletarian Left from politics in a series of lightning, dramatic blows, and with incredible ease: the Reichstag fire brought the end of legal Communism, the imprisonment of its leaders and the crippling of the movement for evermore. By next May Day, the Day of Labour, the Socialists too, had been eliminated, and with them their Trade Unions. Wages were henceforth at the mercy of Dr. Robert Ley, of the middle classes, and of the big industrialists, who enjoyed a community of interests with the Little Men on this particular economic question. In the National cabinet, one portfolio after another was given to brown-uniformed Party men, or their present holders were forced to don brown uniforms and administer their offices according to the interests of the *Kleinbuergertum*.

Now, in every society the two most important elements are Wealth and Force. Those who own much and have great resources can deal out favours and exercise most influence. It is almost proverbial that power goes with ownership, and always has in the history of Society. As for the second element, it is the ultimate authority in every State. A legislature is no good if it has no force to back up its authority. And whosoever controls the Armed Force of a nation can also control the nation itself on assuming power. Hitler systematically shoved the representatives of the Little Man into almost every phase of government. But precisely these two he did not grant them. The middle classes did not even get a smell of real economic power. His economic state Hitler shaped in the form of twelve *Wirtschaftsgruppen*, each "corporation" possessing dictatorial powers of life and death over the industry concerned; the fixing of prices, the granting of raw material import licences, and export subsidies—all decisive factors in the ultimate economic function of a state: the determination of how the nation's wealth, and the power that goes with wealth, shall be shared. The administrators of each *Gruppe* were the wealthiest capitalists in the particular industry it dealt with. In short, the wealthy were made supreme judges in their own case. Such change as this signified was not revolutionary change in favour of the rising middle classes, but reactionary change in favour of those who already ruled economic Germany: the top storey and the key out of the window.

Nor did the Brown Army achieve its coveted destiny of becoming and controlling the Armed Forces of the nation. The army, which Hitler set about rejuvenating and expanding, remained in the hands of the old Prussian caste, the military counterpart of the wealthy dictators of German economic life.

The Little People enjoyed the spectacle of apparent gains in certain phases of power, but the promised millenium was not immediate. In fact, events took the opposite direction from what they had hoped. The more prosperous shops were taken from the Jews in stages, but only to be co-ordinated into the *Wirtschaft* combines. What the independent shopkeepers really disliked was not that the big stores were run by Jews, but that their competitive strength was so enormous that little shopkeepers could not vie with them, and this feature was not changed except in so far as it was reinforced to the disadvantage of the little men. Wholesale prices, which the little men paid for the commodities they retailed, did not fall with lowered labour costs, but rose with bigger profits for the big men, and higher government taxes to build up the army. The middle classes were disappointed, and did not hide the fact.

Discontent among the masses usually first overtly expresses itself in the defection of a section of their leaders. The first overt indication of the disappointment of the small *Buerger* in Germany was the defection of Otto Strasser, one of the Nazi Party's big numbers, and an ardent believer in middle-class socialism. Strasser broke with Hitler and fled from the country. A more serious indication was the projected "revolt" of Ernst Roehm, leader of the Storm Troops, in 1934, which called forth the "blood purge" of the Brown Army. Although the "revolt" apparently did not correspond to the lurid accounts of preparations for it which the Nazis issued to the world, it is generally accepted that the elements of a revolt were there. There was certainly no plan to liquidate the beloved Fuehrer, but there is little doubt that disgruntled Storm-troop leaders hoped to eliminate many of Hitler's direct underlings, on whom they blamed the deception from which they suffered.

The Roehm affair was more than a weather-vane of disappointment; it also marked a milestone in Nazi history. It was the first and last revolt of the middle classes. After the blood purge, which crippled the basis of what Force the Little Men had on their side, the revolutionary element of Nazism, its programme for the Little Men, entered on a long decline. The existence of the *Kleinbuergertum*, as reasonably independent economic elements, grew more precarious each year. The chain-stores increased in power and became ubiquitous; Aryans enjoyed far more rigid monopolies in the retail trade than the hated Jews had ever exercised. Many little businesses were destroyed deliberately by economic decrees issued as part of Hitler's vast, severe rationalization programme. The planning of imports to fit the arms programme, banning certain imports in order to be able to spend more of the national income on imports of war-important raw materials, eliminated the *raison d'être* of many. Others died because, with their own costs rising, they could not compete with the big combines. Not only small shopkeepers, but little industries suffered. According to Nazi statistics, by 1939, just before the outbreak of war, there were only half as many joint stock companies in Germany as there had been in 1933, when many had already been weeded out by depression. In Berlin, hundreds of small retail wine and liquor shops were gobbled up by a large combine which was formed by the Kaiserhof Hotel under Nazi paternity.

The war, of course, only hastened this process. While big industry, the arms and chemical industries, grew bigger, wealthier and mightier, little shops and little industries have died like flies. Where death was caused before by rationalization and the inability of small concerns to compete with the new large ones, it was now caused, at a swifter rate, by the calling up into the army of their owners and their few employees. Still more powerful a causal force has been the dwindling to zero, or near it, of the imports most of them depended on. The Russian war period hastened the development even more, drawing, as it did, many more men, and older men, into the armed forces, and bringing scarcities and disappearances of all kinds of retail commodities. Coupled with this came the fall in the average production of German labourers, and the need to compensate for this by increasing the quantities of workers available for industry.

The significance of this development I have tried to indicate already in another part of this book. It means that the popular basis of Nazism has suffered a diminution. During the Russian war period, the development gathered such speed that it assumed the proportions of a wholesale annihilation. The economic basis of the lower middle classes has been systematically carried almost to extirpation. The social strength of the whole Nazi movement was, in the beginning of that movement, the middle strata of German society, and the people of those strata were Nazis because they had roots in a particular way of life, and saw in Nazism an opportunity to preserve that way of life and make it even better for themselves. Each little family owned a little something, and looked on itself as a shareholder in the German state. But for eight years, Nazism has had the effect of gradually uprooting them from the soil of German society, setting them adrift and removing their interest in Nazism's permanence.

Of course, membership in the middle classes is not purely an economic matter. It is also a psychological one. A little shopkeeper can lose his little shop, but still consider himself higher in the social scale than a mere wage-worker. And though he has descended to the level of a mere wage-earner, he may still act politically and socially according to that pattern of behaviour which the middle classes generally follow. In every respect except as regards his economic status, he thus remains what he was before his economic status changed. Middle-class pride, people call that. In view of this, it is perhaps even more symptomatic of how far the social mutation inside Germany has gone, that middle-class people are ceasing to behave according to their old standards. The matter of Middle-Class Morality, that factor glorified by Shaw's Mr. Doolittle, is a case in point already referred to. Morality has lapsed badly in Germany. Sexual license of people once proud of their respectability has virtually run the prostitutes out of business. In the place of a couple of bottles of cool wine, they are guzzling—the verb is properly descriptive—everything and anything they can get. The aim is not mild titillation in either case, but intense excitement; to get rip-roaring drunk and forget about the unpleasantness of reality.

The shock has come too quickly and been too great for them. That is part of what I meant when I said the pretty red apple was getting rotten-ripe.

They are the only section of the German people who can truly claim to have been duped, and sadly disappointed. The nether millstone knew what was in store for it when Hitler won; and the German workers fought tooth and nail to avoid it, but unfortunately they fought in disunity until too late. The upper millstone was not duped. The hermetically sealed top caste has every reason to be satisfied with the results of Hitlerism thus far. (Uneasiness has crept into their ranks as well now, but for different reasons; but more of that in its proper place.) But the little men have been done in, and they have only just begun realizing how completely they have been done in.

The last apparent hold they had on a lever of influence, after their shops were closed and falling salaries robbed them of any economic weight, was the once glorious Brown Army. The Storm Troops were only an apparent lever, and the polish of their glory had tarnished badly. The old elements had been promoted long since into the *Schutzstaffel*, the S.S., the Gestapo, where they could continue being aggressive and brutal to their own people, and later to other peoples. The more clever of the old Storm Troops got in the lift of economic profits and soared to the top. And the sons of the middle classes were left to their own devices in the Brown-shirted legions. The Storm Troops expanded in size, but deflated in meaning. But the Storm Troops at least continued to exist as the last symbol and the last trace of the middle class revolution.

Then, in August, last year, the axe fell. A tipster told me. He brought to me a copy of the official newspaper of the Storm Troops—the *S.A. Mann*. On its mast-head was the old drawing of a firm-faced, brown-capped man, frowning rays of will-power and holding in his hand the great Swastika banner which the Storm Troops had carried to Power. The newspaper was dated August 22, 1941. The tipster told me this was the most remarkable edition of that newspaper that had ever been published. I looked it over, but could find only the usual emptiness, save for loud editorial boasts and one chapter of a serial novel with the words: *Fortzetzung folgt*—to be continued in the next issue —at the bottom. I asked him what was so sensational about it, and he told me that the serial story was not continued; the story was left hanging in mid-air. I asked him to stop being cryptic and he said what he meant was, the *S.A. Mann* had been banned!

I inquired at my newspaper kiosk on Wittenberg Platz, and learned no issues had been delivered to the newspaper stands after August 22. I went to the Franz Eher publishing house which maintains its own book and newspaper shop on the ground floor. There I told a salesman I had been out of Germany since August 22, and had missed all the issues of the Storm-troop paper since that date, and since I had been reading the serial published in it, might I buy all the back copies? The salesman was annoyed and told me publication of that newspaper had been discontinued; the reason, he said, was the paper shortage. I told him I did not know there was a paper shortage, for the size of none of the twenty or thirty Berlin and provincial newspapers I read every day had been reduced since the beginning of the war. He was very annoyed, and told me, no, but the *unimportant* periodicals had been discontinued. I did not press the point, but I knew that was not the reason. For on his counter, displayed for sale, was the pornographic anti-Jewish sheet published by Julius Streicher— *Der Stuermer*, the least important of all Nazi papers. Lieutenant Dirksen, in the Propaganda Ministry, once revealed to me that since the beginning of the war *Der Stuermer's* paid circulation has dropped to a figure of three integers; that it cannot pay its own way and is a financial burden to the state. But *Der Stuermer* was still being published. But there was no use in pressing the point. It makes no difference if the *S.A. Mann* was banned because it was unimportant, or if it was banned for some other reason. Either way, it was a sad reflection on what had happened to the Revolution of the Little Buerger.

In September, I learned the official newspaper of the Storm Troops was banned for some other reason. This, a storm-trooper, a young employee in a shipping office told me, and other Nazis confirmed later. An anonymous authority, not Hitler or Viktor Lutze, the S.A. chief of staff, by name, but just an anonymous authority issued an order labelled *streng geheim*, strictly secret, to each district group of the Storm Troops. The order stated that the Brown Shirts were to hold no more meetings. There was to be no more drill, no more political lectures and no further political demonstrations of any kind. The brown uniforms were henceforth to be worn only on specific orders, not at will. The man who told me this, dolefully said it amounted to dissolution of the Storm Troops. The Storm-troopers continued to exist in name, but not in any real sense. A handful of men, the top leaders of the Brown-shirts, continued to wear their uniforms occasionally, but they were the reliable aristocracy of the movement. A few others appear in special brown uniforms at Hitler's speeches in the Sports Palace. But these are not Storm-troopers. The uniforms are *nur Attrapen*. They are Gestapo men in S.A. clothing, assigned to keep watch on the audience. Unlike Storm-troopers, each of them carries under his brown great-coat a revolver to shoot, if necessary. The real Storm Troops, the middle class Storm Troops, have been disbanded, save for exceedingly rare purposes of exhibition. Hitler had not just bitten the hand which once fed him; he had devoured it. The middle classes were deprived of every ounce of real influence in the Nazi state, and now they were robbed of even the raiment of power. All that was revolutionary in the Nazi revolution was over for ever.

*   *   *   *

Why were the Storm Troops disbanded? The reason, in its most general terms, is that the Storm Troops were an *organization*. An organization, a number of people acting as a single body with a single aim, is the kernel of political action. Organization can be a dangerous thing. The first political parties in the dawn of the liberal-capitalist social era were vigorously combated by royalty and feudal aristocracy who realized the peril the organization of the rising *bourgeoisie* meant for their position. The bloody struggle to organize trade unions, which has continued down to our own day, is another example of how dangerous an organization can be considered by a ruling group. So long as the Storm Troop organization was Hitler's and entirely his, it was an element of great strength on his side. But for two principal reasons, the Storm Troops were gradually turned into an organization *potentially*, if not actually, opposed to National Socialism. The young Nazi who first told me of the dissolution, blamed it on the *verfluchte KPD*, the damned German Communist Party, legally dead these eight years. Ever since 1933, he said, the Communists, robbed of their own organization, had been following a policy of infiltration into Nazi organizations, and the main object of their boring-from-within activity has been the S.A. He asserted that they have succeeded in capturing high positions in metropolitan Storm-troop units, that some of the units have become wholly Communist, and the members of these units have been using Storm-troop meetings purely to discuss Communist tactics. My acquaintance claimed that forty per cent of the Storm-troop membership consisted of former members of the Communist Party!

Although that figure is certainly greatly exaggerated, there is little doubt that his judgment is partially true. It is virtually impossible, even for Nazis, to wipe out anything but a minority of leaders of a party which once dominated politics in a number of industrial regions in Germany. It is also true that before the war, in 1939, two whole district groups of the Storm Troops were dissolved and their members imprisoned in the Berlin area because they were discovered to be almost all Communists. And it is undeniable that North Berlin, the *Wedding* area, is still infested with Communist sympathizers despite innumerable raids on that working class district of the German capital. I once prepared a story on evidences of Communist influence in Berlin and elsewhere in Germany, but never succeeded in getting it out of Germany. Here are a few items from it: when Molotov came to Berlin, flower shops in *Wedding* and East Berlin sold out of red carnations, and for several days thousands of people in those districts could be seen wearing carnations in their coat-lapels. On last May Day, when rumours of a coming conflict between Germany and Russia were rife, almost every worker in the industrial suburbs of Berlin wore some spot of red in his or her clothing, in hats, in coat-lapels, etc. On the fiftieth birthday of Ernst Thaelmann, the prison farm in Hanover where he is being held, was deluged with thousands of telegrams of congratulations which people had dropped in mailboxes with money attached to pay for transmission; and the German postal authorities transmitted them! Bouquets of red roses and carnations were sent by telegraph from foreign countries, especially from Russia, and one big bouquet bore the name of Molotov. Prison authorities, however, withheld all telegrams, flowers and presents from Thaelmann except a message from Thaelmann's wife, who lives in Berlin. During the few Russian air raids on Berlin, the police had several times to call out riot squads to quell fights in air-raid cellars in the *Wedding* district between Russian sympathizers and Nazi families whom Goebbels has been systematically settling in that area in the hope of diluting its leftism. In the same area, there are at least two beer taverns in whose back rooms workers still give the clenched fist salute instead of the Nazi salute when they enter and leave; and they hum before closing time the *Red Flag*. A man cannot be arrested for humming the *Red Flag*, for it has the same air as *Tannenbaum*, which the Nazi still teach school children as a proud bit of *Volksmusik*. Since the Russian war, the painting of Communist slogans on fences and walls has greatly increased in Berlin, especially in incorrigible *Wedding* and in the *Hasenheide* section of East Berlin. In the hardly proletarian West End, I have seen three such slogans, one on a fence on Lietzenbuerger Strasse just off Kurfuerstendamm, one near the Berlin Zoo, and one on Kalkreuth Strasse, near the restaurant *Roma*, a hangout of the Italian Press. One has to get up very early to see them, for they are, perforce, painted at night, and policemen have strict orders to make their rounds at the break of dawn to discover them and report them to a special "painting-out" squad maintained by the Police Department. The slogan painted on a building on Kalkreuth Straase—*Rotfont siegt!* (Red front will win!)— I saw while walking to the Foreign Office on the morning of the German attack on Russia. It had been painted over when I returned home at eight a.m. Next day, the slogan was repainted on the same spot, and was still there at midday. The "painting-out" squad had apparently had a busy morning and could not get around to it until later.

Communist influence is still doubtless strong in Germany, and that the Communists have chosen the Storm Troops for special treatment is doubtless true. But the assiduous care with which candidates have been taken to the S.A. makes incredible the assertion that that body was virtually run by Communists. The more important reason why the Storm Troops were virtually eliminated is certainly that already indicated. The Storm Troops were the fighting organization of a class that has been destroyed. The roots of the said class have been torn loose from the social system, and they have undergone the process of—no other word fits so well—sheer proletarianization. They have been drawn into the unskilled working classes, into the arms industries and others. Some of them, perhaps even the majority, still deceive themselves that they still belong to a higher class in the social scale. Some of them believe the development is temporary, and that they will go back to their old shops and desk-jobs, if Hitler wins. But many of them, a surprisingly great proportion of the whole, realize what has happened, and that looking backwards is useless. The Nazi economic dictators have already, in their economic and trade journals, made it quite clear that there is to be no return. There have been innumerable articles and essays from the pens of authoritative men to the effect that there can be no return. They attack "splintered retailing" as uneconomical, and openly state that after the war, if Germany wins, there must be still more rationalization, fewer independent retailers, and larger combines which will doubtless yield higher profits to the small controlling clique at the top. The Little Men who realize they have become workers and nothing better are steadily increasing in number. All over Germany last year this bitter question-answer joke was circulated: what is the difference between Germany and Russia? And the answer: in Russia the weather is colder. Germans who had been told for eight years there was no slavery greater than that of Communist Russia, were telling themselves in this bit of bitter-sweet frankness that they, too, were proletarians.

It is an open secret that great discontent has been rife in the Storm Troops and even in the higher reaches of the party itself. I was told in September, last year, that four leading members of the Storm Troops—my informant would not reveal their names, for fear I would publish them and the information could be traced to him—had been arrested, and one of them later was executed for making "treasonable utterances" about the demise of the Little Man under Hitler's regime. It is certainly true, also, that the very prototype of the German *Kleinbuerger*, Julius Lippert, the *Buergermeister* of Berlin has been liquidated. Lippert, a high member of the Nazi Party disappeared a year ago. I have been assured by people who have good reason to know what they are talking about that he has been executed. All municipal decrees are now signed by acting Lord Mayors, and Lippert's name has not been mentioned in the press for a year! There is reason to believe that these are only the few instances that have come to light of a small-scale purge of Nazi party leaders.

One of the outstanding indications that this has been the case is circumstantial, but overwhelming, evidence which the Fuehrer himself laid bare. He did so in his speech on the anniversary of the Beer-Hall putsch, when he spoke to old party comrades in Munich, on November 8, 1941, about a month after the dissolution of the Storm Troops. It was on that occasion that the Fuehrer for the first time threatened his own people. That section of his speech bears repetition.

"Should anyone among us", Hitler said, "seriously hope to disturb our front—it makes no difference where he comes from or what camp he belongs to—I will keep an eye on him for a certain period. You know my methods. That is always the period of probation. But then there comes a moment when *I strike like lightning and eliminate that sort of thing*".

It was then, too, that the Fuehrer declared that the Nazi organization, by which he meant the Gestapo, watches every single house and "zealously keeps watch that there shall never be another November 1918".

The manner in which this particular speech was handled by the Propaganda Ministry and the German press is still more significant. The Fuehrer's speech of November 8, alone of all the Leader's addresses, was not broadcast to the German people. About six hours after the Fuehrer had spoken, the official Nazi news agency issued an expurgated, or better, a slaughtered version of the speech. The version was empty. It was shot through with big blank spaces which the reporter tried to hide with long glowing accounts of the thunderous applause and the enthusiasm of his listeners, the local colour of the beer-hall in which the Fuehrer spoke, and, in fact, everything except what the Fuehrer had actually said. Almost every foreign correspondent in Berlin plagued the Propaganda Ministry with inquiries about the unusual handling of the address that evening. I telephoned twice, to beg for the actual text to use in a radio broadcast that night. In the past, the Propaganda Ministry had been all too happy to provide the texts of Hitler's speeches. In the past, each speech had been broadcast by radio in Germany and all over the world, and the D.N.B. ticker machines issued running texts while Hitler spoke. The Ministry always promptly released, immediately afterwards, official translations in dozens of languages, plus every detail of the setting and the audience's response, and long official commentaries. But on this occasion, for the first time, the Ministry was reluctant; it had no interest. The occasion, it was said, was purely a party occasion, and the rest of the world could have very little interest in what really amounted to a routine meeting of party officials. Two hours after the first version was issued, a second, much fuller version was released, doubtless due to the embarrassing solicitation of the foreign correspondents. But it was obvious that there were gaps even in the second version.

Not having the text of the original speech, in my broadcast script late that night I prepared a long story on the manner in which the speech had been handled. Between the lines—and all radio correspondents had by that time learned to write most of their scripts in the broad spaces between lines—I indicated that the Fuehrer had said many things to his veteran party comrades which the Propaganda Ministry considered it not diplomatic to reveal to the public. Every word was struck out by the censors. I rewrote the script, merely describing the handling, and leaving the implications to the listener. The censors then struck that out. Exasperated, and with only a few minutes left before I was to go on the air, I translated some weak press comment on the speech— the press commented automatically, and on Goebbels' orders, long before the second version of the script was released—and filled my script with it. The censors struck that out, too. They obviously wanted nothing said about the speech, and they had obviously been ordered to blue-pencil every word about it. So that night I went on the air with only half a script. It was the last time I did so. This was the culmination of a series of such incidents with the censors, and the next day I conferred with the two other American radio correspondents, and we decided to send the common protests to our New York offices which resulted in our banishment.

It was obvious that the Fuehrer had said much more than the party authorities considered good for the world's ears. The fact that he was speaking to old Storm-troop comrades, on a Storm-troop red-letter day indicated the theme of his expurgated remarks. The nature of the text which was eventually revealed, supported this impression. Correspondents, in the noon press conference next day, bluntly asked Dr. Brauweiler for the meaning of the unusual handling of the speech, but the old man, with forced casualness, simply waived the questions aside with a weak denial that the Fuehrer had said anything except what had finally appeared in the press. Had he wanted to prove this were all, he might have re-broadcast records of the speech, but this was never done. What Hitler said, and the Propaganda Ministry censored has never been revealed to the world.

It would be false to conclude from these incidents that there was any organized plot on the part of the Storm Troops to over-throw Hitler and the Nazis. Hitler's grounds both for the minia-ture purge and the disbandment of the Storm Troops were, so far as it is possible to determine, considerably less dramatic; both measures were certainly, in the main, precautionary steps. The Little Men, who were the backbone of the party before their Leader evolved from a deified Little Man, to a Man on Horse-back, were seriously discontented when the military leaders became the backbone of his movement. Virtually their only political organization was the *Sturm Abteilung*. As individuals, unorganized, they might be inclined to look upon their mis-fortunes more as individual misfortunes than social ones. But organized, and able to meet together and talk, the common ground on which their complaints were based became clearer to them. And the germ of revolt is the recognition by a group of people of the fact that they possess a common complaint. Hitler disbanded them certainly because discontent, reaching a head, found in the S.A. an organized manner of expressing itself.

For the fact that discontent did reach its highest level last autumn since Hitler came to power, there is a plethora of evidence in the behaviour of the ruling Nazis themselves. In the third month of the Russian campaign, and after it had already drawn heavily on the home front's nourishment and clothing supplies, Heinrich Himmler's assistant chief of the Gestapo, Reinhard Heydrich (the "hangman" as he was known, whom Himmler sent into Bohemia to crush a planned popular revolt there last autumn) published in the Reich Law Journal an article suggesting the institution of a *Volksmeldedienst*, a People's Reporting Service. Briefly his plan was to make every German a spy on his neigh-bour's activities, to encourage janitors and servants to report "treasonable utterances" of their employers, and waiters in restaurants to report immediately, to a central organization of the Gestapo in each neighbourhood, every unpatriotic word they heard expressed by customers. Extracts from his article were published in the *Koelner Zeitung*, but appeared in no Berlin news-paper, where they would be within easy reach of the foreign press. *Gruppenfuehrer* Heydrich's plan, which was eventually instituted in part, spoke volumes about the condition of German morale. In the fourth month of the Russian war, the Gestapo complement in Berlin was augmented by 10,000 young agents, fresh from their training Institute in Bavaria. According to a well informed German source, this amounted to a doubling of the former complement, but later, many of the old, seasoned crew were taken away from Berlin and sent to other lands of Europe more immediately dangerous to the Nazis. Arrests for petty crimes of "hostility towards the state", mainly open complaining on the streets, tripled in number. They were almost all made in the thousands of queues that now constantly decorate Berlin's streets. Of these arrests, the greater number involved disgruntled housewives in market queues. Men are not as bold as women, and cigarette queues yielded relatively small pickings, according to my information. The punishment for a first misdemeanor of this sort was consignment to several days of scrubbing floors in local police stations, but the numbers of arrests increased to such an extent that eventually small money fines or brief confinement in gaols were substituted, for the floors of police stations became saturated with scrubbers. Second offences earned prison sentences.

The omnipresence of the Gestapo became a source of wit in the lighter moods of the population. The habit which almost every Berliner soon acquired of constantly glancing over each shoulder as he talked to an acquaintance, even when the theme was harmless, became known as the *Berliner Blick*—the Berlin glance. Propaganda posters against espionage, pasted on hoardings in tube stations were comically mutilated. On one I saw, a small piece of paper warning, "Take care with your conversations, the Enemy is listening", the paper had been scratched away over the word enemy until only two little paper S's remained, so that the legend read: "Take care with your conversations, the S.S. is listening". Another coloured placard showed a fine, happy Nordic soldier, talking over a glass of beer in a tavern to a civilian friend, while near them an evil-looking citizen with horn-rimmed glasses sat, appearing to read a newspaper, but actually straining his ear to catch the conversation. The caption ran: "Take care with conversations, for WHO is the third person?" Some miscreant had scratched away the big WHO and written in its place, in pencil, "Himmler".

As the Russian war proceeded into winter and the bottom dropped out of the standard of living the Nazis turned from

explanatory propaganda and the fiasco of the Jewish campaign
to the propaganda of Fear. Simultaneously, with this alteration in
propaganda policy, the Gestapo began carrying out actual
measures to meet revolt, to make as certain as possible that
"another November 1918", would not happen: Himmler, who
next to Goebbels is about the only big Nazi leader who concerns
himself with German internal affairs any more, began taking up
positions for battle. What he did was circulated over Berlin by
way of rumour, apparently by the Nazis themselves, with the object
of intimidating grousers; but the content of the rumour was real.
The Gestapo began confiscating buildings, and setting up headquarters in purely residential districts of Berlin. The first buildings occupied were a Catholic convent in West Berlin (the source
of this is a German girl who lived in the convent and had to seek
new quarters after the raid) and a Catholic hospice, or lodging
house. The same girl told me this, and it was later confirmed by a
pastoral letter composed by the Catholic Bishop of Berlin, Konrad
Count von Preising, and read in all Catholic churches in Berlin.
Then—the action was a perfect symbol of the social mutation—
the S.S. black guards began confiscating the shops which the little
middle classes and even upper middle classes, had abandoned as
derelict when the goods shortages came like an epidemic. One
was Meyer's wine shop on Olivaer Platz, across the square from
the home of a colleague of mine, and another was the Singer
Sewing Machine salesrooms on Wittenberg platz just across from
my own apartment. These are the confiscations I have been able
to confirm directly. There were dozens of others which I learned
of by word of mouth. In all the confiscated properties, the S.S.
not only set up information headquarters, but also arsenals, storing
away machine guns, small arms and ammunition. It should be
noted that the confiscated rooms and buildings were all in purely
residential quarters of Berlin; districts with no military importance
whatever. It is also worth remarking that the plan was not only, or
even mainly a plan for Berlin. Even earlier the Gestapo had begun wholesale confiscations in other cities and in the provinces.
The only case of which the outside world has learned has been,
thanks to the audacious Catholic Bishop Count von Galen, that
of the town of Muenster. But I have had reports of similar wholesale seizures by the S.S. black guards in Leipzig, Dresden, Kiel,
and other towns. In Berlin, it is also worth noting that almost all

the confiscations I have been able to confirm occurred in the *bourgeois* West End, which belongs to the *Kleinbuergertum* as much as *Wedding* belongs to the working class. That may be, however, due to the fact that as early as 1933, the Gestapo had already begun building up a network of arsenals in the latter section of Berlin.

Several months later, some of these facts leaked out of Germany, and were miserably exaggerated in some foreign newspapers. At least one newspaper added the embroidery of machine-guns "on the streets and buildings of Berlin", and bunkers for combating civil revolt in the centre of the city! The "machine-guns" were anti-aircraft pom-pom guns which have been sitting on the roofs of buildings all over Berlin since the war began, and the "bunkers" were apparently the huge anti-aircraft-towers in the Tiergarten which are neither strategically situated, nor physically con-structed, for ground combat. The facts are sufficiently sensational in themselves. Less than a month after Hitler's singular threat to destroy any menace to his power, his black Army, specially formed to put down civilian revolt, had done the same thing his green-coated armies do when they prepare to invade a foreign victim. The confiscations, and the arsenals meant simply the *Aufmarsch*, the deployment of his forces for battle. Not mainly for combat against Plutocrats, or Jews, or Communists. But for eventual battle against those who called on him to save them from destruction, and whom he destroyed.

IX

THE ELEMENTS OF CONFLICT

THE RUSSIAN war period has revealed three fissures in Hitler's Nazi monument; three distinct elements of revolt. The dispossessed middle classes do not, in their role as dispossessed middle classes, constitute one of them. Their dispossession has certainly been the most significant development of the war inside Germany. But, in order to constitute an element of revolt, a group or a class must possess some form of organization. When the German *Kleinbuerger* were just beginning to realize what had happened to them, and their discontent was organizing itself in the hull of one of Hitler's own Nazi formations, the Storm Troops, the Fuehrer's moment "when I strike like lightning", arrived and their organization was crushed. The three different elements of revolt to which I am now referring are organizations. None of them has any but the slightest connection or sympathy with the others. But within each different organization, its members have discovered a common complaint, and each group has begun acting against the Hitler regime after its own manner.

How broad the different fissures are, how dangerous to Hitler they are, is difficult to ascertain. But, although I cannot make an evaluation of their absolute importance, I can, on the basis of information which was revealed to me in Berlin, make some kind of estimate of their relative importance. The three in order of ascending importance are: the Communists, the Church and its followers, and the conservative Prussian military caste. That ranking is based on what information I have been able to gather, under the most difficult of circumstances. Here, based on the said information are brief analyses of each.

First, the Communists. It is a testimonial to the strength of Communist fanaticism, that they are the only active purely political opposition to Hitler still functioning in an organized fashion in Germany, although the Nazis have persecuted the members of that political sect far more ruthlessly than any other group or party in Germany. I have already recited evidence of their activity. Their influence among the German labouring classes far exceeds their numbers. I have met hundreds of Communist sympathizers among the German workers in the years I have spent in Germany. Hundreds are not many in a people of 66,000,000, but it must be borne in mind that I was a foreigner, and only the bold dared to make their political faith known, and these only after rather long acquaintance.

All German workers have remained slightly pink-to-red even after almost ten years of Nazi rule. One reason why Hitler called his political party both "Socialist" and a party of the "Workers", was doubtless because he had to make a nominal concession to fetishes which have been popular for the past half-century with a large portion of the German population. For the same reason, no doubt, he attacks Capitalism in his press while sacrificing good German blood to maintain it in its most pernicious shape in reality. It should be remembered that Germany was pink (the people, I mean; not the government) long before any other nation in the world reached that stage in social development. Germany possessed a live and flourishing Socialist Party before the Russian Bolsheviks were born, and while the British Labour Party was struggling for barest existence. It is patently impossible to wipe out this colouration in eight years or eighteen; the more so when Hitler has not solved the problems which make workers pink, but only aggravated them. Another strong point which has won the left-wing many silent supporters in recent years in Germany is the manner in which the pet prediction, made by Communists and Socialists alike, that Hitlerism would mean war within a decade, has been realized. In 1933, none of the millions of middle-class Germans who supported Hitler believed this. But during this war, I have had it told to me like a coroner's verdict, with a bitter shake of the head each time, by many middle-class friends.

Another indication of the strength of the socialist idea among Germans has been the fact that despite years of incessant propaganda—before the German-Russian pact—against Communism, there has been very little real vindictiveness against Russia, even during the Russian war, among German workers; rather, there has been an insatiable curiosity regarding that land and its system. The single most popular show window of the many show windows on Unter den Linden was incontestably, that of *Intourist*, the Russian travel agency. On sunny Sundays, promenaders actually used to line up in rows and wait their turns to study carefully every propaganda photo in the window. Across the street, the Russian embassy building, with its hand-carved hammer and sickle on the door and cryptic Russian characters on the big brass plate next to the door, and, on occasion, an enormous red flag floating over the centre of the building, was the most gawked at embassy in Berlin. Whenever an ambassadorial motor-car, a stream-lined "Zis" parked outside, a crowd immediately formed and people touched it, studied its lines and whispered to one another that the thing could apparently run, couldn't it?

During the Russian war, the Communists have considerably increased their activity. But the ultimate criterion of the effectiveness of any political party is its material results. Hundreds of cases of sabotage, by Communists and others, have been reported from all the occupied territories, but I know of not a single act of industrial sabotage or even of a slow-down strike in Germany since 1937, when a Gestapo agent I met in Heidelberg told me he had in that summer been assigned to put down a minor revolt in the Opel works. That, of course, does not mean they have not been occurring. In Vienna, in the first month of the Russian war, three telephone booths were blown up by Communists in the neighbourhood of Hotel Sacher. But if they had been occurring on a large scale certainly at least several more such incidents would have leaked out to Berlin and the foreign press. It is noteworthy that the Russians in their life-and-death struggle have not once, to my knowledge, appealed to German Communists to revolt; which would seem to indicate that the Russians, who should know, do not estimate the active strength of the German Communists too highly. From what I have been able to learn, the number of organized Communists inside Germany is not large, probably not more than a couple of thousand. The sympathizers are doubtless a large multiple of this, but they are unorganized, unarmed and considerably cowed at the treatment their active comrades have received at the hands of the Nazis. Though Communist activity has increased considerably since the beginning of the campaign in Russia, it remains purely psychological; purely propagandist—slogans on walls and fences, anonymous letters and leaflets distributed in the black-out. The Communist element of revolt offers little hope of development for the present. It must remain, in the main, a coloration among the German working classes, rather than an important directive to action. Their value to the opponents of Nazism can only make itself materially evident after a revolt has begun and made considerable progress. Then, no doubt, they may become important, perhaps even decisive.

Second, the Church; specifically the Catholic Church. The revolt from this unexpected quarter hit the German people like a bombshell. Long before American journalists had succeeded in smuggling out the Bishop of Muenster's historic protests against Gestapo robbery of Catholic property, the texts of his statements had circulated all over Germany. Parish priests, hardly less audacious than the heroic Bishop Count von Galen himself, mimeographed the full texts of his sermons and letters and issued them over the entire country. It is hardly necessary to emphasize the audacity this required in a nation whose leaders brook no expression of opinion but their own. It was an invitation to disaster. And the power of this element of revolt is illustrated in no way better than by the fact that the Nazis have not even yet dared to arrest either the Bishop of Muenster or those who followed his lead, Bishop Bornewasser of Trier, and the Bishop of Berlin, Konrad Count von Preising. It is safe to say that nothing, not even the new senseless persecution of the Jews, caused so much immediate resentment among the German people as the raids of the Gestapo on Church property, which these sermons and letters revealed.

In Catholic South Germany, resentment was directed against the robbery itself. But, in the Protestant areas, the protests found an echo equally as impressive not for religious reasons so much as for social reasons. Discontent was rife, and the Catholic initiative found ready sympathizers. This was the first, bold, open vote of opposition which had been made in Germany since Pastor Niemoeller flayed the new rulers of Germany from his pulpit in Berlin-Dahlem. The protests were against an outrage which cut athwart class lines, affecting sections of the workers, arousing the particular ire of the middle classes, and reaching even into the old ruling class which has its own canons of respectability; and one of them has always been the inviolability of the Church.

How widespread the influence of the bishops' protests was is evinced by the fact that, alone of all the possible opposition groups, Hitler mentioned their organization by name in the first speech in which he threatened the German people. On November 8, in Munich, the Fuehrer, after declaring he would strike down anyone "who hopes to disturb our front", added, "no camouflage will aid them; not even the camouflage of religion".

Religion is dangerous to Hitler; far more dangerous under the present circumstances than any organization which is purely political in its opposition. For one thing the church is still *legal*. For an organization to be declared illegal and be forced to operate underground is very dramatic, but it hamstrings the organization and can even kill it. But the Church has never been broken as the workers' parties have. The roots of religion, too, are far deeper in the consciences of a far greater number of people than almost any political faith which has arisen in the last century. In Germany, religion has drawn the bulk of its following from just those little middle classes who carried Hitler to power. He could not act so promptly and as drastically against the Church, to which the Little Men paid obeisance, as he did against the working-class parties whom his biggest supporters hated. It is significant that it was only when the dispossession of the Little Men economically, the destruction of their little businesses, was virtually completed, that the Fuehrer made his first really determined assault on the Church, to dispossess it, too, economically. He started on the Churches when the veil was down; when he could no longer hide the inevitable demise of the *petite bourgeoisie* from itself, and pretences were useless.

But the encouraging feature is that the Church is not yet broken. The confiscations have assumed national proportions, always on the basis of the law of 1933 for the "confiscation of Communist properties". But the stature of the clerics has grown with each confiscation. Priests have been arrested for fighting with their fists against the invaders, but their defeat has been an added strength to their cause rather than a loss. The moment is not psychological for a blow against an enemy to the State who is bold and scorns punishment and death. Three years ago it might have occurred without embarrassment to the Nazis. But today, every bold action, every arrest, finds an echo among the disgruntled people, who have become all too inclined to take sides with the underdog no matter what his political colour, or his faith. During the past decade, religion has systematically undermined itself all over the world. It has taken sides with wealth and privilege against the people, in Spain against the democratic Loyalists, in America against child-labour legislation, and in England on the side of appeasement. Certainly nothing has served to rejuvenate it so much, to help it reconquer the souls it has been losing fast, as the valour of the German priests in the face of persecution and even the prospect of death. This is truer in Germany than in the rest of the world. Rhineland churches are now filled to overflowing every Sunday by the faithful, and by the hitherto indifferent, who are coming to see some spirit in religion at long last, just as Niemoeller's followers tripled when he took up the banner of protest. But the numbers of the followers now are greater, for the time is psychological—but not for Hitler.

Religious opposition to Hitler is far, far stronger among the German people than that of either of the two other elements I have listed. The Communist opposition does not even compete with it in respect to the numbers of its following, nor to results. It is even stronger than the third element of revolt: the Prussian military caste. The old military caste is too closely tied to Hitler to be capable of leading a revolution. Their fate will be Hitler's fate, and they know that they stand or fall with their leader. But I give them precedence in importance for what I think are good reasons.

The army leaders are separated from the Nazi Party competition for rule over the German state by a gap which is virtually unbridgeable. So long as triumph continues to be uninterrupted, a makeshift *mode de vivre* can be found between them, and has been found for the past eight years, despite many a little and many a big disturbance. But the *Time* is the thing. For the first time in eight years, triumph was interrupted last winter by the Russians, and the gap opened wide for the world to see. There will certainly be other interruptions. Further, the time is not one of revolution, in which the Communist or the Church come into decisive play. The time is the pre-revolutionary stage, when popular discontent is secondary. Popular discontent is secondary because no revolution in history has ever been begun by popular discontent. The people win and lose revolutions, but they do not begin them. The present time is like the period before you start a fire, when the kindling faggots are far more important than the logs which blaze out heat later, when the head of the matchstick which inflames the wooden body is more important than the wooden body itself. No revolution in history has been begun by the people; every revolution in history has been begun by a *conflict in*

the palace. The organizations of the people against Hitler are few—
I know of only two—and, it must be admitted, neither has yet the
proper requisite to decisive, political action. The Church is strong
in spirit, but trains and factories are blown up with dynamite, not
with spirit. There must first of all be a fissure in the walls of the
palace through which the masses can creep into the higher conflict, take it over from their leaders and make a revolution of it.

For these reasons, I believe the third element of revolt, the discontent and uneasiness of the military leadership, is at this moment
the most important of the only three organized elements of revolt
which exist in Germany.

Once upon a time, in the first winter of the war, a German girl I
knew telephoned me and asked if I would join her and her friends
that afternoon to fill out a little tea-party of four. The party would
be made up of her and her fiancé, who was a young Gestapo
officer, a member of what is called the *Sicherheitsdienst;* and the
daughter of a Prussian general from Hamburg, and me. I accepted
the invitation with polite thanks and met the two young ladies
promptly at four in *Kranzler's* café on Kurfuerstendamm. Both
girls were obviously ill at ease and nervous, and the Gestapo
fiancé was late. At four-thirty, the Gestapo-man's girl-friend, after
having nervously torn up two match-boxes and left the splinters
all over our table, begged to be excused in order to phone her
fiancé. After five minutes, she came back, annoyed, and said the
Gestapo-man was not coming. The Prussian general's daughter
perceptibly relaxed and breathed freely, and we had tea *à trois*.
In the course of tea, the Gestapo officer's girl-friend confessed to
me what had been afoot. She had arranged the tea-party for us
four and had not informed her Gestapo-man until the last
minute; she had wanted to present him with a *fait accompli*. It
seems that the girl-friend, the daughter of a Prussian general, and
the boy-friend, a member of the black guards, were not on speaking
terms, and the girl was trying to force them to re-establish friendly
relations for they were both dear to her. She had invited me, an
American, because then the Gestapo-man would have been embarrassed into coming, and would also have been forced to behave
politely to the whole company—Germany was still trying to impress Americans favourably then, and the Gestapo is official
Germany. I learned that relations had been broken off between

the General's daughter and the Gestapo-man about two minutes after they had first met. It had taken them about three sentences apiece to reach the stage of open, mutual insult. The General's daughter had called the Gestapo-man a "prolet" meaning proletarian, and an "upstart", and the Gestapo-man had called the General's daughter an "impudent, haughty aristocrat". So they parted and had never spoken again. On the occasion of the tea-party, the General's daughter, being an aristocrat, had agreed reluctantly to bury the hatchet. But the Gestapo-man had refused, and, no doubt, after reading a few pages of *Mein Kampf* to reinforce his will, had stuck to his guns. So that afternoon I had two dates, plus a clear-cut little example of prevailing sentiments in the royal bedroom of Hitler's palace.

The gorge dividing the Nazi Party, which concept has now come to mean purely the Gestapo, and the old military caste is deep, and such bridges as Hitler has built across it are weak makeshifts. It is a deep and very real fissure. It is not just a difference of opinion between two types of militarism. It is social, and has its roots in long established tradition. And it does not involve only the military men. The military caste is simply the military expression of the old ruling classes, the old capitalists, Krupp, von Borsig, Thyssen and the whole, old gang. On the other side are the upstarts, the social climbers, the Nazis, pure Nazi to the marrow of their bones. To apply the analysis the Prussian General's daughter made in a pertinent joke during our tea-party at Kranzler's: in Germany, life is just a dog-fight; between *Bonzo* and *Pluto*. Pluto means plutocrat, and Bonzo refers to the German word for bureaucrat, by which she meant the Nazis, the upstarts.

Like their economic counterparts, the Prussian generals supported Hitler to the hilt in his struggle for power. They did so because he promised them ascendancy instead of inevitable annihilation by eventual left-wing revolution. But the officers of the *Reichswehr* never lost their distaste, personal and class, for the rising young corporals and sergeants of the world war, now in brown uniforms, any more than the capitalists lost their distaste for the aggressive little Nazi sons of the middle classes who were now coming to sit at their sides at meetings of boards of directors. Soon after Hitler came to power, the mutual distaste of the two cliques expressed itself in two industrial clubs. Both groups were outgrowths from the Koelner Industrial Club, where

Hitler had once spoken and won financial support from the Lords of German creation. One was known as the S.S. Economic ring, led spiritually by Himmler and Ribbentrop but nominally by a prominent industrialist. The ring had for its aim the introduction of the "National Socialist spirit into German Industry". The old men's club, formed in opposition, was called the *Gelsenkirchen* Club, officially just another sort of Industrial Booster's Lodge, but actually aiming to fight off Nazi encroachment in the grand old game of Acquisition. Both clubs have doggedly stuck to their aims to this day, but their competition has become more open and more aggressive. To be sure, there has been some blending of the two groups. A few old capitalists have joined the Nazis quite frankly and openly, and a few generals have become incontestably Nazi generals; General von Reichenau, for example. But, by and large, each group—the radical Nazis and the conservative Old Men and their sons—has maintained itself apart from and against the other in matters of the Palace. The conflict is not only in the Royal suite of the Palace; it extends deep down in the fabric of German governance. The Foreign Office is shot through with young noblemen, sons of the wealthy who compete with, and hate, the young, handsome, so called "prolets" of the S.S. The economics ministry amd the ministry of finance are other battle-grounds. The struggle, mostly a covert one, is not just a conflict between two groups of mutually envious young men for promotion over one another. It is truly a conflict for the future rule over Germany, by the generation which will be the ruling one in the not distant future.

The major struggle between the two elements has been, however, for the Army; for the power that ultimately enforces authority in the German state. To the outside world, the creation of the German *Wehrmacht* in the past eight years has appeared to be the construction of a powerful uniform instrument of destruction with rigidly unified leadership and methods of training. Actually, the creation of this greatest army in the world has been a dual construction. In actuality, not one, but two armies have been constructed simultaneously, and side by side, with different leaders, and totally different methods of training. The development has been one of the oddest in contemporary history. It is almost as though each was the army of a different nation, as though they were fighting temporarily side by side on the battlefield as temporary allies. Throughout their simultaneous construction, they have struggled now covertly now openly against one another. At points in their histories, they have come to serious conflicts, which the Fuehrer has always settled in his *blitzartig* fashion. But the conflict, potential or actual, he has never succeeded in stifling.

Facts about the conflict are hard to get. Regarding the people, and their organizations and conflicts, it is easier for a reporter to get information because he cannot help mixing with them if he merely lives in Germany for a long period. But here we have to deal with the rarified atmosphere of the leadership. Even in democratic countries it is often difficult to delve into the secrets of ruling classes and the leadership of political parties. But in a totalitarian country it is ten times as hard. However, some facts can be unearthed and accepted as certainties, and there is much circumstantial evidence for them.

The first important evidence of open conflict between the two armies, that of the Military men, and that of the Nazi Party, occurred in 1938, shortly before Hitler opened his era of "dynamic" foreign policy by marching into Austria. General von Blomberg, the Minister of War, was forced to resign, and with him went a number of leading Prussian generals. The event was immediately correctly judged by the world to mean a serious disagreement on policy, and after the invasion of Austria, the basis for disagreement became obvious. The conservative generals are not so "dynamic" in their conceptions as the Fuehrer and his radical Nazi followers; they feared the consequences of this drastic revision of Versailles and struggled against the Fuehrer's decision to carry it out. But the Fuehrer knew Chamberlain and Halifax far better than the generals did. After the dismissal of von Blomberg, Hitler himself took over personal command of the whole German armed forces; the event that marks clearly his evolution from the champion of the Little Men, to the Conqueror. The social significance of the event is emphasized by the fact that simultaneously, Goering became personal commander-in-chief of the bright new air-force, and the old-school Foreign Minister, Baron Konstantin von Neurath, was dismissed from his position and replaced by the very Nazi Joachim von Ribbentrop.

Hitler's assumption of command, and his daring successes in no way reassured the generals. Their inborn conservatism led them to fear and counsel against each fresh bold stroke. Their timidity was shared by their industrialist brethren, as indicated by the defection of one of Hitler's earliest wealthy supporters, Fritz von Thyssen, the coal magnate, just before the present war. Von Thyssen's abandonment of Nazism and his flight were widely interpreted to mean that the Nazi millionaire differed from Hitler on internal policy, and the incident was falsely used to support the thesis that the Fuehrer had duped his wealthy friends. Later evidence points to a disagreement on the radicalism of Hitler's foreign policy, which Thyssen thought would destroy Germany. Since the surprising success of the campaigns in this war, there has been much talk in Berlin of a reconciliation between Hitler and Thyssen. If Hitler wins, there may be, for Thyssen is the nearest thing to a pure Nazi-capitalist the old-school has yet produced.

The beginning of the war created an outright panic amongst the old ruling group. The death of General von Fritsch in Poland, where he had gone as a volunteer, after Hitler deprived him of his command, aroused considerable resentment. And, finally, after the conquest of Poland was completed, and the Allies had refused Hitler's offer of peace, it is said that there was a secret plot to rid Germany of Hitler and his immediate followers so as to create a basis for peace which the Allies would find acceptable. The plotters included some of the Generals, the landed Junkers and the most nervous of the Capitalists, according to this version. The bomb-attempt on the Fuehrer's life in the Buergerbraeu beer-cellar on November 8, 1939, was said to be the climax of the plot. It is not improbable that this is true, though it is impossible to say it with certainty. I have been able to ascertain that the feeling among a goodly section of the old-school rulers was certainly appropriate for such an attempt. And it is also true that the official Nazi version of the Buergerbraeu incident—that it was planned by the British Secret Service—has never been supported by any evidence. The Nazis arrested two alleged British Secret Service agents, but the Nazi Press has never mentioned them since the day after the *Attentat*, and the Propaganda Ministry has repeatedly refused to answer any questions put by foreign correspondents regarding their present whereabouts and the possibility of a trial. Certainly, if evidence were at hand for the official Nazi version, the Nazis would have been happy to stage a trial and prove their case to the world.

The best indication that the old Army Generals' corps did not enjoy Hitler's undivided trust was the unprecedented manner in which the Fuehrer at the very beginning of the war ordered unlimited expansion of a separate army—the *Waffen S.S.* The term means the *S.S. in Arms;* the old Gestapo and party *élite* transformed from an internal army to a distinctive National army. Just about the only connection the *Waffen S.S.* has with the regular army is that both are commanded ultimately by Hitler. Otherwise, it is a wholly separate organization. It has its own separate barracks, its own training centres, and its methods of training differ radically from those of the regular army. Its officers never see the inside of any of the old officers' training institutions. Symbolically, it does not even wear the uniform of the regular army. The S.S., the black guards of peace time, wear in war a uniform of a deeper shade of green, and a black collar instead of the army's green collar. On the collar are two S's stylized in the shape of streaks of lightning, embroidered in silver.

More cynical Germans interpreted this act of making the S.S. a separate and visibly distinct army, to mean an attempt by Hitler to stave off criticism of the people who hate and fear the Gestapo and were certain the S.S. would never bear its share of the burden of its own war. In the first months of the war, *Buerger* were humming a little ditty the text of which was:

> *Wir alten Kaempfer sind schon da*
> *Wo bleibt S.S. und die S.A.?*

miserably translated it means something like:

> We soldiers are already in the fray,
> But where's the S.S. and the S.A.?

The interpretation of the said cynics has in its favour the fact that Goebbels has wasted far more hot-air and paper to propagandize and popularize the relatively small S.S. army than he has on the regular army. But, although the formation of the *Waffen S.S.* may have been partially a propaganda affair in the beginning, it has long since ceased to be anything resembling a mere propaganda trick. Its size has been multiplied. For the past year and a half appeals have been published monthly in the press for applicants to enter the *S.S. in arms.* Appeals have also been made on placards and posters in subways and on hoardings all over Germany. The standards for candidates were lowered in order to increase the number of available recruits.

The point that the S.S. was expanded is not nearly so important as at whose expense it was expanded. The additions did not come from the unconscripted civilians, for there are few if any unconscripted civilian men of the age and fitness required by the *Waffen S.S.* They are all in the regular army. But Hitler, through Himmler, decreed that any man of the proper physique and fanaticism who was in the regular army, and desired to join the S.S. had to be released by the regular army for this purpose. The kernel of the matter is this: the Gestapo army was drawing from the regular army its best men. It was not only drawing away quantity from the regular army, but also the best soldiers, creating an *élite* which, though still smaller in numbers, would surpass by far the quality of the regular army. Thus, should a pinch ever come, Hitler would have on his side an army of men who are virtually impervious to defection and revolt. In two years of war he had filtered German manhood to build up a personal army which will support him and the Nazi Party to the death, even in preference to Germany, and against any revolt from any quarter inside Germany. The old army leaders could not but look askance at this development. Every time, in every campaign, a handful of their men distinguished themselves by valour or fitness above the rest, the Gestapo immediately approached them with offers and drew them from the regular army into the S.S.! In the Gestapo army, pay is better, promotion is faster, barracks more comfortable and prestige is much higher. In the regular army the old Prussian code virtually forbids any private soldier ever becoming a commissioned officer. In the S.S. Army, convention and tradition count for nothing, and a private soldier can become a general if he is a ruthless fighter, capable and fanatic. It is small wonder that the *Waffen S.S.* is besieged with applicants every month. Each campaign has made the army of Hitler relatively stronger and the army of the old Prussians relatively weaker.

But Hitler is nowhere near the point at which he can dispense either with the old army leaders or with the regular army. In fact, the deeper he goes into world conquest, the more necessary it is for him to have a large corps of experienced leaders and a quantitatively stronger regular army. For one thing, conquest is not completed by military conquest. A large contingent of soldiers must be left in each conquered country to preserve it for Germany. The elements of a balance, the elements of a checkmate are there.

Neither contestant for supreme rule is winning; both are increasing their influence each day. Circumstances are making the Generals more necessary, and conscious plan is abetting the importance of the S.S. army. It is a strange and precarious sort of balance, but it continues, and neither element can take drastic measures against the other for the simple reason that the old balance does continue. But the balance is, by its very nature, an unsteady one. Though it has never been seriously broken, the gap between the two ends of the fulcrum has deepened and broadened. So long as Germany was winning, the balance could continue. A *mode de vivre*, however unsatisfactory to both, was found, and the conflict between them delayed until after final victory. There have been few disturbances of any moment to the balance between the first winter of war and an indistinct point of time late in the Russian campaign. As factors in the German state, both gained immense power. The leading Nazis abruptly liquidated their possible competitors for power, the middle classes. And the Generals' corps gained ascendance over their economic brethren: the landed Junkers and the rich industrialists. All civil agencies which might compete with them were crushed. No leader of any importance any longer paid any attention to the internal situation in Germany. Civil administration, robbed of its best functionaries by the military, became chaotic. Internal German society rotted. Nobody of consequence in the German Palace was interested. The stakes were now the rule of Europe and the world. The competitors for supreme rule were narrowed down to two: the military men and the party men. And both agreed that their squabble was temporarily less important than final victory over the world. After that they could settle the matter of which of them was going to be supreme.

But quick, easy triumph ended with Russia. The Generals did their job well at first, encircling and destroying Red divisions on the border and deeper inside Russia. But both the Generals and Hitler had underestimated the strength of Russian numbers and war material, but mostly the spirit of resistance of Soviet soldiery. During that aggravating period between August and November, when Russian resistance seemed to grow stronger with each sectional German triumph, the old conservatism stole over the regular army leadership; and they again became disgruntled at having to share command with Hitler's radical second army.

Their uneasiness at the new developments first expressed itself in protests against the management of events inside Germany by the Party. According to one source, they made personal representations to Hitler against the confiscation of church properties, warning him that the Russian war might drag out for a longer period, and that the time was not propitious for any moves which might aggravate the growing discontent among the people at home. Hitler was deaf to their protests, so when the anti-Jewish campaign occurred, the military clique appealed over Hitler's head directly to the people by means of leaflets, distributed all over Germany by post. I have already referred to the leaflets. They declared that the campaign was purely an affair of the Propaganda Ministry and the Gestapo, and that it had been begun without consulting "Germany's real leaders" who were fighting for Germany "at the front". It cannot be proven, but the tone of the anonymous letters, implying in their attacks on Himmler and Goebbels a compliment to the High Command, as well as their timing and audacity, affords grounds to believe the report is correct that they were written and distributed under the auspices of the old army leaders.

In late autumn, the truly serious break came. It resulted, in December, in a wholesale purge of the Prussian military leaders, and constituted one of the most serious crises Hitler has had to face since assuming power in Germany. The information I have regarding the disagreement between Hitler and his Army Leaders comes from a German military source. I cannot prove its truth in any way, except, again, that later developments strongly support it. My informant's sources, further, are reliable members of the German High Command. The facts he gave me are these.

In September, 1941, Field-Marshal General Werner von Brauchitsch, the Commander-in-Chief of the German Army, approached Hitler and told the Fuehrer that in his opinion and his three army-group leaders, Field-Marshals von Leeb, at Leningrad, von Bock before Moscow, and von Rundstedt, in the Ukraine, the time had come to call a retreat. Von Brauchitsch declared he had made as complete a study of the reserve strength of the Red Army as was possible, and had arrived at the conclusion that it would not be possible to take Leningrad or Moscow before winter. He suggested a retreat, first to shorten the lines of supply of the German Army, for winter snow and ice would make serious the problem of supplying the millions of troops on the front; second, to shorten the front and cut down the demand for great numbers of troops, and third, in order to be close to warm winter-quarters for the troops. The time was propitious in September, he said, for the Russians were still retreating, and could not muster for harassing attacks for some time; the German retreat could be carried out in relative peace. Further, he pointed out to the Fuehrer, German troops were in no way equipped for winter warfare.

That was old Prussian conservatism. Hitler promptly rejected, with typical Nazi radicalism, the Commander's suggestions and declared it was possible to take Leningrad and Moscow before winter, and thus to provide the German troops with winter quarters and good positions for defence should the Russian war continue into winter. But he did not believe the Bolshevik Government was strong enough to withstand the loss of its two biggest cities. That is briefly the background of the most serious disagreement between the two ruling cliques that has yet occurred. On November 21, last year, after Hitler's offensive had shot its guns empty, Brauchitsch again approached the Fuehrer and expressed his views more violently, saying that if a retreat were not undertaken at once, no German Army general would feel called upon to bear the responsibility for the consequences. The Fuehrer declared that he and his general staff, the Nazi generals, would assume responsibility. That was the last information I had on the break before I left Germany. Frankly, I doubted its validity at the time. But since the events of December 19, it seems to have a very tangible confirmation. Von Brauschitsch resigned. Hitler personally took over command. All three army-group leaders— von Leeb, von Bock and von Rundstedt—either resigned from their commands or were discharged. The shady manner in which the removals or resignations became known—and doubtless all the removals have not yet been made known—lends credibility to the assertion that Hitler was struggling to hide the full extent of the break. That von Leeb went was revealed in an obscure German military report referring to the northern German Army-group as having been "*previously* under the command of Field-Marshal Ritter von Leeb". That von Bock and von Runstedt were removed or had resigned was first revealed when, on the death of Field-Marshal von Reichenau, it was announced that the late General had been in command of the army-group formerly commanded by von Rundstedt, and that his command would now be taken over by von Bock! There had been a break and, apparently, a partial reconciliation.

Later still, the Propaganda Ministry's military spokesman revealed awkwardly that the purge struck many other big figures in the old Prussian clique, stating that the "catchword invented in foreign countries of 'dismissals of Generals' is false; actually it is only a matter of replacing a number of commands". Then on January 20, this year, the German press unanimously published suspicious stories of the difficulties of life in the snow and ice of the Eastern front, and especially about how the Generals were suffering from illnesses which required them to leave the army, perhaps temporarily!

At the same time that this story reached me, and long before events confirmed its truth, another rumour, which sounds equally fantastic on the surface, was circulating widely in Berlin regarding the conflict between the Party and the Army. Himmler, satisfied with the success of his *Waffen S.S.* in building up a counterbalance to the Prussian militarists, suggested to Hitler a repetition of the process in the other two categories of the armed forces: the air-force and the navy. The Gestapo leader accompanied his suggestion with a detailed outline of plans to form a purely Nazi air-force. Goering got wind of the plan and immediately ordered his right-hand man, the Luftwaffe General Milch, to prepare a memorandum to the Fuehrer opposing the plan to split the Luftwaffe into sheep and goats. Milch prepared a long document, explaining the inadvisability of the plan on technical grounds, and called on half a dozen leading fliers to sign it with him. Then the memorandum was presented to the Fuehrer and Hitler peremptorily shelved Himmler's plan. Those who told me the story said that among the fliers who signed the Milch memorandum were Moelders, Germany's greatest air ace, General Ernst Udet, Baron von Werra and General Wilberg. It may be just accidental but all four have been killed since I heard the story the first time.

Nazi Germany, originally planned as a Little Man's Paradise, bred as a tight little Oligarchy of wealth, has now evolved into an unmitigated military dictatorship. Economically and politically, control of the German State has gone over to the men in uniform. Not even the gilded industrialists, old-school and new Nazi, who ruled in peace, enjoy the full extent of their old power. It is, of course, not easy to distinguish between Generals and Industrialists, any more than it is easy to draw the line between Gestapo leaders and Nazi capitalists. Within each group, the old and the new, both sections tend to become identical. But the balance of power has shifted from the economic rulers to the military rulers within each group. As war proceeded, the Generals, old-school and Nazi, invaded one field of government after another. From having merely advisers in the food ministry, they have now installed rigid controllers of food distribution. From having advisers to Goebbels, they have come to have the power of irrevoca le veto over Goebbels' spokesmen and propagandists. The censorship has become virtually a military matter. And foreign policy is created only with the consent or at the suggestion of the Military men, Hitler at the top of his dual military pyramid. They are the strong, handsome exterior of the rotten apple; they are the new aristocracy, the supermen of Germany and Europe, and potentially the new rulers of the world. They are a very queer lot indeed. As possible rulers of you and me, they bear closer inspection.

The Prussian Generals are fine men to look at; physically, they are exceedingly handsome. Von Bock and von Leeb have today the figures they had when they were sixteen. All of them have passed, or are near, the end of man's normal span of life, but they are all as energetic as adolescents. They do not grow old, for that would make life un-uniform, and uniformity is an inviolable canon of Prussianism. They simply begin living at birth and continue, without any alteration of consequence, until they suddenly pop off and die. Two years before Field-Marshal General von Reichenau popped off and died, he was swimming the Vistula river naked (legend says he carried his revolver between his teeth) at the head of his youthful troops. A year before he died this sexagenarian was taking morning jogs at the side of Max Schmeling in the Tiergarten, and afternoons, was running a leg on a quarter-mile relay team against twenty-year-olds in the Olympic Stadium.

They are charming. Nothing ruffles their composure. Their faces are dead-pan; neutral. From neutral they can shift, as you shift gears on a motor car, in only two directions: from dead-pan

to grim determination, and from dead-pan to the faint trace of a
smile. One is for on duty, on battle-fields; and the other for off
duty, at tea parties, banquets, etc. The change is hardly perceptible in either case. The prototype is Ludendorff, who travelled
in full General's array with decorations, across revolutionary
Germany where mobs were ripping the epaulets off lieutenants
and beating up everything higher than lieutenant, calm and
composed as though he were sipping tea from dainty Dresden
china cups at a royal tea-party. Once, towards the end of the
French campaign, I crossed a battle-field with a young Prussian
officer. I muddied up my shoes in shell-holes, ripped my trousers
on barbed wire, lost my hat in the Rhine, barked my shins on a
destroyed bunker and got my coat black with oil from abandoned
French 75's. But when we arrived at Strasbourg that evening my
guide was spotless, his shiny boots not even dusty and every strand
of his hair in its appointed place.

They are personally irresistible. A New Year's eve party in
my apartment once was graced by the presence of a young
Prussian officer, son and grandson of Prussian officers. He had
lived in the Baltic lands all his life and had thus been bred on a
cross of two rigid military cultures. He drank to the health of a
lady present, drained the glass dry, then turned on his heels raised
the glass high in the air and smashed it against the floor. Un-
ruffled by the awed silence which followed the crash, he marched
a couple of steps to me, snapped his heels together with a bang,
bowed stiffly and low and uttered his profoundest, most heartfelt
apologies. I was overwhelmed with the grace of it all, and soothed
his tender conscience with unmixed forgiveness. The gentleman
then returned to the lady, drank to her, and crashed a second
glass on the floor; then back to me with a click and a bow and
an apology. Since I possessed but fourteen wine glasses and glasses
were hard to get in those trying days, I should, I suppose, have
been angry when he destroyed a total of eleven of them that night.
But his manner was so irresistible that I almost felt he was doing
me a favour. But I did not invite him again.

And drink! My God, they can drink! On a seven-day trip to
and in the Maginot Line, Captain Sommerfeld, the military attaché
in the Propaganda Ministry, and a fine, bloated Prussian Balt,
drank incessantly for seven days and seven nights. He drank
everything, and at all times. I tried to keep up with him, and did

for the first thirteen hours, but the pace was too stiff, and I took my appointed place, under the table, after sharing several dozen bottles of almost as many different brands of liquor with a company of Prussians and newspapermen. Captain Sommerfeld later told me Prussian officers are trained to drink as part of their military education. When he was seventeen, he was made to sit up stiffly at a table with his superiors and drink with them, glass for glass, for hours on end. Afterwards, woozy Cadet Sommerfeld was ordered to stand at attention in the centre of the floor and answer questions, not questions of knowledge but of aptitude of the how-many-two-penny-stamps-in-a-dozen-type. If his rigid body swayed, or he failed to give the proper answers, he was punished. The training is not supposed to be fun, like hazing; it is dead serious. Prussians have always been methodically trained to drink, for it is felt that if an officer were ever seen reeling drunk by a subordinate it would have a bad effect on morale. Dignity, at all times and under all circumstances, is another canon of Prussianism.

They are not human beings, and the passions of the human soul are forbidden them by the tradition of their Prussian military profession. They are machines which function on reflexes. It is said that when a little Prussian is born, he greets the light of day at attention and with a salute, and if the doctor doesn't shout "At Ease", he remains stiff until his heart stops beating. There is no doubt that they are the best soldier-stuff in the world. They live it and breathe it all their lives.

Once I saw a whole theatre-load of them. I welched from the Propaganda Ministry a free ticket to the world premier of *Sieg im Westen*, "Triumph in the West", the German documentary film of the campaign in Holland, Belgium and France. The whole *Generalitaet* came to the premier. The French campaign was just over so I saw the best of Prussia's sons in their and Prussia's most glorious moment. It was a good show; not the film, but the arrival of the officers. Full of gold braid, the scarlet lapels and broad scarlet trouser-stripes of the officers of the Supreme Command; and a sprinkling of Nazi politicians, came to bask in borrowed glory. Of the biggest shots, von Bock was the first to arrive. He has a face like a Texas farmer, hard, thin and with good lines in it. Then came von Rundstedt, the frog-eyed man with a moustache, who first cracked the Maginot Line at Sedan. Von Rundstedt is the general who ran the Socialist government out of Prussia. He hates everything left of Krupp and took a special joy in the Russian campaign, until Rostov, when Timoshenko and fate singled him out for the first attack that began the German winter retreat. Von Bock and von Rundstedt conquered four nations together, and at the premier they sat in adjacent boxes, their shoulders almost touching, but neither said a word to the other, nor, in fact, to anyone else. They just sat there, poker-faced, and looked blankly into space. Once they rose stiffly in succession to kiss the hand of the beautiful blonde-haired woman who is the wife of that chunk of raw, red fat, Dr. Robert Ley. But they only nodded to the grinning Doctor. He is a Nazi.

Von Leeb came in, the man with the piercing eyes, the billiard-ball head and the face of granite. He greeted people for propriety's sake, but did not crease his stony face once. Then he took his place in another box and sat, arms folded, with a ramrod for a back-bone, and looked into space.

Von Brauchitsch arrived with his wife, and he and Dr. Ley kissed one another's wives' hands. The triplets, the von's Leeb, Bock and Rundstedt, rose in unison and saluted their diminutive chief, then all four sat down and looked into space. Not Dr. Ley, who is a Nazi politician. He kept jumping up from his chair to go and greet someone he knew, or thought he knew, and waved and gesticulated, grinning all the time, making sure he was in evidence to us, the public. It was von Brauchitsch's show, and they gave him the central box to prove it. But Dr. Goebbels, who knows the tricks of showmanship best, beat him out for last-to-come by one minute and a half. Then all sat down and the orchestra played the *Zapfenstreich* with lots of tin and trumpets, and the theatre grew dark and the film began. I watched von Leeb through the whole film. His eyes were glassy, and sparkled into space in the darkness; I do not believe he looked at the screen once. Somebody had forgotten to say "At Ease"!

They function on reflexes. They are not trained to think, except in the most elementary terms of time and space on the battle-field, and of quantity and quality of guns, tanks and troops; but this they do perfectly. Thought on a higher, broader level is forbidden. Their minds are closed to breadth at birth. Perspective they never come to know. History to them is static and all its terms fixed. Fatherland is the main concept. But they do draw a rather fine distinction as to its meaning; it means a government chosen and controlled by their own class. If the people elect the government of the nation, then the nation ceases to fit the concept—Fatherland. Good is a word which is synonymous with German, or, better, Prussian (in Bavaria, the members of the Prussian ruling caste are known as *Saupreussen*, the word for pig going together with Prussian in the same manner that *damyankee* used to be one word to an American Southerner); and Bad means foreign or popular, of the people. Decency and dignity, too, are their moral concepts. They permit, however, such manly sins as lecherousness, the maintenance of a mistress, oaths and drinking. They exclude all association with inferiors, prolets, upstarts, social climbers. Two more concepts which they worship and obey with devotion that is admirable are bravery and duty. They never reason why, but they do or die like the stout fellows they are. They are at once romantic as feudal knights and despicable as criminals. They are destructive by the nature of their traditional profession, bored with the works of peace, happy only in war; essentially and inevitably hostile to democracy and affable to regimentation. They are inborn enemies of all that civilization has gained in this difficult century and a half of building democracy.

In their mental make-up one can see at once a great similarity to and a great difference from their partners-in-rule, the Nazis. With the Nazis they believe "War is the highest expression of Mankind" (quoting von Reichenau and Adolf Hitler). Against the Nazis they believe birth is the principal factor in national rule. The Nazis do not believe birth is the main justification of possessing power; they do not care whether or not their followers come from the west end or the east end; they must simply be physically strong, brutal and fanatic. The old Prussians have ruled too long, and become too petrified to accept any such "revolutionary" infiltration into their privileged ranks. The Prussians are stiff and brittle. The Nazis are flexible and opportunistic. The Prussians cannot adapt themselves to new circumstances, and they refuse to violate their rigid concepts of morality. The Nazis will do *anything;* no theory is sacred and no concept inviolable when it suits their ends.

The old Prussians are *old*, individually and as a class. The Nazis are young in both respects. The Prussians, we have read about before in history. Their heyday ended with the world war.

The Russian revolution killed a parallel of theirs in the Russian officers' caste. The Nazis are something new in history. There is no fitting parallel to them in the record of the past. The old German Generals are, in fact, a social anachronism. It is my own belief that the caste is doomed, no matter who wins the war. If Hitler loses, they lose with him. If Hitler wins, they will last a little longer, but they will dwindle in importance, and finally die. The new men on horseback are the Nazis, and if the sons of the old Families want to continue their tradition they will have to do it by entering the Gestapo *Ordensburgen* of Munich, not the officers' institute of Potsdam. It takes perspective to be able to see that, and the old men have never possessed perspective. So they will not yield without a fight to the verdict of history. They will express their contempt for the upstarts now or later, but they will die fighting. That process may, in fact, be what has begun in the first winter of the Russian war.

The Gestapo are the new men on horseback. They are flexible, adaptable, more brutal and unscrupulous, and have no moral code of any kind—not even the Prussian one—save obeisance to the Fuehrer, the means and aim of all their existence. They care nothing about family, upbringing, education or lack of it. The men of the old school have physical vigour but no social vigour. The Nazis have both. The old Prussians could never rule again for long in peace-time; they are decadent. But the Nazis, though the seeds of corruption are buried in their essence, can rule—the most brutal rule the world will ever know—for another half century or more—if Hitler wins the war.

The Gestapo is the most carefully chosen and the most carefully trained army in the world. Not even the Communists, who study at the famous Lenin Institute in Moscow, get such a long, painstaking education in fanaticism as Hitler's *Schutzstaffel*. Postulants for the black guard army are trained from early boyhood for this strange, evil priesthood. In this war, for the first time, Heinrich Himmler, the chief of the Gestapo, has let down the barriers to some extent and admitted young soldiers as old as twenty as members of this priesthood, but these are the men who have proved themselves on the field of battle, which in the Nazi scale of human values is the supreme testing ground.

Every German boy who belongs to the Hitler Youth organization —and that includes ninety-eight per cent of all German boys —is eligible for candidature. Hitler wants a big *élite*, not a small one. He plans to rule Europe and the world, and to make Germany purely a nation of S.S. men, which is what is meant by the word *Herrenvolk*. The world will furnish the slave-labour, and Germany will furnish the rulers, the Gestapo, to rule over them and keep them down. For this reason, the Fuehrer has taken good care of German youth. Of all the elements of the population, certainly the youth has benefited most, and been affected by Hitlerism. They are well fed and receive special rations of cakes and goodies not available to grown-ups even today. They receive healthy vacations at the expense of the state, and their training and schooling is physically good, with the result that the German youth are undeniably virile. Hitler's form of government and his history afford them the excitement youth craves. The only justification I can find for the trashiness of German propaganda and war films is that they are apparently directed at the intellectual and emotional level of children; and alone with the children they enjoy success. Children are barbaric in their very nature, and Barbaric Nazism appeals to them immensely. Hitler gives them excitement and spares them the horror of war. In Berlin, every evening at sunset, dozens of big, grey buses ride over the city picking up children and taking them to the Fuehrer's own chancellery in the Wilhelmstrasse, where they spend evenings and nights playing in the vast, luxurious chancellery cellars, or seeing films or plays for children, safe from bombs. The Great Conqueror, who is inaccessible to high diplomats of foreign lands, then goes down into the cellars and spends half-an-hour talking small-talk at them, whenever he is in Berlin. These are the few children left in Berlin. Most of them from Berlin and other big German cities have long ago been transported to eastern Germany to be spared the experience of air-raids. They live in open-air schools and play on great playgrounds on the countryside. It must be admitted Hitler has treated the *Herrenvolk*-in-being well, when they are physically strong. Hitler issued a decree last autumn banning from secondary schools children who were crippled or who did not show sufficient interest in sports. A boy may be a potential literary or musical genius, but if he does not play football with zest, he is a burden to the state, and the Nazis are not interested. Brains are not important to the creation of a mammoth Gestapo, but physical strength is.

The strongest and the handsomest are placed in "Adolf Hitler Schools". Hitler founded these latter-day seminaries for the new German priesthood in January, 1938. Their curriculum is amazing. Besides studies in doctored German history and the three "R's", the boys are taught to mine coal, build bridges, and are made to undergo physical tests which put the training of Spartan youth in the shade. In a way, the Adolf Hitler schools are a good idea. The boys become acquainted with every phase of life, a little hard labour, a little book-keeping and salesmanship, a lot of militarism and every form of sport. But the strain of the underlying education is warping. They are taught to believe in German superiority to all other peoples, they are rigorously indoctrinated with the racial idea, taught to hate Christianity, both as a religion and as a norm of values, and to believe in the divinity of the Fuehrer. They come out of the Adolf Hitler schools, technically capable, strong, clean and alert, but with a sense of values not much higher than that of an orang-outang.

That is the background of their education. Then they go into the *Ordensburgen*, the Gestapo institutes, to learn the details of their particular task for the rest of their lives. They learn soldiering, how to put down strikes, how to become detectives, and their superiority over all other forms of human life save those who have more silver embroidery than they on their similar collars. Then, they go out into the conquered world and practise their precepts. Their allegiance is to the Fuehrer and to the Fuehrer alone. They will defend him against everybody and everything in the most impossible situations imaginable. The highest goal any of them can attain is to die in battle for the Fuehrer. And they all strive to do so. The only reason they refuse to throw themselves into cannon-fire and die on the first opportunity is to win for him, then die for him on a more impossible occasion. Germans, and the enemies of Germany, who have called them arrant cowards (I have heard it said many times by people who do not know the Gestapo) are deluding themselves. The Gestapo is brave, bold, scorns death, and will never, never yield. Trying to influence them with propaganda against Hitler and against the rulers of Germany under Hitler is of no effect. Their minds have been warped too long and too effectively. As a possible element of revolt, they can be counted out for all time. The Gestapo cannot be won over, though almost every other section of the German population can be won over under certain circumstances. There is only one solution to the S.S. The Russians know it. A German soldier, returning wounded from the Eastern front, told me so. He had found on a dead Russian soldier an order saying that the particular Soviet regiment should try and take as many prisoners as possible, for purposes of gaining military information from them. But, the order said, if you see that the potential prisoner wears a black collar with two S's on it, don't bother to take him prisoner.

Since—if Hitler wins—these will be the future residents of Park Avenue and Mayfair, it is worth while giving a few essential details about them. Most people think of the S.S. as being a uniform body. It was, when Hitler came to power. But it has grown more complicated since then. It is now a whole state, with innumerable departments and divisions, and with different uniforms and different functions. Here is a brief catalogue of the main sections of the future rulers of the world.

The *S.S. Leibstandarte Adolf Hitler*, the personal bodyguard of the Fuehrer. They wear in peace-time, black uniforms with a black band on the sleeve bearing, in silver embroidery, the name of Adolf Hitler. In war they wear a green uniform with the same arm-band. In peace, they guard the Fuehrer's chancellery and the Fuehrer; and in war they fight, and they fight well. Their General (the S.S. word for General is *Obergruppenfuehrer*) is young, swarthy, tough Sepp Dietrich, who lives in the Fuehrer's headquarters at the front. The *Leibstandarte* is the cream of the cream of all German society. In the six years before the war it was built up from a small battalion to regiments of several thousands. Now it comprises more than 10,000, and is expanding steadily. Before the war, it was exceedingly hard to get into the personal bodyguard, but in 1940, the newspapers in Germany suddenly issued an appeal for candidates to the bodyguard itself, to the surprise of almost every German in Germany. According to the official appeal any youth between the ages of eighteen and twenty-one might apply if he had several years of military training and fighting experience. Only those who had been decorated in some campaign were accepted.

The *Regiment General Goering*. These are air-force officers under the immediate command of Goering, and they wear the regular grey-blue uniform of the *Luftwaffe*. They formed the first special military group inside the S.S. and their real origin dates from

1933, when Goering, and not Himmler, was the head of the S.S. which was at that time only a sort of internal political police force. Today the regiment consists of three anti-aircraft battalions who guard personally the *Reichsmarschall's* headquarters, one engineers' detachment, doubtless for the purpose of transferring Goering's headquarters as the front moves forward, one infantry battalion to fight possible enemy parachute troops, and a searchlight battalion.

The *Regiment Grossdeutschland* which forms the mass of the S.S. infantry at the front. It wears the green *Waffen S.S,* uniform, and is purely a war creation. It was founded on September 15, 1939. This section, really far bigger than a regiment, has borne the brunt of the actual fighting for the S.S. Its commander is Himmler, the leader of the S.S., himself. Because it does most of the fighting, it has suffered far greater losses than any other section of the black guards.

The *S.S. Verfuegungstruppe*, the motorized Gestapo. It is not only motorized, but also, to the anger and envy of the Prussian panzer generals, it is by far the best equipped motorized force in the entire German army. Its uniform is black, and it, too, is purely a war-time army. It consists of several whole divisions. schooled in street combat, and house-to-house fighting. The *Verfuegungstruppe* does not function as a unit, but is distributed throughout all the German armies. Its most eminent graduate is General Rommel, who, as a part of it, was the first to reach the coast of the English channel and lock the allied troops in the pocket of Dunkirk, and is now the commander of the German Africa corps.

The *S.S. Totenkopfverbaende*, the S.S. Death's Head formations, so called from the appropriate silver skull-and-cross-bones emblem they wear on their black caps. Uniforms: black, or plain clothes. These are the men you read about when you read about the Gestapo; the real Gestapo. Doubtless, they are the most unscrupulous, brutal organization of alleged humans in the world. Their front is not the war-front, but the home-front. They are the Gestapo Jan Valtin wrote about in *Out of the Night*, who have made nine years of history of brutality. Their immediate chief is Himmler. Before the war, they were assigned to the German workers. Since the campaigns, they are assigned to the occupied countries. For the first time, they are getting a sound licking from the people they are supposed to keep down. Inside Germany, their place has been taken by the *Sichereitsdienst*.

Sicherheitsdienst means, literally, the Security Service. Uniform: grey, with a black square on the sleeve containing the silver embroidered letters "S.D." Leader: Reinhard Heydrich, the "Hangman" who quelled the revolt in Czechoslovakia last autumn, on special assignment. These are the very young and very handsome men who look after internal Germany, and who had their hands so full recently that they had to double their numbers in Berlin. They are the church-confiscators, and the dawn-raiders whose underlings I met in the United Press office. They expect big business soon, and have set up arsenals in cities all over Germany to prepare for it. We shall probably hear more of the *Sicherheitsdienst* in the newspapers before long.

There are many more divisions. These are only the most important. There are, I have learned, at least half a million members and employees, and they are increasing constantly. Their headquarters is an enormous, heavy, grey building on Prinz Albrecht Strasse in Berlin, where I once went to carry books and cigarettes for Dick Hottelet. But they have more than 300 other buildings, filled with card-indexes of every living soul in Germany, and millions of other "enemies" in the outside world, whom they hope to liquidate in time. Every time a name appears in a foreign newspaper expressing dislike for Nazism, they record it and, through their fifth column in the outside world, build up a sizable portfolio of "crimes" which must be atoned for.

An addendum: in the section about the speed with which Hitler is expanding his personal army, I forgot to mention that he is doing so not only to maintain a balance against the growing importance of the regular army; he has had to do so because the bestial Russians have *wiped out almost one-third of the S.S.-in-Arms in six months.*

X

HOW TO WIN WARS AND BEAT NAZIS

IF THE PICTURE is encouraging, it is because the facts are so. I have scrupulously tried to label every statement for what it is; a rumour for a rumour, an unconfirmed report for just that, and a fact, of whose validity I have been able to satisfy myself, for a fact. It is precisely because I am perforce my own judge of what is factual in what I observed that I began this book with an auto-biography of sorts. All people see life through lenses of different kinds and shades. The shade of those through which I saw Germany, I have revealed from the outset. Though readers have, so to speak, been warned, I still do not want to play part father to any illegitimate illusions. German morale is, according to people who have lived there long enough to compare, lower to-day than at any time since 1919. But there is still no readiness among the people to revolt. The fighting strength of the German army is still enormous; better than our own; and the stratagems to which its leadership can resort to ward off defeat are innumerable, and their store of brutality and unscrupulousness inexhaustible save by their own death.

Nevertheless, there are good reasons for us to be encouraged. The war which Hitler expected to end victoriously in late summer, 1940, is now deep in its third year. Under present circumstances, the very lengthening of the war for this period is a serious loss to Hitler. The "campaign" in Russia, to be concluded in two months, has stretched through the winter and Nazi troops have been forced to make the first retreat in their history—another serious loss, not only of prestige but of invaluable material. The core of Hitler's war-objective has been, quite frankly, the conquest of the British isles. Hitler is now farther from achieving that objective than he has been since the fall of France. Tomorrow he will be farther away, and the day after tomorrow still farther. Each day the Russian war continues, whether Hitler advances or retreats, he is farther from winning the war. This is not to be taken as an expression of the attitude that Britain is fighting Germany to the last Russian. If Russia should, by some awful miracle, collapse, however much weaker Hitler would be as a result of having been involved in Russia, he will still be stronger to attack England and America, win the Battle of the Atlantic, and aid Japan, than if Russia and the great Red Army continue to be strong and resistant. More than that, we must aid Russia and help save Russia for Russia's own sake. One of the few happy developments of this war has been that, at long last, the democratic nations have withdrawn completely their psychological *cordon sanitaire* from around the Soviet Union, and admitted Russia to its proper place among the peace-loving nations—an act that could have avoided so much blood, sweat and tears if it had been done at an earlier time.

A short while ago, the war was one between mighty Germany and Italy against isolated England. In little more than a year, the European conflict has become a war of the world against Hitler. The Russian war period has seen one nation after another join the side of the democratic allies. And today the Axis has but two relatively trustworthy supporters in Europe—the two nations who make it up! Aside from Germany and Italy, every nation in Europe hates Hitler with a vengeance, and many of them are fighting against him. What is more important, those who are fighting him on the continent of Europe are doing so not because their governments ordered them to do so, but on their own individual initiative. Hitler has destroyed their governments, but thousands, hundreds of thousands of workers and patriots, have declared war on Nazism since the beginning of the Russian war, from pure conscience; and warriors-by-conscience rather than by government order are always the most effective soldiers.

Look at Hitler's Europe, which he was going to "mobilize to the last man" against the democracies. In Yugoslavia, a year after Hitler's Balkan campaign, the war has not even yet ended. Serbian, Croatian, Greek and Bulgarian patriots have actually wrested towns and whole areas from the well-armed troops of the Axis, in open battle. A member of the puppet Croatian legation in Berlin told me that when trains go through the mountainous area of Croatia, passengers are made to lie on the floor, lest enthusiastic citizens of the new Nazi state should send a volley of machine-gun bullets through the windows from hide-outs beside the tracks. Passengers are warned not to travel at all unless their business is extremely urgent, for the death-rate due to train explosion is terrific. The Croatian Government, months after Yugoslavia has been liquidated, have set up a regular war ministry and have removed government offices from the capital in Zagreb for fear they will be captured by the "red army". I recall one time last autumn in Berlin when D.N.B., the official Nazi news agency, issued a report to the effect that: "Our troops today recaptured from the Red Army, after a long siege and a bitter battle, the town of Lojkovac. Our advance continues." I looked high and low over a map of the Russian steppes to find Lojkovac, and finally discovered it, not in Russia at all, but a thousand miles behind the German front, in Yugoslavia, within the figurative shadows of Belgrade itself! The Italians still give military communiqués about the Balkans as another front in their war, and each communiqué reveals they lose almost as many men in former Yugoslavia as they do on the North African front.

In occupied France, where there are no wilds and no mountains to speak of, last autumn an armed band of workers raided a German munitions dump, killed the German guards and stole T.N.T. which they used the following week to blow up four German supply trains! That was in the civilized west, not in the barbaric Balkans. No single member of the band has ever been captured. On the French Riviera, workers took three towns, arrested the municipal governments and planted their own flag on the city halls. A colleague from Vichy told me one literally takes one's life in one's hands when one speaks German at night in the streets lining the docks of Marseilles.

In Czechoslovakia, though that tortured land has been under a horrible Nazi terror for three years, patriots were able to form the biggest known network in all oppressed Europe for a revolt against Hitler. The Gestapo was forced to kill almost a thousand Czechs to break the back of the plan—if they succeeded in breaking it. More important than the fact that a revolt was planned was the organization's constituents; Marxist workers, moneyed, old-school patriots, and even Nazi puppet governors themselves, who had after three years come to see the light, consciously aided the cause of those who would surely have killed them had the revolt succeeded! The whole Prague town council was arrested, and with them, the puppet premier of Bohemia and Moravia. Reinhard Heydrich, the S.S. man Himmler sent to break the revolt, had even to issue a decree forbidding people, on heavy penalties, from tipping their hats to Jews, which the people did as a sign of protest against Nazism.

It is an open secret in Nazi circles in Berlin that if the Nazis suddenly withdrew their rigid control from the Balkans, open war would break out the next day between Hungary and Rumania. Members of the Hungarian and Rumanian diplomatic staffs in Berlin do not speak to one another, and the Nazis take care never to seat a Rumanian next to a Hungarian at official dinners. On the Eastern Front, Hungarians and Rumanians are not allowed to fight side by side, because if they ever found their ranks contiguous and themselves with guns in their hands, they would forget about the Russians and fight one another.

A Bulgarian Nazi journalist in Berlin once told me that the Communists formed the most powerful political party in all Bulgaria, though they have been illegal for years. Before the Russian war, he estimated, forty per cent of the Bulgarian workers belonged to the Communist Party. Since the Russian war, he said, the figure has risen to sixty per cent. The Bulgarian government had to remove the town councils of two dozen mountain towns recently because they were Red, and were aiding sabotage groups. When King Boris of Bulgaria visited Berlin recently, he did it *incognito* so that his people would not hear about it. On the occasion, I walked from the Foreign Office, where I heard the official spokesman deny rumours that Boris was in town, to the Adlon Hotel where I almost bumped smack into Boris, who raised his hat, and mumbled an inaudible apology for the near collision, at the door of the hotel! The *Portier* confirmed to me that it was Boris.

Up North, the little Nordic brothers have grown fighting bitter. When the Danish foreign minister, Herr Scavenius, went to Berlin to sign the anti-Komintern pact, Copenhagen students revolted, skipped classes and marched through the streets singing *God Save the King*, and threw good Danish eggs at the German minister when he saluted them from his balcony, thinking it was a sign of pro-German enthusiasm. When Scavenius was almost home, on his return journey by train, the government sent him a cable to stop the train, get out and proceed to Copenhagen by motor car, as plans were afoot to give him a rather warm greeting at the station, and the police could not cope with the preparations. A Danish quisling journalist in Berlin told me that his family had disowned him since the occupation of Denmark by the Germans. In Norway, the feeling among ninety-nine per cent of the Norwegian people is so intense against the Nazis that the notorious leader of the Norwegian Nazi *Hird*, Vidkun Quisling himself, has called the situation an internal "war". One reason why the British *commandos* have not had more difficulty with German planes when they have made their raids on the Norwegian coast and on islands is that the Norwegians keep the communications of the Luftwaffe, by which German fighters and bombers are summoned to defence, constantly out of order. As a penalty, the Germans once made the inhabitants of one whole area in Norway give up their normal pursuits and stand guard twenty-four hours a day over miles of Luftwaffe cable. When the cables continued to be sliced, the Nazis made the citizens of the area pay a heavy money fine. When Quisling was named head of the Norwegian State by the Nazis, the people who listened to his "acceptance" speech, all his followers in all Norway, were less numerous than the German armed guard which held watch over the streets outside to keep the Norwegian public out. Quisling's own reputation is so bad, that Germany's other allied leaders shun him. When the B.B.C. listed the Hungarian premier, Count von Bardossey as a European "Quisling", the Hungarian press raged back that they would not stand for their leader being compared with "a man who has been a traitor to his country"!

Belgium has the record of affording the German Gestapo its highest death-rate. More German soldiers and policemen were killed in Belgium last year than in all Occupied France. This was told me by a Dutch commercial man in Berlin, who regretted that his nation was behind both Belgium and France in this respect, but boasted that Holland had prepared the most efficient network of homes and farms to salvage R.A.F. fliers whose planes were shot down, and even to get them back to England.

The two neutrals, Sweden and Switzerland, are neutral only in name. It is estimated that between eighty and ninety per cent of their peoples are violently anti-Nazi. The concessions which their governments have made on occasion to the Nazis in order to prevent occupation and land blockade, have been met with storms of disapproval from the people. Germans say that Sweden is so pro-English, that "when it rains in London, the people open their umbrellas in Stockholm". In Switzerland, the German Government lodges an average of one protest a week against the Swiss press' editorial comments. The most violently anti-Nazi paper, *die Nation*, has enjoyed an increase of circulation in the past six months of three hundred per cent! In a restaurant in Berne, the capital of Switzerland, last autumn, a Jap who, while drunk, began singing the Nazi *Horst Wessel* song, was mobbed by Swiss soldiers, thrown out of the restaurant and found later dead with his skull fractured. Nobody was ever arrested or tried for the murder.

It is true to say that England has never been more popular on the European continent than she is today. Nor has Germany ever been more hated by her European neighbours than right now. And the Germans know it. Once, in Berlin, I ran into an aged German housewife I know; she was holding her almost empty market-bag in one hand and looking wistfully at a faded, ancient propaganda poster headed "Why They Hate Us . . .", referring to the plutocracies, which was pasted on the side of a house. I asked her what she found so interesting, and she said: "I was only thinking. That used to be a propaganda slogan—'They Hate Us' —but now the Fuehrer has fixed it. They do hate us. The Fuehrer achieves everything." The Germans never allowed their famous red pamphlet on the Kaufmann suggestion to sterilize Germans to be published outside Germany. And the reason is probably because too many people would think the idea a pretty good one, sick as all Europeans are of turmoil and starvation which have been initiated periodically for more than a century from inside Germany. If German troops ever withdraw from the rest of Europe, the Germans know best of all what the result will be. England, America and Russia need dictate no peace. Just leave it to Europe. Germany's neighbours will make all too certain on their own initiative that Germany will never again be able to scourge them with war. Quite sincerely, I would not like to witness what would happen to Berlin if the Norwegians, the Poles and the French were suddenly freed of Gestapo terror and given arms. My stomach is not strong enough.

The spectre haunts Germans day and night. They listen to the B.B.C. and Radio Moscow, and what the enemy says spreads over Germany fast as fire every morning. They have grown deathly sick of being a *Heldenvolk*, and would sell their concession on it cheap. They would rather eat well and regularly, and be simple, ordinary people. I have met but few Germans who were not ready, at any juncture in Hitler's progress, to break off the whole thing and go back to scratch, if they could just have peace. They have learned what the Japanese learned in China: that it takes but one to start a war, but it takes always two to stop one. If they could be guaranteed against the white-hot rage of the Poles, the Norwegians and the French, they would become rather hard for Hitler to handle; hard to keep in the war.

In retrospect, the effect of the Russian war on the sentiments of the German people has been almost revolutionary in its proportions. Excepting the very young, who are an element of the future more than of the present, and the Gestapo, I know of no section or category of the German people that is not sick to death of Nazism. They do not all admit it. Since they can do almost nothing about it, why admit it? Why not keep up the empty pretence of being pro-Nazi, for total despair would be unbearable? The intellectuals—there are still many potentially good specimens—are dead tired of it. In the somewhat Bohemian Kurfuerstendamm area, where I lived, I inevitably mixed with hundreds of petty intellectuals, actors, painters, sculptors, musicians, and those I knew were, without exception, weary of the Nazi straitjacket on the development of their talents. One painter of considerable promise told me just before I left that he hoped we would meet again very soon in a "revolutionary Germany". He said, "We missed a wonderful chance after the last war. This time we've got to sweep out every rotten fibre; it's got to be a total revolution". This was remarkable, coming from a man who, when I first met him, had been a perfect ivory-tower intellectual. The professional classes are weary from sheer physical exertion if from nothing else. They have to work unbelievable hours, especially physicians and dentists; far harder than almost any worker. Their ranks have been decimated by the Russian war, and too many of the young have been steered out of the medical and dental schools into the troops and engineering schools, and as numbers dwindle, their burdens increase, what with spotted typhus and trichinosis—from bad meat—mounting each year in the war-swept East and Poland. Last winter, typhus even crossed the border into Germany itself, and at least fifteen cases were recorded in Berlin in one month. In October, last year, the Reich medical authorities had to issue a general warning to the public against trichinosis.

The sentiments of the workers and the former middle classes have already been described. Recent months have only re-inforced the trend of their morale downwards and their indigna-tion upwards. The confiscation of the "People's Car" factories which tens of thousands of Little Men had built up with their subscriptions to buy the little "People's Cars" whenever produc-tion should begin, has caused considerable anger, and even less disposition to save their funds, or invest them. Their people's cars are being produced all right; you see them in thousands, camou-flaged dull brown, on the streets of Berlin. But they have all been taken over by the army, for use in the African war. All the joy derived from getting immediate benefit from the former campaigns in the form of fur-coats and shoes from Norway and France has been cancelled by this winter's nation-wide collection of fur and woollen things for the troops in the East. The "voluntary" collection was carried out by all forms of pressure on individuals to give up their warm things, even with threats of arrest in some cases. Their nourishment has been further diluted by the intro-duction twice a week in all German restaurants of "Field-mess-meals", which contain only a scrap of meat and absolutely no fat. At the end of winter, for the second time, rations of meat, fat and bread were officially reduced. The reductions are only a *de jure* confirmation of a *de facto* situation.

The winter has brought more open signs of the uneasiness of the old ruling and wealthy classes. Inside the circle of the rich industrialists, power and influence have gradually shifted away from the owners of factories making peace-time and consumption goods, to the smaller, tighter clique of arms producers. From the arms producers power has shifted to the military, and inside the military, every day brings new indications of power slipping away from the regular army and its officers to the Nazi army and its officers. It is symbolic of the development, that Hitler decorated the commander of his expanding S.S. bodyguard, *Obergruppen-fuehrer* Sepp Dietrich, with the oak-leaf to the Knight's Cross on the Iron Cross, Germany's highest military decoration, on the first of January, 1942. It has also become conspicuous that Hitler's proclamations and orders-of-the-day to his troops are no longer simply addressed to the "Soldiers of the German Wehrmacht", but to "Soldiers of the Wehrmacht, and of the *Waffen S.S.*". On the occasion of the German Heroes' Memorial Day, when Hitler spoke in the old Arsenal on Unter den Linden, in March this year, the *S.S. in Arms* appeared for the first time in Nazi history as a distinct, separate arm of the German armed forces, on a par with the other three. Hitler reviewed a parade of honour guards of his forces which included not only units of the Luftwaffe, the Navy and the Army, but also one of the Gestapo army. It would appear that not only the old middle classes, but also the old upper classes are gradually being shoved downward in influence; their firm, deep roots are being undermined in the fabric of German society. Of all the conflicts in the Nazi system; this one can bear, at the present time, most watching. A reconciliation of sorts seems to have been attained inside the palace of the High Command, but its precariousness is indubitable. Mistrust between the two rulers can only have been aggravated by the most recent measures.

Enthusiasm has gone from every quarter. The bright decorations with which Nazism, for lack of real solutions, embellished German society, have grown musty and old in a remarkably short time, just as cheap tinsel and cheap toys grow old in a short time. National Socialism, the theory without content, is being outstripped by its own emptiness. Many famous names connected with its happy days of triumph, with the climax of militarism, have disappeared: Prien, the first hero of the war, Kretschmer, Moelders, Udet, Todt, Hess, von Reichenau, and dozens of others. The rapid falling of these names from the roll of the living great have only emphasized the decomposition in the minds of the people. After the death of the most popular of these, 29-year-old Werner Moelders, a letter he is said to have written in defence of Catholicism circulated throughout Germany. Whether the letter is genuine or not is of little consequence. What matters is that it circulated like wildfire and was believed —so much so that the Gestapo offered £5,000 for the capture of its alleged forger. It means that the people are ready to believe such things, whether they are true or not. The German people is unconsciously seeking a hard core around which to build its discontent; a leader to voice its misery. Hitler is winning himself to death not only beyond Germany's borders, but inside of them. Each new conquest takes him farther from his people. The great open space between him and his popular following widens each day he becomes more embroiled in world conquest. Even the Fuehrer himself is showing marks of the transition. He has aged years in the months of the Russian war. The circles under the pouches of his eyes have deepened, his jowls are perceptibly looser due to the strain of worry and work, and his slight double chin is growing into a limp bag of skin. Last year a military cameraman told me the Fuehrer no longer allows close-ups to be taken of his face. The last full-face portrait taken of him was in 1940, the year of greatest triumph. The blue prints for the world's biggest arch of triumph, to be built outside Berlin, are gathering dust somewhere on a shelf in Professor Speer's many offices. But the maps on which the Gestapo records the number and location of its arsenals throughout the Berlin residential district are not gathering any dust.

Revolution in Germany? The question has been put to me so often since I have come out of Germany—How? Under what circumstances? How soon?—that I cannot forbear mentioning the subject. I do not claim to be an authority. But if you want my opinion here it is. I think revolution in Germany, even without decisive military triumph of our side, is possible. I think it is even possible by, or during next winter; but I fear it is not probable, for I do not believe my suggestions to bring it about would be accepted or carried out.

The best possible way to induce revolution inside Germany remains the military way; a decisive allied triumph. The next best thing is a succession of military triumphs which, though not decisive, would be painful in the extreme to the German army and its people. Just look what Russia's successes have done to Nazism in a very brief time. If these could be reinforced by a large scale invasion plan, carried out simultaneously at several points on the European coast, in the West, it would, without being decisive, induce a paralyzing fear in German hearts. I am not a military strategist and I do not know all the factors of relative strengths, so I have no means of adjudging the possibility of this being done.

The third best thing, if either of these is not feasible, is to aid Russia to the hilt in every way, in labour, in arms, funds and spirit. Again, here I do not know all the factors involved, if our leaders are doing all that is possible, or too little, and if so, why too little is being done. But one criticism I think is justified, and it involves both leaders and peoples of the democracies: there is still too much slack in our war effort. We have not yet begun fighting a total war. Regarding spirit, effort, and sacrifice, there are still miles of slack to be taken up in America, and too much even in England. This criticism is all the easier to make, now that we have seen how a truly noble people wages total war: the Russian people in defence of their native soil. We are coming to realize Russia's many virtues, but not yet in sufficient measure. In Spain and China, Russia was accused of the awful sin of "interventionism". Now we learn that a little intervention on Russia's side on our part might have saved us lots, in place of the policy of providing Japan, for twenty years, with just the materials for guns and bullets she is now shooting at us. The purge of the Russian army and state of "Quislings" long before that term was created, but at a time when Quislings and fifth columnists in every nation were working for Hitler, earned volumes of indignation from our side. We now learn that the elimination of a few well-chosen quislings, duly tried by the democratic processes of law, might have saved the lives of thousands of our best sons. Had Russia not "liquidated" a few thousand officers and bureaucrats, there is little doubt that the Red Army *would* have collapsed in two months, and left us holding a bag, many times bigger, containing Hitler and all Europe, and most of Asia. Had we liquidated a few, the war might never have happened. Russia's sole error in foreign policy, the attack on Finland, was, without a doubt, brought about 'by the fear Russians have justly suffered from for years that somehow, through some corner of her borders, the war would be carried into Russia. That, too, we could have avoided had we conscientiously removed Russia's fear of attack by giving her a suitable place among us.

But Russia's proudest virtues have been exhibited not in peace, but in war. The Russians have tried to teach us a lesson in the art of holding towns, but we have not yet fully learned it. The defence of Moscow, Leningrad and Odessa, no less than the defence of every little town and hamlet inside Russia, have been lessons in total defence. Frankly, I do not blame the Russian newspaper, *Pravda*, for growing editorially indignant at the manner in which we have given up Manila and Singapore. If we are going to fight a total war and win it, we have got to learn to fight it with total spirit and effort. When the Germans take a Russian town they first have to remove the dead Russian bodies that block the approaches to the town, before they can get inside. When the Ger-

mans took Minsk, the fact was announced in the Propaganda
Ministry on the day of the occupation. Next day, the Russians announced that they and not the Germans held Minsk. Next day the
Germans announced the Russians were liars and Minsk was in
German hands. This went on for three more days. When the facts
were finally revealed in Berlin, it turned out that both the Russians and the Germans had been telling the actual truth. After a
bitter, bloody battle, the Germans entered Minsk one afternoon.
They slept that night in their panzers and trucks because the
town was too infested with mines to take a chance of sleeping in
the few remaining houses. That night, dead Russian bodies came
alive, and buried Red soldiers unburied themselves. Silently they
stabbed the sentries and equally as silently deposited dynamite in
each panzer, and eliminated the whole occupation force in an
hour! The Germans attacked and recaptured Minsk the next day,
and the Russians threw them out again in twelve hours. In five
days, the town of Minsk changed hands five times! Minsk cost the
Germans hundreds of times its worth. That is defence!

The Russians even fight after death, by means of mines.
They have become the most successful land-mine layers ever
known. After the Germans killed the very last Russian defending
Kharkov in the Ukraine, it was twenty-two days before any German soldier but a handful of engineers, specially trained in removing mines, could enter the city. For twenty-two days, German
panzers had to make a wide and costly detour around the city to
advance further eastward. German soldier-reporters say the Russians mine everything. One cannot even turn on a water-tap
without being blown to Hades. American correspondents who
were taken to Odessa a few days after it fell, said they could hear
an average of two explosions, from different parts of the town,
each hour, although there was not a living Russian in the town.
The correspondents were invited to spend the night in the safest
place in Odessa, a large building where the General Staff of the
Rumanian army had established quarters. They chose, however,
to spend the night in the suburbs, and surely enough, that night
they heard a deafening explosion, and learned an hour later that
the whole headquarters of the Rumanian general staff had been
blown to hell, and with it most of the Rumanian general staff!

Again, it must be remembered that among the most spirited
fighters against Nazism are those people in the occupied lands of

Europe. The concentration camps of Germany itself contain a goodly number of individuals who could teach us lessons in total war against Hitler. These last have been carrying our banner and fighting our battle for almost a decade, through most of which we were sleeping or even making fun of them. I cannot help saying it: we have still not reached their level of spirit; we are still not wide awake. We are still living too comfortably on the time they have all given us to prepare ourselves. We have got to wake up, and fight the Nazis with all the strength of our souls and bodies. We've got to beat them until they scream with anguish and pain. The methods are left to the military men. If they cannot find them, then let us have new military men who can find methods. No personality is sacred. The strength, the spirit and the effort is our job.

In war, the main way to crush an enemy remains the military way—making more and better arms, and fighting harder and better. There is little that is new in the foregoing; I simply want to add my voice to those who believe we are not doing enough for our allies and our cause. However, there is something else that can be done to shorten the war and defeat the Nazis.

In the course of this book I have been driving towards this point and I should now like to make the point clear as daylight: something has happened to the German people. A change of almost revolutionary proportions has occurred underneath the surface of the Nazi state, among the broad masses of the people. The people have lost their roots in the existing state. When a state ceases to serve the needs and likes of the majority of its people, then it is ripe for revolution. The Nazi state has ceased to serve the needs of fully ninety per cent of the German people. In 1933, when Hitler came to power, he was closely tied to a vast number of the people: the wealthy and the broad middle classes and a small, very small fraction of the workers. Year by year, his ties to the people have been attenuated. He paid attention to their affairs less and less as he built up his army. The breach between them broadened slowly for seven years of peace. The war hastened the growth of the gap, and the Russian war has made it a chasm. Today, no Nazi leaders of any importance, except the police and Goebbels, have any interest in the affairs of the people. The Nazis have systematically cut themselves off from their popular basis; and it is only on the people that any state can nourish itself. Nazism is a hard, petrified hull around a coreless fruit, or one which is rotten inside.

This war has graduated almost every nation in the world from potential anti-Nazis to actual anti-Nazis. But the most important single development of the Russian war period has been to graduate the German people themselves into potential anti-Nazis. There are two reasons why they are only potential anti-Nazis and will probably remain only potential anti-Nazis unless we wake up to what has happened inside the land of our enemy. I have already mentioned both, but they bear greater emphasis. The first and lesser of the two reasons is the Gestapo. The Gestapo is mighty and will see that resistance remains potential as long as possible. The second, and far, far more important of the two, is Fear, the stark Terror of what will happen to them if they and the Nazis lose the war.

The minds of the vast majority of the German people are open to suggestion. The evidence that they are ready for an alternative is overwhelming. Why has the Gestapo seen fit to set up arsenals in residential Berlin? Why were the Storm troops dissolved and why does Hitler constantly strengthen his personal army, each member of which is sworn to die, not for Germany, but for him and Nazism? Or why have the Germans who listen to foreign radio broadcasts multiplied in number in six short months? The answer to all these questions is not that the German people are going to revolt tomorrow, for they have nothing to revolt for; but that they are open to suggestion! But nobody makes any suggestions. Telling them in our wireless propaganda that the Nazis are bad is as utterly stupid as the policies of those "Peace Leagues" which used to tell the world that peace is a good thing. Everybody knows that peace is a good thing; what people want to know is how to get peace. The mass of the German people have realized that the Nazis are not a good thing, but what else is there? They are open to alternatives, but nobody offers any. The only alternatives they know are: win with the Nazis and save themselves from the horrors of defeat at the hands of a world which hates them, or lose with the Nazis and suffer those horrors. A fate apart from the fate of Nazism is contained in none of our promises nor our propaganda. Instead, we offer them Mr. Kaufmann and the sterilization of the whole German people. We permit a few High Churchmen to demand in public the total destruction of the German people. And so the German people fight and offer their lives to save their families—and incidentally the Nazis—from total destruction; and they work their hands to the bone to make the guns the Nazis need. And the war will go on for a needless number of years because the German people are afraid.

Our attitude towards Germans is too much governed by our belief in a concept called the "German Mentality". Our idea is that there is a certain twist of mind which is born into Germans, which inevitably makes them warlike and want war. Let jingoists and brass-band-patriots hold their spleen. I am not trying to whitewash the enemy. I agree that there is this kind of mentality which is inducive to war. I agree that wherever it is discovered it should be annihilated by merciless brute force. I agree that it exists, and in the course of this book, I have been trying to point out where it exists and which minds possess it. They are: (*a*) the old Prussians, the militarists and the arms-makers alike. Krupp has it. Von Rundstedt, von Bock and von Leeb, the Blitz Triplets, have it, and with them, hundreds of thousands of other stiff-necked, bemonocoled "von's". My considered recommendation is sudden death by the firing squad, or the noose, or the axe. (*b*) Hitler, Ley, Goebbels, Goering, Ribbentrop have it. Himmler and his hundred thousand young men who would kick their grandmother's teeth out if Himmler ordered it, have it too. There lies the War Mentality. War is their education, their religion and their food and drink. They are destructive, anti-social, diseased, warped, and utterly useless to this world of men. They must be destroyed, and one need not be finicky about the methods.

But I deny that there is any war mentality in the mass of the German people. The German people do not like war any more than we do. Who was scared stiff during the Munich crisis? Not Hitler, Goering and Himmler; they were just itching to hear the heroic music of cannon-fire and bursting bombs. They were probably a wee bit disappointed when we gave in so easily, but, doubtless, they promised themselves to do better next time. But the German people were paralyzed with fear. More than the victimized Czechs or the British. Remember when after the world war our slogan was Hang the Kaiser? Well, however strange it may sound, I am entirely in favour of the Hang the Kaiser policy. It was a good one. But why in the name of common sense, did we not carry it out and hang the Kaiser and all he stood for? Why didn't we hang the Prussian generals, and Krupp, Thyssen, von Borsig, Huebermann and perhaps half a million or so others?

Anyhow, we didn't. We left the hard-fisted old men to thrive, to have their spirits mellowed one day by the creamy words of a brown-shirted paranoiac, and free to start another war. Instead of Hanging the Kaiser, we hanged the German people. We were like the doctor who opened up the side of a patient for an appendectomy, but became confused and cut out the patient's stomach instead of his infected appendix. Let's discover our error before the operation, instead of after it, this time.

I know that it is unpopular to say so at this moment of tension and hate, but it is true that there is still lots of good solid stuff in the German people. If we intend to win not only the war, but also the peace, and set up a new and better world, a lot of Germans are going to be among its best components. A lot of Germans are just aching to help make a better world. In order to win them from Nazism to our side and end the war sooner, we've got to offer them a part in the better world. Thus far, we have not done so. Whatever the virtues of our leaders, Roosevelt, Churchill and Stalin, their 13-point programme, which the two former created and Stalin subscribed to, is not definite enough, and does not make clear enough the inclusion of the German people, minus Nazism, in the scheme. Stalin's recent statement to the effect that the "German People Must Pay" has not helped the situation any, nor has Eden's subscription to that slogan. I repeat again that this is only my personal opinion; but I am convinced of its validity, and, since I am writing for readers in a democratic country, I am entitled to express it and to try and win converts. I know full well how hard it is for the Russians to conjure up an attitude of constructive forgiveness towards people who make the shells and bombs which have wrecked their land and killed their hard-working citizens; and I know how hard it is for British subjects who have suffered torture under Nazi bombing raids to stifle a well-earned desire for vengeance. And, certainly, I am not asking for a softening of our military attacks, by air, land or sea against Germany. In fact, I want to see the Germans beaten until they howl and scream with anguish. I know those things. But also, after long, close, experience with the German people, I know this: unless the British, the Russians and the Americans offer, with deep sincerity, to the German people another way out besides life or death with Nazism, this war is going to last for an unnecessarily long time, and the Germans, to avoid their horrible fate, are going to fight it with the reckless spirit of men who have absolutely nothing to lose but their lives! Every time we call for the annihilation of the German people as our only war aim, we are actually pouring gunpowder into Nazi cannon to be shot at us. I suggest giving the German people something more important than their lives to lose—namely, a better place in a new, better world—and I will wager anything that the European war will be over within a year after we have adopted and carried out the scheme!

What to offer them as an alternative? If we say we have no alternative to offer them, then let's call the whole thing off. Let's quit right now. If we can offer nothing new, then why fight at all? We are simply wasting a lot of good blood and sweat and tears. Shall we offer them what they had before 1933? If we do, we shall not find many takers. After a decade of Nazism in Germany, the world is all too inclined to consider the era before 1933 in Germany a glimpse of paradise, which it was not on any interpretation. Shall we offer them what we had before the war, in 1939, just a few years ago? Not even our own people will accept that, with its millions of unemployed, with those pathetic depressed areas in South Wales. No. We have got to make up our minds right now that, however much it hurts the sensibilities and pocket-books of our wealthy privileged classes, changes have got to be made at home. My propaganda scheme to win over the German people and shorten the war is more than a propaganda scheme. We've got to prove it to them by offering them concrete examples of what we mean to do. For instance—if I may suggest specific details of a plan to knock the Nazis lop-sided without firing a single bullet more than we would ordinarily fire—why not nationalize those Welsh mines we promised to nationalize during the last war, but never nationalized? Why not do it tomorrow morning? The mere publication of the fact would kill more Nazis than a thousand bombs on Germany. You, who have not been in Germany and forced to read reams of Nazi propaganda every day, have no idea how often the Nazis have used those mines to show how few real ideas England possesses for a better world. The Nazis cite them on every occasion (while their own coal capitalists draw six per cent, and two and three times six per cent for every pfennig of coal sold). Or let us go one better than Senator Nye's plan in America, and take the munitions industries out of the hands of private individuals and put them in the hands of the State which is not allowed to draw or distribute private profits per cannon. If we did that today, Krupp would be the deadest man in Germany in a week. Not physically dead, but, like Dr. Goebbels, spiritually dead, which is the main thing. We can shoot them both later. But let us make our war aims to shoot Dr. Goebbels and Krupp known now as war aims. Let us make all our war aims equally specific.

I know there is a large school of opinion which maintains, "Let's not confuse things by working out war aims now. Let us defeat Hitler first. That is the main thing. If Hitler wins, our war aims are no good anyhow. So let's worry about beating Hitler first, and talk about our New Order after Hitler has been beaten".

That is an argument which has too wide an appeal. There is a fallacy in it which may be decisive as to whether we shall win or lose the war. The true feature about it is this: the main job before us is to defeat Hitler. The fallacy about it is contained in this: one of the best ways, if not the best way of all, to defeat Hitler is to *make our war aims, our blue print for a new world, known as definitely and clearly as possible to our own people, to the German people and to the world right now!*

Nothing will take the wind out of the Nazi sails so quickly as that. More than that, the publication of a detailed revolutionary programme for democracy, both political and economic, will inspire our own people. It will take up the slack that remains between us and a total effort to win the war. It will make our allies, both those who are free and those whose lands are occupied, more vigorous warriors for our cause. Once, when I was in France, after France had been defeated and occupied, I visited an old Alsatian priest whom I have known for years. It was before the Russian war offered its spark of hope of salvation to the French. The old priest, shaking with fervour, told me: "Go back and tell them. You can; I cannot. Tell them we hate the Nazis; but we are not going to fight because we like plum-pudding better than we like *Apfelstrudel*. Give us a lead; give us a slogan and an idea. Give us something to fight for, and I promise you the armies will form; they will rise out of the very earth"!

We have a golden opportunity before us. We have a chance to rally all Europe to our side, including the Germans. This is no exaggeration; I know it. People were saying rather nasty things in

France about the English and the Americans, after the fall of France in 1940. For witnesses I can call specifically on Joseph Harsch of the *Christian Science Monitor*, Percy Knauth of the *New York Times*, and Edward Shankey of the *Associated Press*, who walked with me and talked to the French people with me in those days in Northern France. They were calling us "hypocrites", and adopting Nazi propaganda slogans themselves. They do not want to go back to what France was. They, too, want something new; an idea, but one with real content. Since the Russian war, some of them have changed, and have begun fighting. If we can now offer them an idea and a slogan with meaning, the armies will, I am sure of it, rise out of the very earth. Inside Germany, it would break the hearts of the last believers in Nazism, and can turn potential anti-Nazis into actual anti-Nazis. Real proof of our democratic intent, like the nationalization of the mines, the socialization of the munitions and heavy industries, the banishment of privilege, the placing of less developed colonies under a truly international mandate—not a British or an American mandate—would convince Germany and our own people we are fighting a true war to make the world safe for democracy.

I know Germans and I know hundreds of German student-friends who are in the mighty German Wehrmacht well enough to visualize the general sequence of events after that. The people cannot start a revolution spontaneously as spontaneous combustion. For you have to have guns in order to revolt with effect, and the German people have no guns. But the soldiers have. The reason Hitler is hastening the process of constructing a purely personal army is because the soldiers, who are human beings and susceptible to suggestion, do have guns. Visualize what happens, yourself (and there is good reason to believe that this is almost exactly the way Hitler has visualized it): the soldiers fight at the front, and they fight hard and well. They do not want to lose, for they know what it means to lose. Excepting the *Waffen S.S.*, German soldiers are human beings and worry seriously about their families and wives at home. Then, they go home on leave, tired, weary and perhaps wounded. Home-leave, which should be restful and rejuvenating, is not. For people at home are hungry and discontented. (This is no hypothesis; this is fact right now.) Also, the families at home, who listen to the B.B.C. and Radio Moscow, are talking about a possible alternative to Hitler. Or, if they do not listen to the foreign radio, they have heard it by rumour; it is remarkable how fast rumours circulate in Germany; it is in fact a sign of the times, a further proof of the decay of German morale. The soldiers need not be convinced. But they go back to the front with the trace of a doubt in their minds. The only ray of hope, which was that of Nazism, has a competitor for their minds. Beside Nazism, in their mind's eye, there stands another image. They are inevitably less willing to die for Hitler so long as that other disturbing suggestion is in their minds. And a soldier who is less willing to die for his leaders and nation than before is a soldier who fights less efficiently than before. The soldiers who experience the sensation mention it, off-hand, to their comrades in arms. Doubts—very mild doubts—spread, but they inevitably express themselves in audible words from time to time. Officers grow afraid and arrest soldiers for "defeatist utterances". This makes other soldiers angry, and increases the ranks of those who doubt. For it is true that there is no *Kameradschaft* so strong as the comradeship of common soldiers who have been through fire together. Meantime, other soldiers are going home on leave, and coming back disgruntled because home-leave wasn't so pleasant, and they, too, are worried by doubts. Eventually, some officer, on the look-out for defeatism, gets his nose bashed in by a dyspeptic soldier, and the soldier is shot as an example. The other soldiers get mad, and a couple of other officers get their noses bashed in, or an insolent young Prussian lieutenant gets stabbed in the back one night while nobody is looking, and tension increases on both sides. Note that all the time, defence is less effective, and we have chances to get in a few good hard blows. We can even make them retreat, perhaps in confusion, because so many are less willing to hold their ground and die for their leaders. Anger and differences grow in a retreating army, unless the retreat is as thoroughly planned as the Russian retreat was. There are more nasty remarks by soldiers, and more reprisals by officers. So the process goes on. It is familiar, because it can happen in any army which is composed of human beings with an empty cause, *but who are offered an alternative cause.* One can trace its path right back to isolated revolts of detachments and battalions; then to regiments and divisions, from thence to national revolt, civil war, and revolution.

This is no day-dream. It is possible now as never before. It means not only the creation of clever propaganda slogans on our part. It means inducing our privileged classes to sacrifice their privileges. If they are not willing to make the sacrifices right down to, and beyond, the last yacht, and the last ten race-horses, then they must be forced. And if our leaders do not want to force them, then let us have some other leaders. The only thing that is sacred is the lives of our soldiers out on the front, and their future—the future of all of them, whatever their nationality—in our world to come after we have defeated Hitler.

The slogan for our campaign to beat Hitler's Totalitarianism, might be *Total Democracy*. But Total Democracy must also be an idea plump with meaty content. Total Democracy means both political and economic democracy. Let us clear up terms. Democracy, the system we have been fighting for a century and a half to gain, protect and perfect, is a system of society in which each individual citizen represents approximately one unit of power. *Political* Democracy is a state of affairs in which each individual possesses one unit of *political* power; which is just another way of saying each person has one vote to use in all kinds of political elections and on political issues. In America and England we have achieved, with some imperfections, a system of political democracy. We have fought a long time to get it; the English fought their way through the three great Reform Bills; the Americans won part of it in the revolutionary war against George III, part of it in the Civil War between the states, and part of it in individual struggles within each state of the American union. But we have obtained it, and it is worth preserving, for it gives us a lot of real power to protect our civil rights, and real power to make and break governments, and, at least, theoretically, the right to alter the whole system of society.

The other constituent of Total Democracy is Economic Democracy, which is a state of affairs in which each individual has approximately one unit of *Economic* power. That means, a state of affairs in which there are no vast differences in incomes. There can be differences; differences of as much as 10 to 1 are not too great; but the differences cannot be as great as they are in America and England today if we are to become Total Democracies. For instance, Mr. J. P. Morgan possesses several million units of economic power, in the form of funds left over after he has satisfied his bare necessities, and these he can use to influence state and national governments on big issues. On the other hand,

my friend, Steve Smith, a dock-worker in New Orleans, possesses
no units at all of economic power. After he has paid the rent and
bought food from his pay-check, there is nothing left to influence
governments on big issues. Now, to show you how economically
undemocratic this is: there are in Mr. Morgan's group of citizens,
perhaps 10,000 people who can rank anywhere near him in
economic influence; 10,000 rich people who live by owning things
and drawing profits from what they own. But on the side of Steve
Smith there are between fifty and eighty million citizens, who live
by hard labour and own nothing, and have no units whatever of
economic power. The 10,000 Morgans can use their vast
economic power to influence and run governments in many ways.
Take the single example of electing a national president. In
America a president is elected not by votes alone, but also by
money. It takes upwards of ten million dollars to elect a president.
After the Steve Smiths have taken care of their necessities, they
have little or nothing to contribute to the fund to influence an
election. But the Morgans can pay ten millions and more, and
they do. (This is not meant to be specifically a criticism of
President Roosevelt's election. For once in our history, we have
got in our present leader a man who is not only not entirely
dependent on wealth, but has also had the courage to oppose
wealth and privilege on innumerable issues. However, it remains
an actuality in respect to every one of our past presidents from
Lincoln's day on; and it remains a potent factor in future elections.) They can also entertain senators and "lobby" for con-
gressional acts which are beneficial to their own accumulation of
more wealth. They can influence all the means of moulding
public opinion; buy big newspaper concerns or influence them
through advertising, get time on the wireless, and so on, to
increase their power. Neither in England nor in America do we
possess Economic Democracy.

We in America and England have actually possessed a hybrid
system of Political Democracy alongside Economic Autocracy for
the past century and a half. We are not Total Democrats, but the
time is ripe to become Total Democrats, and beat Hitler in the
bargain. In fact, we must make up our minds as to which of the
two systems we are going to follow. Political Democracy cannot
live for long in the same state with Economic Autocracy. Their co-
habitation is illogical, unstable and, in the long run, impossible.

Either the political side of life must give up its democratic content and adjust itself to the Autocratic Economic set-up, or the economic side of our social life must cease to be autocratic and adapt itself to the democracy of our political system. Adolf Hitler writes in *Mein Kampf* his agreement with this analysis. He writes that, if Political Democracy in any state is allowed to develop to its logical conclusion, it will develop into Economic Democracy—Socialism, which he calls by his favourite scare-word, Bolshevism. The essence of the Hitler system, of Nazism and all forms of Fascism is to prevent Political Democracy from achieving its logical consequence; to destroy political democracy and align the political side of life with the Autocratic Economic side of life—that is so that the masses of the people shall have neither economic nor political power. If you want to know what Hitler said in his speech to the Ruhr Industrialists in the magic Dusseldorf meeting where he won the support of wealth, he promised them just this. He said, in effect: Gentlemen, your way of life is in a state of crisis. Things are so bad that the people are going eventually to make use of their political power to destroy you and your economic power; unless you destroy their political power first. Now, with your financial aid, I can destroy their political democracy. Fot I have a set of ideas and slogans which will be popular with a large section of the people. But I need money for propaganda, money for uniforms and weapons. So, gentlemen, take your choice: eventual destruction of you and your way of life, or rescue, by me, and a flourishing arms business to revive your dying industries, and the conquest of markets and colonies in the outside world to keep your industries going later. Why Dr. Dietrich expressed surprise at the way the hard old faces of the hard old men softened up and became wreathed in smiles I cannot understand; there is no ground for surprise.

The same crisis has presented itself in every nation in Europe, and in most of them elsewhere. The history of the world since the last World War has been, in fact, a chronicle of the struggle between Totalitarianism and Total Democracy. At first, the elements in favour of Total Democracy gained the upper hand, and socialist governments established themselves in each nation and began trying to make the economic side of life democratic. They were, alas, too weak, and did not work in unison. In their disorganized, timid condition, the wealthy and the Men on Horseback were able to eliminate one weak-kneed socialist government after another. The trend was reversed in favour of Totalitarianism. Dollfuss killed political democracy in Austria, the socialists died in Hungary, Mussolini smashed them in Italy, Hitler in Germany, Franco in Spain, and so on. The lights of Democracy went out all over Europe. But Totalitarian Fascism offers no solution to the problems their states were suffering from except blood, destruction and world conquest. That, in a word, is what is happening! But the whole point of this book is that, now, the people of the totalitarian countries are coming to see they were badly deceived. They have lost interest in what is a false solution. The time is ripe to offer them Total Democracy, now that they have tried Totalitarian Fascism and it has failed. The people keep on fighting because they fear loss of the war to a world that hates them, more than they fear the loss of their individual lives. But they are sick and they are susceptible to suggestion. Total Democracy, including them as full-fledged members, would have an enormous appeal. They must be told in a detailed programme that after the war, they will have the support of every Total Democratic nation, with raw materials and all else, to make useful things; but arms will be taboo, for they are useless and only form another incentive to war.

While we offer them the slogan, we must hit and bomb hard to break the hearts of those who are not yet ready for revolt. While we offer them the slogans we must carry out a series of dramatic actions in our own lands to prove to them that we mean what we say about Total Democracy. Make the Welsh coal mines national property tomorrow morning. Don't worry that the German people will not hear about it. They will. The fact will be on everybody's lips by noon. Nationalize the arms factories. Don't just begin buying up a few shares for what is called "gradual socialization". That is not dramatic enough. Pass one single law commandeering the arms factories for the state for evermore. Call a conference of colonials—the Filipinos, the Indians, the Sudanese, the Egyptians—to discuss which shall become completely independent next month, and which shall be placed under real international mandates with the aim of educating them to independence within a year, or perhaps five years. Call a conference of the nations which will educate them, and make it include everybody: the Russians, the Chinese, the British, Americans,

Portuguese, Mexicans; everybody! Do this and more. And just watch the morale of the Welsh, the Indians, the Egyptians and the English and Americans rise; and watch the fighting power of Hitler's armies decline.

The time to preach and achieve Total Democracy is now. It will not only win the war for us, but it will also win the peace, which is more important. Accept the suggestion, and watch the Nazis decompose. Hitler will probably sacrifice himself in some manner of *Heldentod* at the front. There will be weeping and gnashing of teeth among the enemies of civilization. We have nothing to lose but a handful of parasites, and we have the world to win. Or don't accept it, and let's continue fighting a lot of frightened Germans and Italians for the next three or four years of hunger, disease and destruction; unless the Germans win sooner than that.

A reporter is a person who is paid a salary—a high-toned name for wages—to go places and see things and write about them or talk about them. He is not paid to say what he thinks about what he sees and hears; he just sees and hears and describes. To get facts reporters risk their health and necks in Mississippi floods, bar-room brawls, and in Nazi Germany. They see and learn an amazing lot of things. But the canons of their profession decree that they shall only tell what they see, rather than what they learn. Drawing conclusions from events, and suggesting action on the basis of these conclusions is reserved to what are called editorial or "leader" writers, or radio "commentators", who are all men who have their own offices separate from the rest and learn what they learn by reading the reports of reporters. But, now and then, by some mischance, an ordinary leg-reporter gets his hands on an opportunity and a typewriter and writes not what he has seen but what he thinks about it. That is a rare moment, and the reporter enjoys every luscious syllable of it. The foregoing is my first editorial.

EPILOGUE

A FAREWELL TO BERLIN

THE LAST MONTHS in Berlin were an odd experience. For all of us—the eighteen remaining American correspondents from an original corps of about fifty—life was exasperatingly temporary. We never planned for the week-end nor even for the day after tomorrow. The Gestapo might come any day. Some tense days when American ships had been sunk in the Atlantic, we lived from hour to hour. Jack Fleischer took to greeting me at the breakfast table each morning when dawn, the visiting hour of the Gestapo, was safely behind us, with the observation that, well, that was one more night behind us, and here was one more twenty-four hours ahead of us. Living that way is not good for the nerves. But Jack had an amazing knack of finding stray bottles of schnaps in strange places even after the shops were emptied, which helped the nerves considerably.

Excepting our dispatches and scripts, we wrote nothing. All stray scraps of paper were destroyed, and notes were torn up as soon as their immediate usefulness was over. My desk I emptied of everything except a few pencils and pens and a bottle of ink. I even erased notes and pencil-marks from books in our bookcase. There was nothing suspicious in any of them, but the precaution might have saved days of answering questions to Gestapo men, should they ever have decided they did not like the colour of our ties and picked one of us up one morning. When we talked to friends over the telephone, we could occasionally hear the grinding of an intermediary dictaphone in the receiver. Telephone conversations were curt and to the point, composed with respect for the rampant imagination of the Gestapo, so as to avoid suspicion, arrest, and further tedious investigation.

Pretty much the same spirit pervaded the American Embassy. Not even the Embassy escaped over-close Gestapo attention. Once last year, Gestapo agents entered the Embassy and demanded to see the ladies' rest room. Puzzled Embassy officials readily showed them the room, and the Gestapo men went away disappointed. The grounds for the raid were blue-prints of the

Embassy building on which an architect had designated the ladies' room as the *Pulverkammer*. To the architect, the word *Pulverkammer* meant the room where women powder their noses. To the Gestapo, which had studied the blue-prints and knew German better, the word meant "Powder-magazine"! All unnecessary papers in the Embassy were destroyed, and the most important files and equipment packed away in wooden crates to wait for the inevitable day. The Embassy staff was reduced to a skeleton. Actually, there was little for the Embassy to do. Diplomatic relations with the German government were, in actuality, broken off many months before. They could not protect the interests of Americans in Germany, for the Germans refused to concede that the Americans in Germany deserved any protection. When they approached the Foreign Office on some matter, they were seen by some petty official, who listened to them as a matter of form, then, on orders, forgot about what they had said. Lodging a protest with the German Foreign Office had the same effect as dropping the protest in the nearest manhole and forgetting about it.

We were outcasts, and a friendly enemy in the Propaganda Ministry told me: "Your situation is anomalous. We do not want you here and you do not want to stay. Why don't you leave"? That was very blunt, but there was never an official suggestion to that effect, and we stuck around to see and write whatever we could see and write. The situation inevitably produced some of the best cases of Berlin Blues of the whole war-period. Men, grown men, separated from their wives, and sick of dull, grey Berlin and longing to see a few bright lights, actually wept real tears of anguish. In hotels, bar-tenders remained friendly and shook their heads futilely when we talked together about the unavoidable break.

One fruit of the miserable situation was the growth of a strong *esprit de corps*, which is not easy to develop among competing correspondents. The agency men began moving together. For two years, Pierre Huss of I.N.S., and I had maintained a little personal feud. But when the pinch settled down we buried the hatchet and forgot the past. Alex Small of the *Chicago Tribune*, who is generally willing to develop a feud with anybody and with as many anybodies as possible, became downright sentimental and friendly. The American Embassy commiserated with us and, for the first time, supplied us with foodstuffs from America. For, even on our own doubled rations, German food was not too nourishing or tasty. As a result, we took to eating at our homes and abandoning the restaurants and press clubs. I, in fact, became one of the few regular visitors to the press clubs I loathed; I got a nasty pleasure out of watching the insolence wear off the faces of the little bureaucrats who ate there, as the Russian war proceeded.

Aside from food most of our other needs went unsatisfied. The clothing crisis was severe. I was almost in rags. I was saved from being totally ragged by the kindness of a few departing friends. Steve Laird, of *Time* magazine, left me a suit when he returned to America. From departing agency men I bought a few shirts and several pairs of socks (most of which had been patched and re-patched several times). Mrs. George Axelsson, the wife of the *New York Times* correspondent, brought me a pair of shoes from Stockholm. From the wife of a Gestapo man, who had just come from France, I bought an overcoat, and I inherited Bill Shirer's sweater. Oddly, I was earning ten times my first wages as a re-porter, and three times as much as I had earned when I had first arrived in Berlin, but I had the appearance of a beggar. There was simply nothing to buy in Berlin.

Others were hit hard by the housing shortage. Alex Dreier was forced to give up his apartment and begged the United Press to allow him to sleep on a cot in the U.P. offices, until he found a room resembling a stable hay-loft. One American arranged to share a corner of a room with German friends. Jean Graffis made arrangements to sleep in his car, when he lost his apartment on Olivaer Platz, but was saved when he found a chance single room in a pension. Fleischer and I kept our apartment, but the furni-ture was sold out from under us, so to speak, and for months our only furniture consisted of two beds, a couple of straight chairs and a broken wireless set. When friends came we simply dropped a few pillows on the floor and sat there. Our crockery was in a pitiful state and it was impossible to buy any more. We possessed exactly one water glass, and treated it with love and care as though it were the Holy Grail. I bought a few forks and knives before the shops stopped selling them, but they bent or cracked in half after a little pressure. So, we proceeded to live temporary existences, planning nothing, doing nothing except our daily labours, and hoping the end would come soon. But circumstance was stubborn and neither Roosevelt nor Hitler seemed willing to take the final, formal step.

In intervals, when I was not banned from the air for some misdemeanour or another, I continued writing radio scripts and broadcasting to America. But every day, the censors grew more sensitive, and the Propaganda Ministry tabooed one category of stories after another. We were forbidden to mention the anti-Jewish measures. We were not allowed to report the execution of Czech patriots or of French "communists" and hostages. The suggestion by the assistant Gestapo chief, Heydrich, that a "people's espionage service" be instituted in every building in Germany was struck from our scripts. We were not allowed to mention the beating up of Americans for talking English on the streets of Berlin. We were not allowed to say Nazi, but had to use the full title, National Socialist, and it was forbidden to say any German source *claimed* or *asserted* something were true. The censors even complained when we wrote that the German High Command *said* something was true. They argued this amounted to casting doubts on the High Command's veracity. Most good stories I did not even write, for I knew from the outset it would be impossible to force them through the censorship.

In the studios of the German short-wave station, on Adolf Hitler Platz, where radio correspondents worked, the directors of the station carried on a petty nuisance campaign against us. I was suddenly removed from my rather commodious office one night and consigned to a cubby hole. One of Lord Haw-Haw's assistants took over my old office. My good typewriter was given to the hireling and I was loaned an ancient, rickety machine with one key missing. Twice, when other keys dropped out of the old apparatus, I had to write my scripts in long-hand, until a sympathizing secretary in one of the offices loaned me her typewriter. Another secretary, in the offices of Dr. Schotte, the director of the American department of the short-wave station, once informed us Dr. Schotte had suggested to the general director of the German radio that we be thrown out of the building entirely.

One day, one of the Propaganda Ministry censors, one Dr. Krauss, presented us with a handout penned by Dr. Schmidt, of the Foreign Office, attacking Roosevelt, and made known the Ministry's desire that we use the material. With Alex Dreier of N.B.C., I agreed not to use the material, since we had thus been served with a sort of order to make use of it. Dr. Krauss declared indignantly he would "report you gentlemen to Dr. Goebbels". We thanked him for the undeserved compliment and remained adamant. On the heels of this distasteful little incident followed the slaughter of my scripts on Hitler's speech of November 8. About the same time I complained to the Propaganda Ministry because I was not allowed to visit the Eastern Front, although press correspondents had been taken on four trips to the front. I called on five different departments of the government but none was even willing to hear my protest, and none had any suggestions to make as to whom I might see about the matter. The other two radio correspondents had, of course, the same difficulties. So we conferred on measures to be taken. Reading over past scripts, I remarked how utterly vapid they were, and that they not only failed to give a fairly accurate picture of what was occurring inside Germany, but even gave a false impression. In the pressure of writing each script to pass between the straits of newsworthiness and what the censors would allow, I had not noticed how completely I had failed to report Berlin with any degree of fairness. We all three agreed that it was purposeless to continue in this manner, and decided to make an exhaustive telegraphic report on the situation to our companies, and request that we be recalled. We deposited our cables at the proper cable offices, but the cable censors refused to send any of them. Next day, we telephoned our New York offices and read the texts of the cables to them. The following evening, the official German news agency issued a brief message to the press to the effect that the three American radio correspondents in Berlin were banned from the air in view of our protests, which were "singular in the history of journalism". The message declared that we had never complained about our conditions to the proper authorities, and therefore we were doing an injustice to the Reich Radio which had shown us "years of hospitality" (the old song and dance) by going over their heads. That we had never complained was a blunt lie. We had lodged at least one complaint a week, written or oral, for several months, but none had ever elicited any kind of response. However, it was probably true that we never complained to the "proper authorities". When I complained to the Propaganda Ministry, I was told the affair belonged to the Radio authorities, who in turn, flatly rejected responsibility and instructed us to return to the Propa-

ganda Ministry. One evening, Dr. Froelich frankly revealed to me
that he did not know who was responsible, and he did not think
anyone else knew! In any case, each of us received brief, two-line
letters from the head of the German radio, Dr. Glasmeier, to the
effect that the "Reich Radio rejects further co-operation with
you".

We applied for exit permits to leave Germany, but the permits
were not forthcoming. Instead, the German Foreign Office sent a
special envoy to Switzerland to interview our representatives there,
and to request them to send substitutes to take our places in
Berlin. The tactic was miserably transparent. The German government was, in plain language, requesting hostages. If our companies sent hostages, we would be "released" from Germany, but
we would not be able to report on the new German situation when
we were safely outside, for it would mean reprisals of one kind or
another against our substitutes inside Germany!

I waited for an uncertain month in Berlin, able to do nothing
but twiddle my thumbs and go walking. Columbia backed me up
admirably. Paul White, Columbia's director of news broadcasts
in New York, cabled a response to the Reich Radio company's
announcement to him that I had been forbidden to work in
Germany, asking the Nazi radio director, since when had it become "singular in the history of journalism" for a correspondent
to complain to the company which employed him? The Propaganda Ministry had apparently hoped that Columbia would fire
me for being "indiscreet", and White's message took many cubic
metres of wind out of the Ministry's sails. Dr. Froelich made it
known to me by way of a go-between (having broken off relations
with me, he could not approach me, himself), that he was willing
to "talk things over". I sent back the message that I was sorry,
but relations were broken off by an official D.N.B. dispatch. If
another D.N.B. dispatch were issued, I said, stating that I was
reinstated, and apologizing for the untruth of the first announcement, I would be glad to meet Dr. Froelich. The attitude was
rather audacious, perhaps unnecessarily so, for one who, like myself, was entirely at the mercy of the German government. And I
am sure it made the bureaucrats more than a little angry. One
evening, the same Wilhelmstrasse tipster who had once told
Richard Hottelet that he was growing dangerously unpopular
with the Gestapo, came to me and suggested, "My dear Smith, if I

were you I would get out of Germany as fast as I could. If you do not leave soon, you will have reason to regret it". I assured him I agreed fully, but I could get no visa to leave. Next day, I visited the Foreign Office and learned that Columbia had agreed to send a substitute to Berlin, and I was granted an exit visa. Relieved, I went home and packed my single bag full of shabby clothing.

The visa had come unexpectedly and late in the day, and I had said goodbye to none of the boys. After I had packed, I told Fleischer, perhaps I had better hang around for another day, bid my farewells, arrange my affairs quietly, and leave the following evening. Jack peremptorily disapproved, saying he was going to put me on the train for Berne that night if he had to do it by brute force. Something might happen, he said. I told him he had a case of nerves; nothing would happen overnight. He reminded me that I, too, had had a case of nerves until I had gotten that precious visa, and if I stayed in Berlin an hour longer than I had to stay, I was screwy. He went out on the streets with a little bag of coffee for bait and conjured up a taxi, and we went to the Potsdamer Station.

Word got around quickly that another deserter was deserting and a goodly clot of friends met us on the *Bahnhof* platform in the blackout. Besides a gang of agency reporters there were a few German friends there, bearing sandwiches and a bottle of home-brewed *Weizenbier*. Fleischer, too, gave me a fat bundle of sandwiches, stuffed with big chunks of imported sausage which he directed me to use for "propaganda purposes"—i.e., to eat them within the view of as many Germans as possible, walking up and down the corridors of the coaches, and maybe droppng sizable pieces of sausage out of the corner of my mouth, with American abandon from time to time, to irritate them. Pat Conger of U.P., told me he would see me in Switzerland in a couple of days. He had applied for an exit permit and should get it after the week-end. Departures from Berlin were always bibulous occasions and some of the boys were mellow already. Jean Graffis suggested giving the quartette a last exercise. Though I sing badly, I was one of the sturdiest legs of the quartette, making up for absent harmony with lots of the proper spirit. We hit off a mean Swanee River, then not a bad rendering of "Lili Mardeen" so the German friends could join in. With me I had a fat bottle of champagne I had been saving for the departure, if and when that event should ever mature—it was Russian champagne which Steve Laird bought in Moscow a year before and willed to me when he left. We popped off the cork and had a community sip. I was enjoying myself more than I had for months, and suggested to Fleischer that maybe it would be a good idea to stay just another day and celebrate the way these things ought to be celebrated. The others overheard me and poured me into the train and it left. The German friends waved white handkerchiefs in the blackout until I was out of sight, and the Americans went across the street to the Press Club bar to wash away the Blues which always settled down with a vengeance when those who had to stay said goodbye to those who were escaping.

I felt very sorry for them, but I was very happy for myself. It was good to hear the train wheels clicking under me again after two years that seemed like two decades. The train was jammed with humanity, and I had to share my sleeping compartment with a German. He was a pretty nice fellow, though talkative, and, like every German I know, worried and grim. He struck up a conversation, asking me if I thought America was actually coming into the war. I told him it was inevitable; we were not going to let our ships, containing precious guns, be sunk in the Atlantic, and Hitler was not going to stand by and watch them delivered to England. He tried a little propaganda on me to feel me out—they always do; I'm so accustomed to the routine that I have become a master of it—asking me why didn't we use our heads and stay out this time; we didn't get anything out of it last time. I said maybe we were using our heads and defending ourselves while we still had means of doing so; that if France had defended herself when the Nazis crossed into the Rhineland in 1936, maybe Frenchmen would be eating a lot better right now. By way of being nasty, I added that also maybe Germans, too, would be eating a lot better —would you like a bite of my sausage sandwich? Be careful how you hold it, or the sausage will fall out from between the bread; it's cut too thick, really. He said: but you don't really believe little Germany is going to cross the great big ocean and attack rich, powerful America? I said I certainly did believe it. He said, fantastic! I said yep; it was very fantastic, about as fantastic as one man conquering the whole of Europe and part of Africa in two years. He shut up a while and ate half a sausage sandwich.

Then he said, but the German people don't want war with
America. I said No; and I respect the German people for it. But
since when have the German people been running Germany?
I had a third of a bottle of champagne left, and I offered him a
sip. He said it was good, so I pointed out it was *Russian* champagne; they still have oodles of it. I was talking through my hat,
for I have no idea whether the Russians have or not. But my
friend was impressed. Then he said *schlafen Sie-wohl* and went to
sleep. I felt too good to sleep so I removed the blackout curtains
from the window and stared out in the blackout all night, listening to the rhythmic clicking of the wheels under us. Dawn came up
surprisingly swiftly. On one side of us was the Rhine. Across it I
could see the green bunkers of the Maginot Line, with their guns
removed. On the other side of us I could see the grey bunkers of
the Siegfried line, the *Westwall.* The railway tracks ran right
between them.

When it was light, I could see how seedy our coach was. German sleeping cars used to be the best in Europe. Their trains used
to be among the fastest. Ours was creeping along slowly; I bet to
myself that the boilers of the locomotive had not been cold and
cleaned for months. In the coach, the carpet was threadbare and
spotted with brown cigarette burns. The mahogany panels were
scratched and the varnish on them was flakey. On the window-
sill there was a hole in the wood with a broken screw in the middle
as a reminder that a shiney brass ash-tray had once been there. The
coach porter, an imported French worker in a porter's worn
uniform which was too small for him, came in and asked me with a
French accent to his German if I wanted some *Malzkaffee*. I said
yes. He returned a quarter of an hour later and said I could not
have any. The chef had gone on strike because he was an old man
and his rheumatism was hurting, so he refused to prepare anything
for anybody. I said it was all right, and I drank my bottle of
Weizenbier for breakfast.

At Freiburg, I climbed out of the coach and bought the morning
Voelkischer Beobachter. There was a note in it, issued by the Supreme
Command, that due to the unprecedentedly early winter this year,
the German troops were shortening their lines on the Eastern front
and preparing for winter defence. I showed it to my German
friend, who shrugged his shoulders and repeated "unprecedentedly early winter". I though it very strange that the arrival of

winter in December, in Russia or anywhere else, should be unprecedented, but I did not say anything. My friend was sufficiently worried already. The date on the top of the newspaper was
December 7, 1941.

Peace, brother; it's wonderful! Peace is unbelievable. You
cannot take somebody's word for it. You must spend two years in
the Berlin blackout some time when you have nothing else to do,
and then go to Switzerland suddenly, if you want to love Peace
the way Peace deserves to be loved. Whatever the dead hand of
Hitlerism touches—whether it comes as friend or foe—it kills,
dulls, greys, deadens. It kills in allied Rumania and Hungary just
as it kills in hostile England and Russia. Wherever it passes, it
leaves a streak of grey death, spiritual and physical, to mark the
path of its progress. Berlin is the colour of cadaver I once saw
preserved in a big jar in a medical school: grey, lifeless and
sickening to look at. The moment you cross the Swiss border the
atmosphere changes, as if by a miracle. There was life, and there
was colour in everything. It was the life and colour of normality,
which I had forgotten. People's faces downright beautiful. They
would have been I suppose, ordinary to anybody else, but to me
they were lovely, tinted with the colour showing there was life
going on inside of them. Colour in cheeks and eyes. No red rims
around the eyes. Facial muscles were relaxed and they smiled
easily, as though there was no particular reason why they shouldn't
smile. December 7 was just one more day in Switzerland, but it
marked an epoch in my young life; the way eyes sparkled, not because people were happier today than yesterday, but just because
they were healthy, at peace, with clear consciences and normal.
Houses were bright and painted in various fresh colours. I think
house-paint must be part of the blood-stream of society. When
society is sick, the exteriors of houses grow pale and grey; and
when society is well, houses are colourful and nice to look at.
Shops were clean and neat with bright Neon signs and clean
windows just chock-full of everything. No *Attrapen:* oranges and
apples stacked in pyramids, canned goods with white, printed
labels on the shelves, quadruple rows of bottles of everything,
ketchup made of tomatoes and not of acid chemicals, and there
were bars of soap in paper wrappers which you could smell the
perfume of; there was everything.

People's clothing, even the clothing of workers, breathed good quality, and shoes had the hard, clean lines of good, new leather. I sat in the *Bahnhof* restaurant in Basle gawking at things like a country visitor in the big city. I have never had such a kick out of just looking at plain, ordinary people, and ordinary things. I almost tripped a waitress with my ankle by accident, and instead of cursing me, she said "Pardon, M'sieu". I think I must have frightened her when I stared back in amazement. Along one whole side of the restaurant there was an endless glass show-case filled with things to eat, cakes with coloured icing, chocolate, sandwiches, with large slices of ham in them, fish, lobster, and at the end three beer-taps which flowed beer almost constantly. On the counter by the beer-taps were about three dozen bottles of all kinds of liquor, including whisky. The menu was filled to the margins with hors d'œuvres, entrées and desserts. There were exactly fifty-two entrées. German menus offered one entrée. I asked the waitress if it were all there for ordering, or was it only *Attrapen* to impress visitors. She said it was there to sell, and to test her I picked out the most unlikely dish I could find in the middle of the menu. And, surely enough, it was brought to me in fifteen minutes on a big platter brimming over with luscious green peas, red carrots and potatoes, fried crisp and brown in good fat.

The cigarette girl came by pushing a big double-decker tray with packages of cigarettes of all the colours in the rainbow. There must have been more than a hundred packages of cigarettes on that tray, and some of them were shiny in cellophane. They were beautiful. I bought a package. Then I bought a cigar. I do not like cigars, but whenever I feel prosperous—usually on pay-day night—I always buy a big cigar and smoke it because it seems to fit the occasion. Then I called for two fingers of whisky and settled back and waited for the train to Berne. I enjoyed smelling the aroma of the whisky more than I enjoyed drinking it.

In Berne that night, the street-lights were on. Now that is a sight to see. It made me feel naked in front of an audience, and downright giggly, as a thirteen year-old girl in her first two-piece bathing suit. It makes every street-corner look like a stage-setting. Berne, of course, has the most beautiful streets in the world, night or day. But street lights do the same thing to any city that expertly applied cosmetics do to a woman's face. Street-lights give streets and buildings a new colour, a new sheen. I am convinced of it that the man who invented electric street-lights did as much towards the furtherance of aesthetics as Beethoven or Rembrandt. I walked the streets for hours. Not on the sidewalks, but in the streets, grinning and happy. A six-year-old girl with a new doll could not have been as happy.

In the brightly lighted shop windows there was rich red meat and big, fat sausages hanging from hooks. The candy shops had many boxes of chocolates all done up in yellow and pink ribbons in them, and a big department store was exhibiting plaster models in woollen suits and dresses. I grinned the whole time in spite of myself. I imagine many people must have thought me a bit balmy, shuffling up and down the streets in my lumpy, worn suit and my dirty hat with a crooked brim, grinning the whole time.

I had a room in the *Schweizer Hof*, across from the station. In the hotel bar, I met a couple of newspapermen I had known in Berlin. They treated me to welcome whiskys, then we had dinner. I had a T-bone steak big as a ham and almost two inches thick, garnished with six different vegetables. Afterwards I had a bicarbonate of soda, and went to my room to be alone and think. I filled my pipe with good American tobacco I had bought, and turned out the light. I sat before the window, looking down on the streets outside and smoked a long time, until the telephone rang. It was the *Portier* downstairs whom I had asked to let me know if a Mr. Conger from Berlin should arrive in the next couple of days. He said he was only calling to tell me, because I might be interested to know, that Mr. Conger was not coming, because ten minutes ago the Japanese, Germany's Ally, had bombed Manila and Pearl Harbour, and no more Americans could get out of Germany. I asked the *Portier* to get Berlin on the phone to see if the lines were still open. They were, and I talked briefly to Fleischer. Fleischer said the situation looked critical, but everybody was glad the waiting was over. They might get other brands of Blues, but they would never have the Berlin Blues again.